# EPISODES FROM A FOREIGN SERVICE CAREER

Charleston, SC
www.PalmettoPublishing.com



Hardcover ISBN: 979-8-8229-4915-7
Paperback ISBN: 979-8-8229-4916-4

# EPISODES FROM A FOREIGN SERVICE CAREER

## Africa, Democracy and Public Diplomacy

ROBERT LAGAMMA

The cover photo depicts the author as he began his diplomatic career in 1962 at age 22 shaking the hand of Edward R. Murrow, legendary journalist, and named by President Kennedy as Director of the United States Information Agency.

To my beloved wife of 58 years, Anita Vitacolonna LaGamma
whose poetic spirit inspired my life of prose.

And to our children Alisa, Matthew, Therese, Adrian and Florence
who not only put up with the life of the Foreign Service but
thrived and taught me lessons in relating to other cultures.

# Preface

This memoir is an episodic journey across six decades of a life lived in pursuit of three goals. The first was an effort to convey a vision of America abroad, a vision defined by President Kennedy. The second was promoting democratic values globally. The third was working in Africa, with Africans and forging relationships between the United States and Africa. At the age of twenty-two I leapt from graduate school and chose diplomacy focused on Africa with the United States Information Agency in the waning days of the Kennedy Administration.

In the years to follow my wife Anita and I and eventually our five children experienced the odyssey of living and representing the United States in Southern Rhodesia, Zambia, the Congo, Ivory Coast, Togo, Senegal, Nigeria, and South Africa (at the time of Nelson Mandela). My African years coincided with the early unsuccessful efforts to win majority rule in Rhodesia to the excitement of attending independence ceremonies in Zambia. They also included years in a Nigeria ruled by the military and the Congo in chaos. Those assignments concluded with my time in the euphoric post--Mandela South Africa as it sought to deliver on the promise of its freedom from apartheid.

In between our eight African sojourns we spent six years in Milan and Florence and experienced the world of our ancestors. My focus on Africa during its formative post-colonial period eventually led me to serve as USIA's Director of African Affairs. That and other roles at USIA allowed me to work with and direct the work of our desk officers and other specialists in support of some fifty USIS African posts from Washington. And it enabled me to visit most of those offices firsthand.

What follows then is an anecdotal account of the highlights of my experiences in chronological order from 1962 through my retirement from the Foreign Service in 1997. It also recounts my experiences working on a project of the National Democratic Institute in the Congo and the Carter Center as their monitor of the 2000 Nigerian elections.

Finally, I document my work with a unique democracy promotion NGO, the Council for a Community of Democracies (CCD), first as Executive Director and later as President from 2003 to 2017. In that capacity we sought to create an international nongovernmental dynamic in support of a group of democratic states that had formed the worldwide Community of Democracies. Throughout every day in my thirty-five years in the Foreign Service I was inspired and supported by my wonderous wife Anita who was both a source of ideas, inspiration, and a moral compass for our joint adventure.

# Table of Contents

# I. The Bookcase

As I reached down to take *Moby Dick* from the bookcase in my home in Reston, Virginia, a story from more than a half century ago came flashing back.

That memory was of another perfect day in early 1964. Anita and I, just married for a month, had recently landed in Salisbury, Southern Rhodesia. It was our first week in Africa and we were settling into a newly found cottage surrounded by a field of roses and exotic flowers whose names were unknown to us. We were catching our breath on the veranda after three weeks of traveling and unpacking when the silence was broken by the sound of a bicycle clamoring up the driveway. On it rode an African teenager in tattered clothing. Perched on the back of his bike was a wooden object.

"Good day," he said. "Would you wish to buy my bookcase?" Looking closely, we saw it was a meticulously crafted, single shelfed bookcase, one that would meet our need to store some of our only half unpacked books. "How much are you asking?" I responded. While the price he quoted sounded reasonable, our money was tight and having been taught the imperative of bargaining for everything in Africa, I offered half his asking price.

He stunned us with "is that fair?" Clearly half was not but recalling that used clothing was a currency in Africa, my wife proposed we add some of our least needed garments. To that offer he replied, "I must ask my uncle," and rode away.

Two days later the boy returned, and the sale was consummated. We learned his name was Joshua Sithole, ironically a composite of the names of the colony's two African nationalist leaders, Joshua Nkomo and Ndabaningi Sithole.

Joshua was a handsome boy and seemingly quite bright. We asked why he was not in school, He replied, "my family needs my work." He informed us that the bookcase had been made by his uncle, Goliath, to whom he was apprenticed.

The next week he returned asking if we needed another bookcase. Casting a glance at the rags he wore, Anita suggested an expedition to town. The three of us got in the car and I asked my wife where we were going. She responded, "downtown." Once there, she directed me to park in front of a department store. Anita led us swiftly to the shoe department. When Joshua was asked to remove his shoes, we learned that the holes in them were stuffed with newspaper and the socks were threadbare beyond belief.

The astonished saleslady, not knowing whether to serve a Black ragamuffin and his bizarre accompanying Americans, finally took out her measuring stick and Anita ordered her to provide the best pair of sneakers available as well as several pairs of socks. We then headed for boys' pants and shirts before exiting with Joshua's newly acquired wardrobe. The boy was simply stunned as he stammered words of thanks.

On the way home we peppered Joshua with questions about his aspirations. We learned he yearned to complete his education. He had excelled in school until he had to abandon it to work. We also learned that he had developed a fondness for carpentry and wanted to pursue it as a career. This rang a bell for us. We knew that education was rationed for Africans in this replicated apartheid colony and that vocational training was scarce. Coincidently, we had recently travelled south to a Catholic Mission run by a Swiss order, the Bethlehem Fathers, where we had stayed and come to know some of the priests. While there we learned they ran a school, named Gokomere, after an ancient African settlement. We learned the school provided both academic and job-oriented education including carpentry. In short, they had exactly what Joshua wanted.

A great bonus of our discovery of Gokomere Mission was the added discovery of its related and stupendous Serima Mission station described as an African Chartres by Evelyn Waugh in his *A Tourist in Africa*. We learned that it was created by Swiss missionary, Father John Groeber. He was both a sculptor and carpenter who trained local African carpenters, transforming them into sculptors. He had them adorn his church with sculptures depicting biblical scenes. While they were based on classical biblical tales, the imagery reflected Africans and their surroundings. Their artistry led to a school of religious sculpture, works that were acquired around the world. Gokomere contained a spark of creativity it sought to pass on to its students.

During the following weeks we sought to enroll Joshua in its program while at the same time seeking permission from his family to do so. The school's principal agreed to test him to determine his qualifications and aptitude. After some hesitation, Joshua's family agreed. Happily, the school indicated he seemed qualified. We then drove him to Gokomere. Along the way we stopped at the World Heritage Site of the Great Zimbabwe ruins. Joshua explored the mysterious collection of stone structures that had been created by a bygone kingdom more than a millennia ago. Despite the systematic propaganda by the White minority government deprecating African accomplishments and attributing the ruins to an improbable Chinese settlement, Joshua recognized Great Zimbabwe as the creation of his ancestors. His reaction was one of enormous pride.

After settling Joshua with our Swiss friends, we returned to Salisbury. Two weeks later two letters came, one from the school, the other from the new student, both announcing their optimism.

Soon after dropping him at Gokomere, we were assigned to the Congo and lost contact with the boy who sold us the fine bookcase that has served us for the last five decades. For all those years, to no avail, we sought to reestablish contact, during which prolonged years of bloody violence finally led to majority rule and Rhodesia became Zimbabwe. While searching through piles of old correspondence many years later, I found a composition notebook that Joshua had sent us containing his autobiography. In it he wrote of the time before we had met. He told of his responsibilities back home before he had come to Salisbury, recounting that his life had consisted of taking care of the garden and herding the family's goats. It was our hope that the Swiss school had enabled Joshua to survive the bloody transition to majority rule and transcend the limitations of his past to lead him to a better life.

In my early days in Salisbury, I found that our Cultural Center had sponsored a nationwide art contest for school children. A portrait of a ferocious leopard by a young boy, Ribbie Chimucheka, was selected as the winner and Anita and I were charged with caring for him while he was in the city. It was all wonderous for Ribbie who came from a rural area. He stayed with us and for the first time in his life had the experience of a shower and a modern kitchen. We took Ribbie to tour what for him was his first modern city.

The National Gallery which had hosted the competition was a remarkable institution. Its dynamic founder and director, Frank McEwen, who had a distinguished background in contemporary art history in Europe, was most interested in generating and reviving an indigenous African art form that transcended the modest collection of European art he inherited at the museum. His genius drew its inspiration from archeological findings of soapstone sculptures including the sculpture of a fish eagle from the ancient and mysterious Shona kingdom of Great Zimbabwe. McEwen identified the source of deposits of soapstone which he arranged to have mined. He then recruited Africans, former police officers, and trained them in the basement of the Gallery to carve soapstone sculptures.

They later formed what was known as the Zimbabwe Workshop School. Since racial laws would otherwise have prohibited them from living in town at the museum's dormitory, to continue their training and encourage their work, he hired a dozen of them as museum employees. Their art school became world famous. Some, serving as guards, combined their artistic skills by providing visitors with highly imaginative commentary and African perspectives on the European art of the museum's traditional collection. The sensation of the early sculptural creations led to their exhibition throughout the world, but subsequent mass production and commercialization in the form of "airport art" has diminished their acclaim.

My passion for traditional and contemporary African art which I thought of as a window into a culture's imagination began in New York. As a student I particularly enjoyed New York's Museum of Modern Art. One day I wandered down the street from MOMA and discovered a second Rockefeller founded museum, the Museum of Primitive Art. The collection of that museum included the art of Oceania, Ancient America, and Africa. Rockefeller later donated that museum's collection to the Metropolitan Museum. Decades later, my daughter Alisa would earn a PhD from Columbia University in African art and archeology and later went on to serve as Curator in Charge of those galleries that form the Michael C. Rockefeller Wing at the Metropolitan.

Another early influence on my relation to African Art occurred at the beginning of my Foreign Service career while in Washington. In 1963 my Foreign Service Institute area studies course on Africa exposed me to a lecturer on African art, Warren Robbins. While a State Department officer in Germany, Warren had begun to collect African art that he came across in Hamburg antique shops. When he later returned to Washington, he purchased the former home of Fredrick Douglass, the great African American abolitionist. Warren decorated his home with the works of African art he had acquired and his home soon became a local attraction.

As this was the time of the Civil Rights Movement, it occurred to Warren that he might establish a museum in the Nation's Capital which had a majority African American population. As the Civil

Rights Movement was inextricably linked to the African diaspora, Warren successfully attracted African American school children in order to connect with their ancestral heritage. After his lecture to us at the Institute, my colleague David Wilson and I stayed on to talk to Warren. He told us he was at the point of painting his new museum and asked if we would help him. David and I spent the evening there painting, eating pizza and listening to an address by President Kennedy. Robbins decades later donated his collection which became the basis for the Smithsonian Museum of African Art. African Art and artists, and the historic art of ancient Africa became an important interest in my future assignments.

One mindless task I was asked to perform in Southern Rhodesia was the bane of the Cultural Affairs Officer's existence. Numerous borrowers had failed to return the books loaned by our library. Mailed notices failed to get results. Our Cultural Affairs Officer's solution: send the new junior officer to their houses to collect them. The problem was most of the missing books were in the African townships where white pigmentation usually was equated with racial adversary. One of our drivers and I went to Highfields township and when we arrived glanced at each other wondering about the absurdity of the task. He then suggested an alternative destination, the local beer hall. Going there with an African colleague did in no way signify "enemy" and we were greeted warmly and even treated to our first mug of beer. It was an acquired taste but one I got used to.

Although Southern Rhodesia did not live up to my professional expectations of an experience to work in newly independent Africa, it did provide insights into the difficult struggle confronting those who sought to be free of colonial or apartheid type oppression.

Unhappily, the dominant result once Southern Rhodesia became Zimbabwe was the heritage of a bitter struggle and the quest for revenge. The rule of Robert Mugabe was brutal and unleashed a long period of violence and a failure to achieve the reconciliation that characterized Mandela's vision for South Africa. A different experience of independent Africa would come soon enough. Years later, our Ambassador to Zimbabwe once told me that Mugabe came to be characterized by his ministers as a pedant, citing the textbooks he had read as if they were absolute guides to economic policies.

# II. Beginnings

Early days in Rhodesia

**"One person can make a difference and everyone should try."**

John F. Kennedy

The idea of the Foreign Service came upon me one day over coffee in the Brooklyn College cafeteria. My good friend, Richard Erde, told me offhand about taking an exam administered by the Department of State. I had never for a moment dreamed of a life in diplomacy but we were both students of international relations and what better to do with the subject than to attempt to apply our study in that way. I thought of it as a remote long shot but I had always been reasonably good at exams, so I joined Richard in applying. It was a long process. After passing the written exam, then came an oral exam. I approached it believing it was still beyond the realm of possibility but found myself before a panel of kind, easy to converse with examiners. A year later after an FBI agent had interviewed friends and neighbors, I got the letter that changed my life.

My start in the Foreign Service of the United States Information Agency (USIA) dates to 1962. I came to it after growing up in a Bronx tenement and graduating from Brooklyn College while working for New York's 42nd Street Library. My career began during the Kennedy presidency. It coincided with two great overlapping historic developments. It was the time during which the Civil Rights movement was taking off. Initially my dream of international service began with the idea of joining the recently established Peace Corps. I was in the process of filling out an application form for it when I received the news that I had been accepted into the Foreign

Service of the United States Information Agency. Being stationed in Washington for my USIA training program that first year allowed me to witness Dr. King's *I Have a Dream* address on the National Mall in the shadow of Abe Lincoln.

Simultaneously, decolonization was at its zenith, transforming the entire African continent. Sixteen new countries came into existence in 1960 alone. As a student I was able to observe that process via the subway on my way home from college when I could attend United Nations debates in which proud African diplomats in flowing robes began articulating their countries' views on world affairs for the first time on the international stage. I recalled the Roman historian Pliny's observation: "Always something new out of Africa" and wanted to be part of that.

I like to say that "I got my job through the *New York Times*," an oft quoted *Times* slogan. Each day I read it religiously for news and op-eds, often featuring both Africa and Civil Rights. I imagined being present at that turning point in history and witnessing the struggle of what I saw as the unraveling of the twin evils of racist and colonial domination. The other inspiration to be a participant in a changing world came from the powerful influence of John F. Kennedy when he declared: "Ask not what your country can do for you--ask what you can do for your country."

After graduating from Stuyvesant High School, I joined three friends for a summer drive across the United States, Canada and Mexico traversing sixteen thousand miles. That awesome experience was enthralling, especially that of the marvels of our national parks. A highlight was hiking across the Grand Canyon. The grandeur of the American West filled me with wonder that I somehow conveyed at the Foreign Service oral interview, and that I'm convinced helped me persuade the interviewers that I might effectively represent our country abroad.

My training year in the Foreign Service began in late 1962. I found it thrilling to be part of what I considered to be the charismatic Kennedy administration. That was enhanced by serving under our boss at the U.S. Information Agency, the great American journalist, Edward R. Murrow. The motto on the doorway of the headquarters of our Agency, one block from the White House was "Telling America's Story to the World." Murrow was expected to be a close advisor to President Kennedy. He was quoted as telling the new President not to do anything he would not like to see in the *New York Times*. Murrow's vision of the world and USIA's role in it transcended propaganda. He told a Senate Committee: "we have no choice but to try to tell the truth about ourselves." To those new idealistic officers among us, that was exactly the message we wanted to hear from our boss.

I very much wanted to be one of our nation's storytellers. The Washington year was invigorating, a tour that consisted of visits to Congress, and the State Department. Most exceptional was an appointment at the Supreme Court, where we met with the extraordinary Justice William O. Douglas, an early environmentalist and equal rights proponent, whose opinions had been of monumental importance. We also were exposed to many other relevant institutions. Those of us headed for Africa concluded our training with a week of African Studies at the Foreign Service Institute with our State Department counterparts. I then underwent five months of intensive French language training. After all that training I realized that the real test of whether I had what it took to be successful in the Foreign Service had not yet begun and would have to await my first overseas assignment.

What I failed to witness during those initial months was that we were in the process of inventing what came to be known as Public Diplomacy. The reason I could not understand that was the Cold War had clouded our vision of what eventually would be a very different kind of diplomacy. The Cold War caused a portion of our officers to focus on combatting the Soviets, Chinese and international Communism. To some it meant countering their propaganda with our own propaganda, as well as countering what came to be known as disinformation. Some of that was clearly necessary in what we perceived of as a life and death struggle for the survival of democracy and Western values. But with the passage of time and the reduction of the threats of the Cold War, I saw the emergence of a new and more effective diplomacy, one especially geared to Africa.

Public Diplomacy then contrasted with traditional diplomacy for which our ambassadors, political, and intelligence officers aimed at influencing a head of state and senior officials to support our policies, and to vote our way at the U.N. With the emergence of democratic institutions, the new diplomacy, the one best practiced by USIS, was to support civil society and develop an array of exchange programs that could in the longer run influence the people of a country to support leaders and develop representative institutions that would be in tune with Western democratic values.

Halfway through that first year, while enrolled in my intensive French language course, I learned that my request that I be assigned to Africa had been granted. Ironically, however, it was not to be the newly independent Africa, but to one of the remaining colonial outposts, the then Federation of Rhodesia and Nyasaland where I would be based in the capital, Salisbury. Rhodesia's mile-high capital had a climate and flora and fauna that made it a paradise, but to quote one critic "a malignant paradise" because of its politics. "A challenge" in the parlance of the Foreign Service is an assignment to a problem post, and although it boasted a paradisical environment, Rhodesia's politics were a loose equivalent to that of Alabama's in the 1950's and closely mirrored those of neighboring South Africa. Africans were restricted to living in townships and rural areas while white farmers controlled the productive farmlands.

Before the professional challenge was the challenge that was Anita. We had been dating for more than four years and it was clear to me that the most important decision of my life was impending. Either we would shortly be married, or our relationship would unwind. So, for what seemed the tenth time, I proposed marriage as the time of my departure drew near. She at first was hesitant and suggested that maybe after I began my career overseas, we could decide. When I was adamant and said it was now or never, she said yes to my proposal. We had a ridiculously short time for preparations, less than a month. But it all came together by the most important date of my life, November 16, 1963. Once married we moved to my apartment off Columbia Road and began the process of medical clearance, shots, passports, visas, and then the painful vigil of the Kennedy assassination. It was especially somber since Kennedy had inspired me to sign up for the Foreign Service and his vision had inspired the world to such an extent that his photo coupled with those of Pope John and Gandhi often hung on the walls of huts abroad.

But the dreadful grief was mitigated by the beginning of fifty-eight years of marriage to the most extraordinary of women. Anita and I started off with a phenomenal three-and-a-half-week voyage on the way to Africa. I had never been to Europe so it was especially remarkable to share it with my bride. It began magically in Paris. We had planned to stay just a few days, but there was no leaving it, especially after midnight mass on Christmas Eve at Notre Dame. Many years later my eldest daughter Alisa presented us with a photo of Paris taken on the precise date of that first visit. It depicted the Seine and a dreary, rainy city. But if it rained, I wouldn't have noticed since we walked on clouds. Our Left Bank hotel, the St. Pierre, was run by a French family who were kindness personified. Who could ever forget their first breakfast croissant?

That hotel we stayed in had been recommended to me by my USIA desk officer, Blake Robinson, or so I thought. Years later I learned that what he had suggested was not the Hotel St. Pierre but rather the Hotel des Saints Peres which I, with less than perfect French, had misinterpreted. Blake was a remarkable model of a Foreign Service Africanist. He had served before the independence of many African states as Public Affairs Officer in both Dakar and Brazzaville and was responsible for both francophone West and Central Africa. I came to regard him as an American Lawrence of Arabia. Yet another desk officer that I related to and later worked for in Zambia was Phillip Dorman, one of the kindest and most effective officers I had known in the Foreign Service.

The time Anita and I had in Paris was spent covering great distances on foot when not learning to master the Metro. My Foreign Service Institute French was enough to impress the natives but not enough to navigate *Le Monde* very successfully. We were able to digest too much of the fine food, not enough of the great art, and to begin to savor a dynamic culture.

Sadly, after ten days we had to leave Paris and continue on our way to our second destination, Rome, where we were guests of a colleague and his wife who were gracious hosts and guides to the eternal city. After several days we concluded our European adventure in Athens where again we were hosted by a colleague and his wife who occupied an apartment that looked out on the Parthenon. After a few days of contemplation of that city that shaped the history of our Western world, we were on our way to begin our twenty-three years in Africa and our thirty-five years in the Foreign Service.

**Anita and Bob in their garden in Rhodesia**

My concern was how my wife Anita would adapt to life in Africa. It was a Sunday when we first arrived, accommodated at the Jameson Hotel in central Salisbury. That evening, I suggested we leave the hotel and wander the town in search of dinner. Salisbury was dark and deserted. All we could find was a greasy spoon place to eat. We returned to the hotel and entered our room. Above the bed was a picture of the Acropolis which we had seen the night before from our Athens window. Anita burst into tears, asking why it was that my friends had landed in Paris, Rome, and Athens, and we had to come here. I tried inadequately to console her. The next morning after breakfast we wandered out, crossed the street, and found ourselves in a wondrous public garden the like of which we had never seen. This was an Africa Anita could gladly relate to. Never again, in all our years did she regret our being in Africa, loving its flowers, its forests, its birds, its wildlife and most of all its people.

While Anita was totally new to world affairs, diplomatic life, and the challenge of Africa, she quickly adapted to every challenge and proved to be a remarkable resource to me and to everything she touched. Aside from raising five children, she was an outstanding teacher. She taught adults in Rhodesia, secondary school in Zambia, English as a foreign language in the Congo, and elementary school in Togo and Senegal. Not only did she teach, but she adapted so well that she frequently provided me with wise advice that many times guided me in the midst of professional troubled waters. I owe whatever professional advancement I had in large part to my brilliant wife.

Britain had linked Southern Rhodesia to its northern neighbors, Northern Rhodesia, and Nyasaland in a federation with the latter two about to join the ranks of the increasingly large number of newly independent African countries. Northern Rhodesia would soon become Zambia and Nyasaland, Malawi. But the third part of the Federation, Southern Rhodesia, dominated by a white minority, wished also to be free of Britain while emulating South Africa. Rhodesia's Africans, like their brethren elsewhere on the continent, sought majority rule, but were struggling against that obdurate, imbedded White minority. In 1961 a former Assistant Secretary of State for African Affairs, G. Mennen Williams, in assessing its future declared: "Rhodesia is a volcano ready to explode."

My disappointment with the assignment was somewhat mitigated by the thought that my own government, in tandem with Britain, might serve as change agents in the decolonization process and the move towards majority rule. While Southern Rhodesia was still a British colony, however we soon learned that Prime Minister Wilson was not inclined to risk bloodshed in the cause of a Black majority government and with the death of President Kennedy, Johnson was similarly disinclined to intervene in any way.

# III. Where the Banished Ones Sleep

In October 1964, the final month of my first diplomatic assignment in Salisbury, Southern Rhodesia, I was summoned to the office of the U.S. Consul General Paul Geren. What could he want with a junior officer like me, I wondered? I was ushered in to find that besides the Consul General, I was welcomed by the Political Officer, Phil Cherry. They greeted me with the news that they were sending me on an unusual mission. I was to travel to Gonakudzingwa, the remote prison/restriction camp near the Mozambique border, created by the white racist government, to which the African Nationalists who sought majority rule for Rhodesia were confined.

The objective of the mission, approved by the State Department, was to show the American flag and indicate sympathy for the cause for which the detainees had been arrested. Gonakudzingwa in Shona means "where the banished ones sleep." I learned that the camp was in a once forested, but currently semi-desert wasteland, far from any urban area. I was to deliver a cargo consisting of books, canned food, some alcoholic beverages, as well as USIS documentary films together with a projector and a generator.

Our gifts were intended to alleviate some measure of prisoner hardship. I was to be accompanied in a Consulate van by a USIS employee of my choosing. The camp had only the most rudimentary facilities, so we brought a tent and sleeping bags. I was both stunned and exhilarated to have been chosen for this assignment since I identified with the goals of the detainees. They were being punished by a minority White government, a regime increasingly emulating South African apartheid.

I was especially gratified at having been given this opportunity since I had had little meaningful work up to then in Salisbury. I saw the Ian Smith regime, unimpeded by its British colonial master, moving toward a unilateral declaration of independence. Just a few weeks earlier a representative of Rhodesia's Minister of Interior visited our American library to request a copy of America's Declaration of Independence. Clearly, a Rhodesian declaration was in the wind and was pronounced a year later.

To accompany me on the journey I chose Alex Munongo, known to sympathize with the Nationalist cause. Our destination was close to the Mozambique border post of Songo in the rarely visited Gonarezhou National Park. I hoped that the van we were given gave us a patina of invulnerability as it bore diplomatic plates. A day was spent loading the van. Primed to embark on our mission, I spent the night dreaming of what might lie ahead.

Early the next morning, with Alex at the wheel, we headed south on a major highway. Perhaps highway is not the proper word. The road, as did most Rhodesian highways, consisted of a clear dirt path with two ten-inch-wide paved strips in the center for tires. The rule of the road was that when encountering an oncoming vehicle each vehicle would have to move so that only one set of wheels was left on the pavement. The confoundedly tricky part of driving came when two cars driving in opposite directions approached a one lane bridge. Then the rule was the closest vehicle to the bridge flashed their headlights and would be given the right of way. The problem came when both drivers thought they were closest and both flashed. Then it was a game of chicken, sometimes ending in a deadly crash. In that case a tie went to no one as attested to by the many wrecks in the gullies under the bridges. But fortune was with us, and we safely left the highway and reached an unmarked dirt road that we believed might lead us to our destination.

The vagueness of the instructions I had been given led me to recall Elbert Hubbard's tale, "A Message to Garcia" in which a soldier is simply sent to deliver a message to a freedom fighter during the Spanish-American War without any details on how to find him.

By mid-day we were driving down our dirt road adjacent to railway tracks which confirmed we were heading in the right direction, east to Mozambique. After an hour of roller coasting, going over miles of potholes, a tire blew. We exited the vehicle and found ourselves in a flat, torrid, desiccated landscape. After off-loading half of our cargo to get our spare, we changed the tire. Continuing on the road we began to feel the oppressive heat. Our car was not air conditioned since the U.S. Congress at that time considered air conditioning to be a luxury. Our only recourse was to open all our windows to let in air to cool, dry, and cover us with reddish sandy dust.

Another hour further and we found a second tire had sprung a slow leak. As we had no other spare, we ran the risk of becoming stranded in that harsh land. It was then that we spied ahead what looked like a huge boulder with a flock of birds resting on it. As we approached the object, we saw it to be the body of a dead elephant whose body was covered with vultures. We speculated the great beast had died of thirst.

Soon after, to our relief, we saw what looked to be our destination, a camp of ramshackle, disheveled zinc huts, the detention camp. We had made it. Our arrival was greeted with a well-meaning frenzy. I was aware that my friend Alex was supportive of the majority rule cause, but the welcome he received was that of a close friend, or in the words of the movement, "a comrade." I recognized only one detainee, Josiah Chinamano, second in command to the ZAPU party's leader, Joshua Nkomo. I had last seen Josiah at a garden party in Salisbury. On that occasion we had spoken of his love of American music, and he had borrowed several records from me including *West Side Story*.

I spoke to Josiah and explained our mission. I told him of the support of the United States for majority rule in Rhodesia and explained that we brought some modest gifts. He thanked me for coming and appreciated what our coming signified but noted that while it was fine that the U.S. backed the ideas of majority rule, it was not sufficient. He asked me to tell my leaders that the detainees considered America to be a leader that stood for democracy. He argued that if President Johnson placed the power of America behind his movement, Zimbabwe would be free and the African people would remember their friends.

Josiah argued that the movement he represented wanted America to do a good deal more, especially to pressure the British to exert control and end repression. He told us that the camp was a harsh place but a fitting one since the settlers who put them there were the same ones who long ago had robbed the land from their people.

Another detainee, one with a strong Christian background, spoke up arguing that the Rhodesians "say we represent godless Communism" and added "is that what they taught us at the missionary schools we attended or spent our time discussing in church or Sunday school?"

Josiah then took me aside and asked for a favor. He said the detainees had a vehicle and were permitted to drive within the National Park, but they lacked fuel. Could I, he wondered, cross into Mozambique and fill their jerry cans with gasoline? I responded that I would try and in return asked if his people could fix our two tires lest we become permanent members of their camp.

Dinner was served to us in pots brought from the cooking fire by one of the old men. The food was blessed by a minister among them, and we shared dinner with the detainees. Josiah welcomed us by toasting our arrival, raising a bottle of orange Fanta. We proceeded to consume a meal consisting of a big bowl of *sadza*, a corn porridge covered with tomato sauce and some vegetables.

We then distributed precious mail we had collected from family members in Salisbury. After dinner we unloaded the van and out tumbled a load of books falling out of the back and stirring up a cloud of red dust lit by the campfire. We unloaded drinks and canned food and Josiah's senior aide commented that it was all good. But of all the things we had brought, books seemed to have the most value.

Then exhausted, we retired for the night to the music of not-too-distant roaring lions, fellow inhabitants of the park. We awoke the next morning to find our tires repaired and drove to the Mozambique border post manned by Portuguese soldiers. We told them of our need for gas and they directed us to a nearby station. A half hour later, the jerry cans had been filled and we were back in camp. I was pleasantly surprised at the friendliness of the Portuguese colonial border guards who had been so accommodating given their country's support for the white racist Rhodesian government.

Upon our return detainees filled their vehicle's gas tank and we were invited to join the nationalists on a journey in their Land Rover. We crossed bone jarring, trackless wastes for an hour before coming to a small settlement. Villagers gathered round our car and were shouting and pointing, some of them at me, in their local language. I asked Alex if he knew what they were yelling about. He laughed and said, "nothing serious," they just wanted to know if they should kill the White man. Since I was the one being pointed at, I asked why. He told me that the last Caucasians they had seen were tax collectors and they had chased them, firing arrows. Josiah told the villagers no; they were not to kill me as I was a friend, and our fellow travelers had a hardy laugh. I was left with the indelible impression of the intense hatred the common people of this country, even in remote areas, had for people of my pigmentation.

While in their settlement we noted how very precious water was to these villagers in this desolate area. We were shown a nearby dry-as-dust riverbed. In its center was a hole that had been dug to a depth of eight feet. A trickle of water seeped from its base and was being laboriously collected by a young man with a calabash. I was told that the smell of water attracted elephants at night and that when they found the well, they would cave in its sides, and it would have to be laboriously dug again the next day.

To celebrate our visit the villagers passed around a container with an unknown beverage. Alex told me I had to take at least a sip, lest our hosts be insulted. I did and then made a major effort to hide my grimace from imbibing in the fermented bitter liquid.

Upon our return to the camp, we discerned two rhino-like Land Rovers, purveyors of four white Rhodesian police officers. They were unloading the prisoners' weekly provisions of corn meal, chicory coffee, sugar, vegetables, and large jugs of precious water. One of the officers came directly to me and asked: "and who do we have here?" I offered him my diplomatic passport and he took note of its details. He said, "you have the right to be here, but I can't say the government's too bloody happy about your being with this lot." I responded, "they're friends." At that the policeman made another note. He returned to his vehicle for an animated conversation on his radio. Then he snapped at me: "carry on." And off they drove in a cloud of dust.

Before leaving the detention camp, Josiah invited us for a cup of late morning tea, with his inner circle: a professor, an editor, and a pastor. Samuel, the Oxford educated editor commented on our trip to the village. He told us we had witnessed a foray to a settlement amid desolation, calling it the first stone upon which his party wished to build the new Zimbabwe. He called the dialogue with those people, a dialogue with his ancestors. He noted that those villagers were representative of a vast number throughout the country who were largely untouched by the white settlers and deserved help from a government to provide a reliable water source, health clinics and an opportunity for education. He went on to describe how the white settlers had taken over most of the country's arable land, the land of his ancestors. African urban dwellers, he noted, were reduced to servitude and menial tasks. And he spoke of the daily trek endured by workers from the remote overcrowded townships in suffocating buses, on bicycles, and on foot. He concluded by stating: "such hardship is exhausting, but it toughens our people."

The professor added, "call it what it is, slavery pure and simple." He recalled America's Civil War that ended slavery in the U.S. at which time British journalists promoted the opportunities available to British urban masses who were lured by ocean steamers, not to the Americas, but instead to the African Cape and on wagons across the Limpopo where they carved out great Southern Rhodesian farms for themselves. Confronting their great fortune, they thought themselves God's chosen people.

Speaking to a young man among us I asked: "what do you hope to achieve?" He responded with one word: "revenge." Ultimately, there was a heavy dose of that when majority rule was finally attained more than a decade later. Because of the bloody, bitter struggle for majority rule, racial animosity prevailed once independence was achieved. Unlike South Africa, Rhodesia was not blessed with a Mandela or a Bishop Tutu who had managed a peaceful if imperfect transition. That outcome is described by former Zimbabwe leader Robert Mugabe in Martin Meredith's book, *Our Votes, Our Guns: Robert Mugabe and the Tragedy of Zimbabwe.*

The pastor reflected on the heritage of white domination, calling it the exercise of raw power. He noted the European devotion to an idea of democracy was abandoned when dealing with Africa. He called their relationship toward Africans one of conquest, upheaval, control, repression, and the daily humiliation of racial insults enshrined in law. He concluded by saying: "we so much want majority rule that most of us care little for what comes next." And he added that while their struggle was noble, they faced repugnant choices that compromised their fundamental Christian beliefs. His views proved prophetic as a result of the prolonged, racially bitter struggle.

At the end of our two days, we dismantled the tent we had slept in. Each night before bedding down we had carefully surveyed the ground for scorpions and snakes as directed. We then said our goodbyes to the detainees and headed home. The ride back was nowhere as fraught with anxiety as the trip out. I left with the feeling that I had been privileged to spend some time with the future leaders of Rhodesia. I knew their struggle might be long and hard and that some would not survive.

I left hoping that our government could do more than sponsor my symbolic mission but did not expect it would. Upon my return to Salisbury, I briefed the Consulate staff on our mission and was told by the Consul General that Prime Minister Ian Smith, the leader of the White minority regime, had said he was prepared to expel me from Rhodesia. Consul General Geren told him that it would not be necessary as I was to be transferred in a few weeks, suggesting that both sides should regard my trip as if it was at my own initiative. Clearly, I had been chosen for the mission since I was regarded as expendable. A year later after we had been transferred to the Congo, the White Rhodesian settler regime broke with the United Kingdom and issued its Unilateral Declaration of Independence. It would be 15 years and thousands of deaths later before an agreement was reached to bring majority rule to the newly named Zimbabwe.

Years after we left Rhodesia when we were in the very different world of Milan's La Scala, a package arrived one day. Its wrappings were tattered and torn, and it had signs of having travelled from Africa to America and now to Italy in search of us. We opened it to find a shattered record accompanied by a note from Josiah Chimamano's wife. She wrote: "Dear Bob, by now you know that Josiah is dead. He died from the hardships of prison. But he died confident of the righteousness of his cause. I know he wanted to return this recording of *West Side Story* you kindly lent to him. We both enjoyed listening to it many times and hope we did not wear it out. Best wishes to you and your lovely wife Anita." The note ended with: "Zimbabwe shall be free!"

There were some in the United States that strongly supported majority rule in Southern Rhodesia. I was assigned to assist one of them. Distinguished American sociologist and professor at Columbia University, Amitai Etzioni, came to Salisbury on behalf of Americans for Democratic Action (ADA). I arranged for him to meet with two academics at the university with ties to the nationalist movements. When he asked them what they most needed to advance their cause they answered, "weaponry." Etzioni explained that while his group could not provide guns and bullets, they might be able to offer other forms of political help that could be useful.

While in Southern Rhodesia, near the beginning of the space age, we were drawn to a new frontier when our Agency sent an exciting NASA project our way. Two African American lecturers were trained by NASA to tour Africa to lecture about the American space program. The lectures were designed to explain the basic science that made space travel possible and the potential rewards for mankind of our space program and President Kennedy's pledge to reach the moon. The lecturer assigned to Rhodesia was a journalist, John Twitty, who was a skilled and congenial speaker.

We arranged a tour for John carefully assuring that the places we went would have hotel accommodations for Black guests, as most in Rhodesia at that time did not. Twitty's lectures were enhanced by exploding rockets and other spectacular experiments to demonstrate how we planned to go into orbit and eventually to the moon. The demonstrations were particularly exciting for students and designed to encourage their pursuit of science.

Soon after our arrival in Salisbury we encountered a young American journalist. Charles Gusewelle, a reporter with the *Kansas City Star*, was to become a lifelong friend and eventually syndicated columnist and foreign editor of that paper. He came to us stricken with malaria after arriving from Congo Leopoldville. His hotel reservation there had been cancelled by a Belgian manager, furious with America for having opposed the Katanga succession. Gusewelle was obliged to spend the night sleeping on a chair of an outdoor café where he was food for malarial mosquitoes.

As he clearly needed some care, we invited him to stay with us and be healed with the aid of Anita's home cooking. Charles had been told by his paper's editor that something important seemed to be going on in Africa and asked that he cover what was for most Americans, the mysterious continent. He was granted a letter of credit that he could use as needed and developed his own itinerary of the continent. We spent hours in insatiable conversation with him exploring ideas, especially about the Rhodesian situation in the context of the demise of colonialism throughout most of the continent. Our dialogue was to be continued on and off across the decades both in his hometown, Kansas City and in other African countries that he later visited for extended periods, including Senegal and Nigeria.

Towards the end of my time in Salisbury my boss, the PAO Dick Erstein, was transferred and I was left in the hands of an Acting PAO, the Cultural Affairs Officer, with whom I could not get along. As a consequence, he wrote my evaluation in which he assessed that I was "unfit for the Foreign Service." Fortunately, Phillip Dorman, the newly named PAO, assigned to the soon to be independent Zambia, had been a good friend and mentor in Washington and did not agree with that judgment and gave me a chance to prove myself.

The next stop for us was the former Northern Rhodesia which was about to become independent as the Republic of Zambia. Before I was formally assigned to Zambia, I was asked to assist a USIA film crew to document independence ceremonies of the newest independent African state. Anita and I set off for Lusaka in our car and made it halfway before an explosion of the engine caused us to be stranded in the middle of nowhere. After arranging to sell the car for junk, we called the USIS office in Salisbury, and they provided us with another vehicle. As it arrived late in the day, we drove to Lusaka in darkness passing many signs warning of elephant crossings. Despite my lifelong love of pachyderms, we prayed fervently not to come across any in the darkness on the road to Lusaka and our prayers were answered.

We were welcomed to Lusaka by USIS PAO Phil Dorman and his wife Leslie who had befriended me in Washington prior to my departure for Africa. A bad scare shook us shortly after arrival when Anita was hit by a miscarriage. The Dormans were quick to find us medical help that led to her recovery. Soon after, we were able to attend the October 24, 1964, Zambian independence ceremonies which included a State Department provided jazz band. The highlight of the day was the darkening of the stadium and the illumination of the flag of an independent Zambia, a flag composed of a field of green with a hovering eagle, which was raised as the British flag was lowered.

Zambia was off to a fine start with a popular President, Kenneth Kaunda, and rich copper resources. Our main USIS office headed by my boss, PAO Dorman was in the capital, Lusaka. We also had a branch office in Kitwe, the country's economic heartland, its northern Copperbelt. That office had been manned by an officer who was a Japan specialist and had been reassigned to Tokyo, leaving a vacancy.

At that time a PAO conference was held in Lusaka for our USIS officers in the southern Africa region. As I had recently left Salisbury, I was asked by the Director of USIA's African office if we should continue our presence in Rhodesia after a Unilateral Declaration of Independence was declared by the racist government as was anticipated. I answered that I believed we should shut down our USIS presence in Salisbury if that happened in response, much to the fury of the recently installed PAO. Ultimately it was decided that we should keep the office open for the time being. Then I was told it had been decided that I would serve as interim Branch PAO in Kitwe as a temporary replacement until a more senior officer could fill the position. So, after winding up our affairs in Salisbury we set off for Kitwe, Zambia for what would be an eight-month assignment.

Holding the fort in Kitwe was an utterly unique experience. While we inherited a fine house with an attached office wing, I had no staff or cultural center to manage. My mandate was to cover that vital territory consisting of mining towns, among them Ndola, Chingola, Mufulira and Chilliabombwe. The heavy presence of British and South African engineers and copper company managers hadn't changed with independence as they were considered essential to the operation of the mines and central to Zambia's economy. Africanization of key positions was still a long way off. What was palpable was the exuberant mood independence had created with an expectation of good things to come in the wealthiest region of the country.

My beat, in addition to the key mining sector, contained several of the country's national newspapers, headquarters for the key unions which had played an important part in the independence movement, and other institutions of national significance. It also was the site of a major initiative to relocate and provide support for the Zambian youth that had been on the front lines of the independence movement, but subsequently were thought of as "the rock throwers," seen by leaders of the Kaunda government as a potential menace or disruptive force. The youth camp was twenty miles from our Kitwe base. It was clear that while the government owed much to the young radicals, they wanted them in a remote area where they could not make trouble. The problem with the camp's location was that most of those twenty miles of road needed to be negotiated on muck and mire, especially when it rained, and became something that could hardly qualify as a road. Making it a serviceable road was a task assigned to a young British volunteer, Andrew Owen, who had no previous roadbuilding experience. We got to know and like Andrew and encouraged him to do what he could to improve the road, but to no avail. Nevertheless, I decided that a camp of politically active young men could be important and vowed to get to know its inhabitants.

To do so required bone crushing rides in our Chevy carryall over cavernous potholes. My contribution was a generator, films and a 16mm projector that I brought to the camp on numerous evenings to provide much needed diversion to the otherwise neglected youth. Showing American documentaries became a regular occupation on the Copperbelt. On one occasion, we were asked by a Catholic mission to project a series of Disney health documentaries to their community. The audience had never seen a film before, and initially they mobbed the screen and went on its reverse side to see where the images came from. Only after the screening did we learn that much of our audience consisted of lepers.

As Ndola was equal to if not of greater importance than Kitwe, I found I had reason to drive there fairly frequently. The two towns were merely 40 miles apart on a decent two-lane highway. However, during the rainy season the rain came down with fury, flooding the road and limiting visibility to a mere few feet. Complicating the drive even further were the fast-moving trucks carrying heavy timber. Anita and I felt fortunate every time we got home alive.

Not far from our Kitwe home was St. Francis College, a Catholic school run by American Franciscans. When they learned that Anita was a teacher, they pressed her to join the faculty. She agreed. The school was a good one and President Kaunda had sent one of his sons there. When the end of the school year came, Anita had to recommend that the young Kaunda, an outstanding soccer player, but a very poor student, repeat the year since he was failing. His mother, the country's First Lady, came to discuss his situation with my wife who found her understanding and agreeable to the boy's repeating the year. Several years later we learned to our great sadness that the young Kaunda boy had been an early casualty of the AIDS virus.

President Kaunda was a man known for his integrity. One example was reported in the newspapers while we were there. It was recounted that he had sent his car to the homes of several of his Cabinet Ministers who had chosen to abandon their wives in favor of women they considered more appropriate to their newly elevated station in life. Kaunda sent each of them letters urging them not to abandon their former wives.

I was never replaced as USIS representative on the Copperbelt. It turned out that the Soviet embassy had asked for permission to establish an office there as we Americans had. Unwilling to have a superpower competition in that important part of the country, President Kaunda decided that he would not allow any diplomats to have offices there. The U.S. then closed our Salisbury office and I was off to the neighboring Congo.

# IV. The Theft: Our Two Years in Katanga (1964-66)

In late 1965, Elisabethville, capital of the former breakaway Congolese province of Katanga was the next step that followed my first diplomatic assignment in Rhodesia and an interlude of less than a year in Zambia. My wife Anita and I found ourselves transitioning from the euphoria of a newly independent Zambia to the dysphoria of the Congo where we would spend the next two years.

In writing about the many difficulties confronting Nigerians after independence Chinua Achebe took as his title for his classic novel *Things Fall Apart* the words of W.B. Yates from his poem "The Second Coming." While it might describe aspects of Nigerian society the Yates' quote more completely captures the Congo after independence:

> Things fall apart; the centre cannot hold;
> Mere anarchy is loosed upon the world;
> The blood-dimmed tide is loosed and everywhere
> The ceremony of innocence is drowned;
> The best lack all conviction, while the worst
> Are full of passionate intensity.

So much of the violence of Congolese history is best described as anarchy triggered by human greed. The curse of mineral richness has been pervasive both during Belgian rule as captured by Conrad's *Heart of Darkness* and has continued after independence without interruption. The brutal Belgian colonial legacy and its failure to properly prepare the colony for independence left the Congo arguably the least ready for that complex transition. The 1960's were characterized by the presence of mercenaries and rebels as well as a kaleidoscope of foreign interventions motivated by greed without end. There was, in Yates' words, "a passionate intensity" in the search for power in order to control wealth. Endowed with untold mineral wealth, Katanga was famed for its exceedingly rich copper deposits. Copper ore was refined in Elisabethville. Once separated from the copper ore, the waste was piled in a mound that soared over the city like a small mountain. That slag, or discarded ore, was judged to be richer in copper than the ore we mine in Arizona.

Katanga also boasted what was called a geological embarrassment of other mineral deposits. Included was the uranium mined in the western Katanga town of Shinkolobwe, known to be the richest deposit in the world. Uranium from that source was used by the Manhattan Project to produce the first atomic bombs, which not incidentally "loosed a blood-dimmed tide everywhere."

Our arrival in the provincial capital of Elisabethville came at the zenith of the Cold War. For the Congo this engendered continued violence in the struggle between rebels and government forces bolstered by European and South African mercenaries on one side and Soviet support on the other. The country's violent heritage was evident in the faces of those in the streets. Upon our arrival we were housed in the Grand Hotel Leopold Deux, a hotel that had known much better days. It was in no sense grand. It happened that while we were there its employees were on strike. The strikers had broken the windows at the hotel's entrance, and the broken glass remained strewn on the sidewalk, which was patrolled by Katangese gendarmes with automatic weapons who had not been paid. We noted a strange array of people coming and going from the hotel and later learned it was an entrepot for diamond smugglers.

**Bob and Anita with pachyderm**

The involvement of the Soviets and Chinese in support of the various rebellions led to an intense effort on the part of the United States to counter the rebels. We supported the central government in order to assure that the Congo had good relations with us and with our Belgian NATO ally, the past colonial ruler of that country. Former Congolese leader Patrice Lumumba had been assassinated and Moise Tshombe who had led the failed Katanga succession, then surprisingly became the Congo's Prime Minister. American support aimed at unifying a fractious country the size of the U.S. east of the Mississippi was located smack in the center of the African continent. Given its geographical centrality, Congo's instability had implications for at least seven of its neighbors. The turmoil of Congolese politics was dizzying. Such was our experience during our two years there. A semblance of stability, at least at the center of government, was established when U.S. backed Mobutu came to power in 1965.

Promotion of Congolese unity was a central theme of the American Embassy in Leopoldville, roughly a thousand miles from us in Katanga. A motion picture unit was created by USIS in Leopoldville to produce documentaries on that theme entitled *le Congo en Marche*. Furthermore, mobile units were armed with generators and projectors to show the films. A "witch" who had been working with the rebels purportedly with the power to turn the regime's bullets to water was captured by the government. Once in government hands, at our behest, Mama Onema turned her powers against the rebels. Posters were produced, to be scattered by airplane throughout the rebel-controlled areas proclaiming in multiple local languages: "rebels abandon your weapons. Rebels who fail to do so are dead men."

This is an example of the propaganda war waged by the U.S. on behalf of the Mobutu regime. In many ways this campaign proved to be a rehearsal for Vietnam. Such was the chaos of the Congo during our time there. An example of the chaos and the literal mindedness of Congolese officialdom is illustrated by a problem we had in Elisabethville. All hell broke loose after independence. Many Belgians fled the country's chaos abruptly, leaving their dogs to roam about the city. The dogs formed dangerous packs. An order was given to the police to shoot the dogs on sight. We had a dog that we took for walks in the evening. When a policeman encountered us, he raised his rifle and was about to shoot it. I jumped between him and our harmless animal and stopped him, perhaps unadvisedly because we later realized he could have pulled the trigger. Another example was told to me by the Swiss UNESCO representative. In his travels around the country, he distributed books to schools. At one stop the school director accused him of racism. Why? Because he accused him of donating a *la Petit Larousse* which because of its title, he incorrectly assumed was a children's book. A phrase was coined to capture difficult to explain events. With a shoulder shrug one would simply say: "c'est le Congo." Notwithstanding all our problems, the birth of our daughter, Alisa, assured that the Congo would be one of our life's joyous moments.

A crippling event seriously risked harming an already shaky Congolese economy, especially that of the rich mining region of Katanga. The white settler government of Rhodesia was subject to sanctions. Those sanctions starved Katanga of fuel oil since its supply depended on southern Africa. To solve that problem the United States rented Pan Am jet airliners and emptied them of passenger seats to load them with barrels of fuel oil. That fuel was flown from Leopoldville to Elisabethville and was sufficient to compensate for the gasoline blockade by the Rhodesians. The Pan Am flights allowed room for a few passengers. That enabled me and other staffers to hitchhike back and forth across the thousand miles, a distance that was not possible to traverse otherwise by road or rail. Given the cargo, it was a stinky flight. I was pleased, however, that for the months it operated we were able to receive the treat of the Sunday *New York Times* and more importantly, diapers and baby formula for our newborn.

While we were in the Congo, USIA produced a French language version of the film *Years of Lightning, Day of Drums*, a brilliant Hollywood depiction of the three years of the Kennedy administration which was written and directed by Bruce Herschensohn. We arranged to rent Elisabethville's largest theater for the first showing of the film. After the viewing we held a reception for the invitees at our nearby cultural center. Among the attendees was Katanga's governor Godefroid Munongo, a major adversary of the late president Kennedy who had supported United Nations efforts to reintegrate Katanga into the Congo. I was curious to learn of his reaction to the film given that adversarial relationship. His comment: "President Kennedy, he was a man who knew how to use power."

Life in Elisabethville was somewhat more stable than in the rest of the Congo given the powerful control exercised by the Belgian mining company, Union Miniere, and its Congolese supporters. Still there was uncertainty. Our security officer spoke of the prospect of potential evacuations. Only partially tongue-in-cheek, he suggested that in time of trouble we should keep our eye on the local beer factory's chimney. When it stops emitting smoke, he said, it would be time to get out of town.

One delightful dimension of life in Elisabethville was the art scene. I discovered several painters whose work appealed to me. The most interesting was the artist Mwenze Kibwangw. He painted traditional scenes with backgrounds consisting of stripes representing the thatch of the house in which he grew up. Several of my consulate colleagues paid regular visits to his home to collect his work. More than 50 years later an exhibition at the Fondation Cartier in Paris featured his work as part of the development of modern art in the Democratic Republic of the Congo beginning in the 1920's.

The Congo was also noted as among the most important producer of traditional art. Elizabethville had a branch of the country's national museum. During the time when United Nations troops occupied the town, a contingent of its Ethiopian United Nations peacekeeping troops looted the museum. There followed a desperate attempt at retrieval when the museum's Belgian director raced to the town center attempting to buy back his most treasured pieces.

One of Congo's most serious problems was its lack of well-educated people to manage things. At independence, the huge country had among the fewest college graduates of any country in the world. To address this need, USAID decided to provide undergraduate scholarships. It happened that the first wave of successful candidates included students from an American missionary school in the northern Katanga region. As we were the nearest U.S. diplomatic office, the students were asked to travel to Elisabethville to be processed. The first batch consisted of eight students. As most came from a rural area, for them coming to Elisabethville was like coming to a major city like Paris. Our task was to work on their medical and security clearances and have them apply for passports and U.S. student visas before going on to Leopoldville and then to New York where they would disperse to various colleges.

It was a wonder to be with the young men during that period and to imagine how their lives would be transformed. They would have the opportunity for a good university education in a stable environment away from the anarchy of the Congo. The program was designed for them to return home, perhaps at a time when their country was stabilized to enable them to make a meaningful contribution to it. In short, we believed they were the hope for their county's future.

Preparations for their departure might have seemed to be straightforward but proved to be a minefield of difficulties. Those difficulties were heightened when one morning one of the students, Jean Mutamba, ran into my office shouting: "Mr. LaGamma, Mr. LaGamma, they've arrested Mephie." "What happened?" I asked. He told me that a Belgian women had her purse stolen while in the open market. She identified the thief as an African wearing a white shirt. While Mephie and Mutamba were at dinner with a Congolese official after having attended a movie, gendarmes entered carrying automatic weapons and stated that a Belgian woman had her purse stolen by a Congolese wearing a white shirt. Since Mephie was wearing a white shirt, they concluded he was the thief and arrested him. I thought it absurd that the boy I had gotten to know to be honest, one with a golden opportunity before him, would stoop to stealing a purse.

A quick review of Mephie's background convinced me even more as to why such an accusation was totally out of character. After all, he was a student always at the top of his class. School officials and teachers trusted him as evidenced by the many responsibilities that they had bestowed on him. In 1961 he was one of two students selected by the faculty to serve as a YMCA camp counselor in the United States. Having received a scholarship to study in the U.S. a brighter and promising future lay before him. Mutamba and the government official confirmed that they had been with Mephie during the period in question. Notwithstanding, Mephie was thrown into a wretched prison cell, his impending travel to the U.S in jeopardy. We learned that any food he needed would have to be provided from outside the prison, so we got to work on establishing a pipeline to provide him with food. The fundamental problem was that the clock was ticking and without a quick and favorable resolution, he would probably miss his chance at the scholarship.

My priority was to seek an expedited trial that would prove his innocence. At that point I was summoned to our Consul General's office. Consul General Arthur Tienken had heard a version of the story and admonished me for what he charged was "interfering in the internal affairs of a sovereign nation." After explaining to no avail, I held my tongue. To my astonishment, a senior representative of the U.S. government, a government that had ousted Prime Minister Lumumba leading to his death in Katanga and the installation of Mobutu as President of the Congo, had accused me of interfering in that country's internal affairs; or was it "infernal affairs?" It was a time and place in which the concept of human rights held no sway over the doctrine of realpolitik. Full of fury I returned home and told the story to my wife Anita.

Adroit at solving many of my problems, Anita suggested the solution. "We'll ask the Deals." The Deals were American missionaries who had been held hostage by Congo rebels and were recently evacuated to Elisabethville. They had been involved in education and were naturally inclined to help. We contacted them immediately and found them willing to take the plunge and ask the authorities to hold a swift trial.

That day came a week later. The Belgian accuser sat on one side of the courtroom, the accused, Mephie Ngoi on the other. The back door of the courtroom opened and in walked the berobed Congolese judge. The Belgian woman erupted. Rising from her seat and pointing directly, mistakenly, at the judge, she bellowed: "he's the one, he stole my purse." At that it was clear all Congolese looked alike to this Belgian woman. It was evident that she could not identify the culprit. End of trial. Mephie is declared innocent and set free. Two weeks later we put the group on a flight to Leopoldville and presumed all would be well. We were wrong.

To add to their chaotic venture, key documents necessary for their travel to the U.S. including their passports and health and security clearances had been placed in one suitcase which had been lost upon arrival at the airport in Leopoldville. Luckily the lost bag with the vital documents was recovered after having been taken mistakenly by a passenger with an identical bag. Unluckily, once in Leopoldville they were mugged and the money they had been given to tide them over for the week was stolen. Somehow, they found ways of surviving but instead of flying to New York, the Congo government responsible for their travel put them on a freighter. Halfway across the Atlantic the ship was hit by a ferocious storm that lasted three days. The captain, after sending out an S.O.S. somehow managed to keep afloat and on they went to New York. All that misfortune must have seemed to the boys like the fate of Odysseus as he sought to return home. They must have wondered if their misfortunes would never end.

Once in America they did. The tales of what happened to some of the boys after that was told to me many years later by our agricultural attaché to the U.S. Embassy in Pretoria, South Africa. Besa Kotati had been one of the students we sent to the U.S. Besa had earned his PhD, became an American citizen, gone to work at the Department of Agriculture and then had been named Agriculture Attaché to Southern Africa. Mephie after having earned his B.A. from a small college, earned a Master's and PhD in Chemistry, and taught at the State University of New York at Buffalo. He concluded his career at Northwestern University designing a science program for gifted American high school students.

After years of attempting to contact Dr. Mephie Ngoi, I finally found his phone number in Evanston, Illinois. We were at last connected after a half a century and reminisced during an hour's conversation. I learned that he had returned to the Congo. He attempted to find meaningful work in that chaotic environment and was given a position as chairman of the chemistry department at a college in Kinshasa. The college reneged on its promise to provide him with housing. It took eleven months before he received his first salary payment. After all that time of not having been paid Mephie decided to ask his American wife to accompany him to the college business office. After joining him in the office, the agent suddenly claimed to find Mephie's salary in an office drawer. After two years on the job, he and his wife decided to return to the U.S.

The saga of African students coming to America is exemplified by a book written by Legson Kayira, a student from Malawi, entitled *I Will Try*. The title is taken from his response to friends and family who were skeptical of his ability to attain his dream. Inspired by a book about Abe Lincoln, in 1958 he embarked on foot on an epic 1800-mile journey across Africa to seek a college education in America. After crossing the African continent by land, he had found a way to win a scholarship. He eventually graduated from the University of Washington and then went on to the U.K. for graduate study. Subsequently, upon his return to Malawi he became a minister in its government.

President Obama's father tenaciously found his way from Kenya to a scholarship in Hawaii. Ghanaian educator James Kwegyir Aggrey was a pioneering advocate of having his countrymen go to the U.S. for college education. Aggrey, the Booker T. Washington of Africa, was a passionate believer in the fundamental importance of education to investing in the success of African countries. He was responsible for arranging for the education of Kwame Nkrumah, the founding father of Ghana's independence, and Nnamdi Azikiwe, Nigeria's first President among others. Aggrey's African American son, Rudy Aggrey, remained in the U.S. and went on to become a distinguished American Ambassador.

The quest for an American university education was widespread across Africa. In 1960, Kenyan labor leader Tom Mboya appealed to then Senator John F. Kennedy to arrange for scholarships for Kenya students. That request led to what was called "the Kennedy airlift "which brought more than 200 East African students to the U.S. where they were provided with financial support and tuition waivers to attend college. In subsequent years, thousands of Ethiopian students arranged to study at American universities. Furthermore, in later years the Nigerian oil boom also made it possible for that country's government to fund and place a large body of students in U.S. colleges and universities.

USAID ran an excellent African scholarship program beginning in the 1960's which evolved from the undergraduate to the graduate level, and USIA managed a smaller, highly selected Fulbright program. Yet the U.S. government failed to significantly meet Africa's much larger need and appetite for higher education in America. Since our Fulbright program was worldwide in scope, it placed African candidates in a greatly inferior position in such a highly competitive academic selection process. For that reason, I later proposed a program for young African government officials that would provide them with a year of combined academic courses blended with a hands-on practical work experience in a relevant field. It was adopted by the U.S. Information Agency. It was called the Hubert H. Humphrey program and while it initially focused on Africa, it later was expanded worldwide.

While back in Washington, after our Congo years, I was assigned to what USIA called its Phase II training and familiarization program for officers who had completed their first overseas tours. Bur prior to beginning that program Africa was again calling.

# V. Niamey Interlude: A Turning Point

Following my assignments to Rhodesia, Zambia, and the Congo, I returned to USIA headquarters to be based initially at its Office of African Affairs, only to learn I was needed for a short-term job in Africa. It seemed there would be a vacancy in Niamey, Niger for some ten weeks and Robert Ryan, our ambassador to Niger, a poor country on the edge of the Sahara had asked for a replacement until a Public Affairs Officer was available. I accepted the assignment even though I would have to leave my wife Anita who was pregnant with our second child.

Our African Office, always committed to saving a dollar, booked my flight to Niamey accordingly. Since the U.S. provided substantial assistance to Tunisia, it had an accumulation of Tunisian dinars that could be partially reimbursed by having American officials use Tunis Airways. So it was that itinerary that took me from Washington to New York where I would get a flight to Paris. The next morning, I had to fly to Tunis where I would overnight before flying back to

Paris and from there on to my destination. I would not recommend that routing to anyone. Landing in Niamey utterly exhausted, I did enjoy seeing Niger's gracefully grazing giraffes and camels on the way from the airport to town.

Having experienced some of southern and central Africa, what I first saw of Niger's desert terrain contrasted with the moderate mile high climates of Rhodesia, Zambia, and Katanga. It gave me yet another understanding of the incredible diversity of the continent. I was intrigued to have the opportunity to explore the Sahara's edge. What I most looked forward to was the opportunity to manage a USIS post for the first time. Previously, I had reported to senior USIS officers. After meeting and being briefed by Ambassador Robert Ryan, I found I would be working for a consummate professional, an ambassador who appreciated what USIS had to offer, one who also shared my own enthusiasm for the work in Africa. This was especially the case since I was replacing an officer steeped in East European experience, one nearing retirement and not fond of a country that he considered to be at the end of the earth.

Niamey was not yet even close to being a high U.S. priority (the discovery of rich uranium deposits later increased its importance to us). USIS was nonetheless a small but well-rounded and appreciated operation. It consisted of a heavily patronized American library located across from the central market, an educational and cultural exchange program, and an English language program for the country's French speakers. One of our students was the country's President, Hamani Diori, who previously had been taught by Peace Corps volunteers but was preparing for a visit to the U.S. and at that time

The author in Niger

lacked a teacher. I volunteered to fill the gap and was rewarded by having one-on-one weekly meetings with one of Africa's finest statesmen and a kind and generous individual.

The population of Africa was afflicted with many illnesses but in the 1960's the World Health Organization launched a campaign to eradicate the scourges of measles and smallpox. It arguably proved to be one of the most profound successes in public health history. The U.S. Center for Disease Control (CDC), with the support of USAID, played a major role in that campaign with the help of newly developed jet injectors, instead of feared vaccination needles. I learned that northern Niger and nomadic caravans that crossed the

Sahara were thought to be one source of spreading those diseases. A CDC team was at that time vaccinating nomads in that region. Together with a United Nations pilot and a Peace Corps photographer, I flew north to Agadez on the Sahara in a small private plane to produce photos and film the vaccination campaign. Halfway to our destination I asked the pilot how he navigated. He pointed at a narrow dirt road below and said, "I follow it." As we approached the town, we spotted a landmark, a mosque known as the world's tallest mud brick building. Rather than landing directly, the pilot had to radio the airport tower to ask that they kindly remove the cattle and camels grazing on the runway.

The next morning, we met with the CDC team after a scorching drive across the desert on a hundred-degree day. The team explained the difficulty they had confronted in vaccinating desert nomads. Initially, they set up camp in a place the nomadic herds would ordinarily pass. But they found that the nomads would simply alter course to avoid them. They ultimately succeeded in attracting them by making it known that in exchange for getting painlessly vaccinated they would provide aspirin and malaria pills. It worked! Clearly these doctors were among the most courageous in their profession, working as they were under the harshest conditions. Without doubt, their success saved countless lives.

After a flight back to Niamey I took some time to visit its renowned museum. It had been developed by an Italian architect who understood that a traditional Western style museum would have little appeal to Africans. Instead, while he did build a pavilion in which there were artifacts in cases containing objects of the local culture, the main attractions of the museum were an outdoor theater where local musicians would perform on weekends, and a small zoo containing giraffes and other indigenous animals. Another ingenious highlight was a half dozen traditional mud structures each containing traditional dress and woven textiles of ancient and more recent vintage, as well as spears, swords and other fine metal and leatherwork of the region. I was much taken by the concept of the museum and how it successfully attracted local citizens as well as tourists and educated them about Niger's diverse cultural heritage. Yet another feature of the museum was a craft village where artisans were housed and produced artifacts that were available for sale.

Throughout my days in Niamey, I received a steady stream of letters from my wife Anita who I missed intensely since it was the first time since our marriage that we were separated. Our time in Africa had sensitized her to racism beyond anything we had previously understood, an issue which was dominating the news back home. She kept me informed about the dynamic Civil Rights movement and some of the protests and rioting that were taking place in reaction to discrimination. She said she felt the Americans we had known in Africa, especially those in white dominated Rhodesia and neocolonial Congo needed to better understand the impact of racial discrimination. She informed me she was assembling a collection of news items that reflected racist terms and insensitivities to share with those Americans who were out of touch with offensive terms and behavior. She also wrote to me about one-year-old Alisa who missed me and called her missing father BobBob. She related how curious and focused Alisa had become, and how she had mastered the art of walking. She also gave me a status report on her pregnancy with what was soon to become our second child, Matthew.

The Niger experience was a turning point in my career. That assignment confirmed my long-term commitment to serving in Africa. It led to my decision to request a year of African Studies at Boston University where I earned my Master's degree in International Relations with a focus on Africa.

At the end of my ten weeks in Niger, Ambassador Ryan asked me to stay on in Niamey as Public Affairs Officer. I was honored to be asked and it would have tempted me had I not needed to return to my wife Anita and meet our new son Matthew.

Hugh Masekela in the U.S

Upon return to Washington, I was assigned to a rotational training program to learn how various Agency elements provide support to our overseas posts. Its aim was to convey an understanding of all aspects of the Agency over the course of two years. The program cycled us for a month in each of the major elements of the organization. Among my most vivid memories was my time in the motion picture division. There I helped put the finishing touches on Agency produced documentary films. One of these films aimed at instilling an understanding among foreign audiences of American political processes. It featured the 1967 election of mayor of Cleveland, Ohio's, Carl Stokes, one of the first Black mayors of a major American city. One of my contributions was to give the film a name. I called it "Cleveland Makes a Choice." My main job in the film unit was to help produce a documentary on the young South African jazz trumpeter, Hugh Masekela. He was performing in Los Angeles where he had a home in Malibu. Masekela had sought refuge in the U.S. to avoid arrest because of his vocal opposition to apartheid. We filmed his concert at a leading nightclub in L.A. which became part of a documentary film series telling the story of successful Africans in the U.S.

Another stop on my USIA rotation was a month with the Voice of America's Africa Service. That time fired my imagination with the understanding that our broadcasts had an impact on daily audiences of millions throughout the African continent with not only its broadcasts in English, but also its French, Portuguese, Arabic, Swahili, Hausa, and Amharic services. At the conclusion of my rotations, I opted to spend a full year at VOA. My job there was to serve on the Africa news desk where together with three journalists, we prepared the news programs based on wire service materials and reports from our own Africa based correspondents. It was a thrilling experience, to write news stories that we then heard broadcast less than an hour later to listeners in more than fifty countries. I found it required severe discipline and adherence to fact.

It was the time of the Nigerian Civil War. The tragic happenings, the loss of tens of thousands of lives and the massive starvation of civilians in breakaway Biafra, too often led our newscasts. But we were also aware national unity was vital to African countries. The provincial succession as had been attempted in the Congo, could inspire others throughout the continent where borders had been arbitrarily drawn by European colonial powers. The head of our desk was a seasoned journalist, Fred Brown, who skillfully avoided the pitfalls of the propaganda from both sides. The omnipresent propaganda often maligned and distorted the U.S. posture on the war. That posture was that the U.S. remained neutral and was working toward a peaceful resolution while providing food aid to the starving Biafrans. Writing news that I could hear broadcast a half hour later was an exhilarating experience. With the help of Fred, an excellent editor, I learned more about writing in a year than I had in four years of college. During my time at VOA, we experienced the tragic assassination of Dr. Martin Luther King Jr. Of course, it dominated the news that we broadcast to Africa. At one point one of our colleagues on the news desk left me dumbfounded by asking: "why are we giving so much attention to him?" I never spoke to her again. When I left the office to get my car I found its windshield had been broken by rioters who swept the neighborhood.

Toward the conclusion of my time at VOA, I still had one more year before going back overseas. Since I had determined I would seek another African assignment, I applied for a year of university study to be enrolled in an African studies program. I chose Boston University which had one of the country's oldest, most venerable programs. It was headed by Professor Alfonso Castagno who I had met while in the Congo. Professor Castagno helped me map out a program for the academic year.

Since the African Studies Program at Boston was linked to Harvard and MIT, he suggested and I agreed, to take a graduate course at Harvard offered by two eminent Africanists They were, a veteran historian of colonial Africa, Rupert Emerson and a younger political scientist, Martin Kilson. As it was the time of Vietnam protests our seminar had a number of radical members from the SDS organization. At one point during an Emerson lecture, I recall he was interrupted by one of them who challenged the professor as being too understanding of the colonial powers. Emerson, without missing a beat, rejoined that the student had made an interesting point. But he suggested he might wish to read... And then he reeled off a number of works and their chapters. That student and others would henceforth no longer interrupt his lectures unless they were very sure of themselves.

Castagno helped me structure my studies to aim at what I could accomplish in two semesters and one summer. Castagno also asked if I had ever taken a course on the philosophy of Aristotle which he urged I take to broaden my knowledge of political theory. I could see that the year would be challenging, even exhilarating. Another invaluable resource at the Boston African Studies Center was Édouard Bustin, a Belgian Africanist and foremost authority on the Congo and francophone Africa. Having recently served in the Congo, I found him to be an excellent mentor and someone I continued to interact with for many years. Exhilaration at spending a year in Boston was greatly enhanced by the birth of our third child, Therese Ariana.

A dominating theme of my Boston year was the anti-Vietnam war movement. Boston, a town of notable academic institutions, was at that time boiling over with anti-war protests. To understand that movement better, I felt compelled to study with one of its leading exponents, Howard Zinn, a leading anti-war activist historian. Zinn a most congenial individual who often had students to his home, offered a leftist course in contemporary American history that I signed up for. His position on American history was expressed in his *People's History of the United States* which looked at history from the perspective of the minorities and the working class. I found Professor Zinn to be a dynamic scholar who sought to rediscover our history in innovative ways. He was in the forefront of the Vietnam anti-war movement and his mild and congenial manner would erupt into a charismatic personality when he left the classroom to address packed college stadiums.

My year in Boston was a year during which anti-establishment protests erupted forcefully into my Africa field of studies. During that year I attended the Montreal annual African Studies Conference. During that conference North American scholars of Africa were challenged by African American protesters who sought to disrupt panels and questioned the legitimacy of white professors whose field of study was Africa. It was ironic that this challenge was directed at many progressive professors, some of whom had been leaders in the anti-colonialist and anti-apartheid movements.

While at Boston University I learned that I had been assigned as Public Affairs Officer to Conakry, Guinea, a most challenging assignment given Guinea' radical regime. It had been the only former African French colony to break with France at independence. Two months after learning of that assignment I received a call cancelling it and assigning me instead to Abidjan as Cultural Affairs Officer. It seems that our Ambassador to Conakry insisted that the PAO had to be an African American. While I regretted not getting the Conakry assignment, Abidjan had the virtue of having become the most prosperous of the former French colonies in the immediate post-independence period.

# VI. American Legends Come to Africa (1970-72)

We arrived in Abidjan, Ivory Coast in 1970 where I was to serve a two-year assignment, as Cultural Attaché. Anita was expecting our fourth child and I was accompanied by Alisa, Matthew, Therese and our teenage niece, Diane. That job involved managing a variety of educational and cultural exchange programs. Our dwelling, which originally had been intended for the PAO who rejected it, was spacious and set upon the top of a hill with a long sloping lawn. Early on our gardener brought me a dead black mamba he killed in our garden. Without foreseeing the consequences, I asked him to alert other gardeners in nearby houses that I would give the equivalent of ten dollars for every dead snake they could bring to me. Two days later our gardener brought me a half dozen. I realized that this trade in dead snakes could accelerate without my knowing for certain where the corpses came from so I ended the system of bounties.

Besides the exchange programs, my responsibilities involved arranging activities for Americans coming to the Ivory Coast for public lectures and encounters with Ivoirians. Notable was the visit of a group of American civil rights activists including several close colleagues of the recently slain Dr. Martin Luther King during a time of racial turmoil in the U.S. The group was headed by Hosea Williams of the Southern Christian Leadership Conference (SCLC), a man who claimed he had been arrested for non-violent protests more than any other civil rights activist. Another visit was that of the ten-day tour of the large Amherst College Glee Club, one of the finest American university choirs.

Hosea Williams and his SCLC colleagues had obviously been recruited before the tragic assassination of Dr. King when it was thought they might present a picture of progress of the movement to secure equal rights for African Americans. Instead, their presentations to Ivoirian audiences were predictably bitter and pessimistic. As a result, the audiences heard, and the press coverage reflected an unattractive picture of an America still struggling with racism. Our one positive result from their visit was that we credibly portrayed a time of reversal and a sad chapter in our history which we sought to overcome in the wake of a martyred Dr. King.

Perhaps the most impactful and unusual set of visits were the coming to Abidjan of some of the most acclaimed all-time U.S. Black athletic stars: one of our tennis greats, members of a championship National Basketball team, and one of the most celebrated American athletes ever to compete in the Olympics. I was awed and honored to have been responsible for those visits to Abidjan.

27-year-old Arthur Ashe came to Africa to stimulate interest in tennis. Ashe came across as a consummate professional, a great champion and not incidentally, an icon of our civil rights movement, and arguably our most outstanding male African American tennis player

The author with Arthur Ashe in the Ivory Coast

of all time. To the young Ivoirians he met, he was clearly an inspirational figure.

Not long after two other visits by American sports heroes followed Ashe to Abidjan. They were the soon to be crowned NBA champs, Kareem Abul Jabbar, Oscar Robinson, and coach Larry Costello of the Milwaukee Bucks. Kareem had only recently starred in professional basketball and had just converted to Islam. Further, he was traveling with his new bride. Robinson was an all-star veteran and a gracious individual and was especially keen to interact with young Africans. They also conducted training sessions with young Ivoirians in a sport that was to become more popular in Africa in years to come. Both Robinson and Kareem also exemplified the centrality of African Americans in sports.

While the visits of the tennis and basketball greats made an impact, a third visit was immensely historic. It came about when the United States moved into a new embassy in downtown Abidjan. The new site was on a short street with no name. Our ambassador, John Root, thought it a good idea to ask the Ivoirian President if he could propose the name of a particularly revered American for the street.

Jesse Owens in Abidjan

President Houphouet-Boigny responded that he agreed and would put it on the agenda for his next cabinet meeting.

A week later he contacted the ambassador and provided a name. The consensus of his cabinet was that the street should be named Rue Jesse Owens. The ambassador agreed that it would be an appropriate choice and asked why it had been chosen. The President responded that many of his ministers had been young village boys in 1936 when Owens stunned the world. They always remembered his gold medal victories in Hitler's Germany that undermined the doctrine of Nazi racial superiority and its concept of the Master Race. We were surprised to learn that news of that triumph had reached the huts and villages of Africa in an age when world news was not known to spread so widely. Once the name of our street was decided, I was asked by Ambassador Root if we could arrange for Owens himself to come to Abidjan to preside over the naming ceremony. I responded that I would contact my friend Mal Whitfield to invite him.

Whitfield who had himself been a three-time gold medal winner in track in the 1948 and 1952 Olympics, had been engaged by USIA to serve as its sport's ambassador to Africa. Jesse Owens had been Mal's mentor, arranging for his athletic scholarship to Ohio State University. After a distinguished career as a Tuskegee airman in World War II, Whitfield took on the role of the U.S. Africa Sports Ambassador based in Egypt, Uganda, and Kenya over a 47-year period during which he was instrumental in developing African track stars. In that capacity he arranged for over 5,000 scholarships for African athletes to be trained at American universities.

Mal welcomed the idea of honoring Owens in Abidjan and quickly came back with his acceptance. The visit of Jesse Owens to Abidjan was front page news for a week. His story was celebrated by a vast array of Ivorians from the young to the President. Jesse Owens himself was especially gratified that Africans would value his reputation for his anti-racist accomplishment. This was important to him since his reputation had been tarnished among Black Americans in the U.S. because Jesse had criticized the symbolic black power protest at the 1968 Olympics, because of his conviction that politics should be left out of the Olympics.

Another rather remarkable visit to Abidjan in 1972 was that of choirmaster Bruce McGinnis who led the Amherst College glee club, one of America's oldest and most outstanding university choral groups. That visit was part of a world tour. It presented several unique problems especially that of keeping a group of some several dozen young men healthy and safe when travelling in Africa.

First and foremost, I had to ensure that none contracted malaria. Further, since the tour would include the northern city of Korhogo and the president's hometown and future capital, Yamoussoukro, logistics were critical to the tour's success. We were faced with the need for transportation, housing and critically, bottled water and safe food. We were lucky that since school was out, Korhogo's student dorms were made available to us. Inspecting them, I found the windows were not screened and so we had to provide and install screening and thoroughly spray the dorms with insecticide. Despite our best efforts, we had no ability to prevent a case of appendicitis and had to arrange for the medical evacuation and hospitalization of one student that came down with a case.

After a successful concert in Korhogo it was on to President Houphouet-Boigny's hometown, Yamoussoukro, a city of monumental public buildings and schools where we would be housed in American style motels. In its vast airconditioned Catholic cathedral, reputed to be larger than St. Peter's in Rome, the students performed at a Sunday mass attended by President Houphouet-Boigny. Finally, we arranged for the choir to perform at a meeting of the Parliament in Abidjan. It turned out, despite my concerns, that we were able to overcome many barriers to create a uniquely successful visit.

Yet another musical event not on the scale of the choir's multitude, was that of Barry Fulton, an African American singer of Negro spirituals. Barry was based in Paris and had mainly sung in a number of European countries before being discovered by our African Regional Service office in Paris. He subsequently toured a number of African countries under USIA's auspices. One of Barry's concerts was to be held at the Ambassador's residence. Ambassador Root asked that I scope out and arrange the room and position the piano. I arrived to find that the piano needed moving and together with a local staffer, we proceeded to attempt to position it. Never having moved a piano before, I believed we should simply glide it across the floor. One push led to catastrophe. One leg of the piano was not fastened to its frame. The noise as it fell was not out of Mozart. I believed that not only was the concert to be cancelled, but that the piano was dead. We managed to raise it off the floor and connect the leg properly. I then had an inspiration. One of the ambassador's sons played the piano. He was outside in the garden. We called him in, explained what had happened and asked him to play something, anything. He did and said the piano was fine. That evening Barry was in fine voice and the spirituals, with their African roots, was enjoyed by all.

While gratified at the three exciting visits from the world of sports and that of the musical ambassadors, world politics intervened to threaten my career in the Foreign Service. Just before leaving for Ivory Coast, we had a neighbor in Arlington, Virginia who invited us for dinner. That neighbor was a lawyer who happened to oppose the war in Vietnam. As we were leaving after dinner, he offered me a bumper sticker for my car in the form of a peace symbol. It seemed acceptable to me to display it there and I thought nothing more about it until our embassy's DCM in Abidjan asked that I come to his office. DCM Cunningham, a rather conservative and authoritarian diplomat, had been told of my peace symbol and considered it a critique of U.S. policy. He ordered that I remove it. I refused and responded that I had a right to my own opinions, noting there was nothing controversial about the universal sign for peace. I told him that no Ivoirian to my knowledge had raised the issue or interpreted that bumper sticker as a criticism of my government.

Aware that my refusal could lead to my expulsion from my position, I was uneasy for several weeks until an inspection team from the State Department arrived in Abidjan. At a reception we attended for the inspectors my wife, Anita, spoke to the two lead inspectors about my dilemma. The next day I was told by the inspectors that they had advised the DCM and the ambassador that they should not pursue the issue. End of problem.

Three weeks of the entire U.S. Abidjan Mission's time was devoted to an unexpected visitor. We learned that as part of a tour of Africa, First Lady Pat Nixon was coming to Abidjan. The White

House apparently made the rather unusual request that the visit should be treated as if she was a head of state. The Ivoirian government at first evinced reluctance to accord that status, they eventually relented and pulled out all the stops. The main event was a picnic offered in a rain forest not far from Abidjan. To prevent any risks to Mrs. Nixon, a substantial area of the forest was sanitized to banish insect life and other critters. While it was designed to convey Africa's environment, the event was typical of Ivoirian distaste for their traditional habitat. A second theatrical event staged during the visit was a cocktail offered at the top of the twenty-third floor of the iconic Hotel Ivoire. To add a touch of Africa to the event, traditional Ivoirian musicians would play for Mrs. Nixon. A sign of the rapid changes underway in Ivoirian society was apparent as I ascended to the top of the tower on an elevator with several of those musicians who apparently were unnerved by the contraption that they had never experienced before and that raised us to the top of the city.

Perhaps the most enduring memory of Abidjan was the intense post-colonial grip of the French on an independent francophone African country. The Ivory Coast had not begun to be prosperous until a few years before independence when the French opened the lagoon to the sea. At that point Abidjan became a major West African port and production of coffee and cocoa thrived. Exports of timber and agricultural products expanded rapidly. Given this burst of economic growth, French priorities in West Africa switched to Ivory Coast from its previous favorite child, Senegal.

As Ivoirians at independence had a relatively low educational level, the French sought to meet the county's many needs by providing expertise needed throughout the government. That was reflected in the great number of French technical assistance experts known as *cooperants* including schoolteachers at every level as well as at the university. Cooperants were ensconced in every key ministry as well as the presidency. They were seen as purveyors of the orthodoxy of French culture, which was not to be deviated from.

One attempt to do so came to me in the form of a French cooperant who asked if the American Cultural Center would host the production of a play he planned to produce by the French playwright Eugene Ionesco. When I asked why he wasn't offering it to the French Cultural Center, he explained that their schedule was full. I agreed with the condition that they would cover whatever costs were involved and handle the administrative side. He returned to tell me the play was off. He had been told by the French embassy that if he produced the Ionesco play at the American Cultural Center, he would be expelled from the country. It seemed odd to me. Even if the French felt Ionesco was not a good symbol of their culture, I felt the main reason for their opposition was that the young man had involved the Americans in something they had rejected.

We found the reluctance to deal with aspects of American culture at the University of Abidjan reflected in the efforts to introduce African American literature into the curriculum of the University's English Department. Its head, Professor Christophe Dailly, had encountered resistance when he attempted to teach African literature. He expressed his frustration to me because there was a stranglehold of French culture throughout the curriculum. After many years when Dailly became Dean of his faculty, he was able to make the breakthrough. While I was in Abidjan, I offered to provide Fulbright professors to the University. It seemed that the one field they were interested in was computer science. We were able to find Dr. Ernest Chabot, a young French speaking American, to teach that subject.

The domineering presence of the French occasionally went too far for the Ivoirians to tolerate. One example was a strike of university students. President Houphouet-Boigny ordered the police to occupy the university to put down campus demonstrations. The University of Abidjan's Rector was French. He called the President and reminded him that in the French tradition police were not allowed to violate the sanctity of the campus. He then told the President to kindly remove his police from the university campus. The President's response was to remind the Rector that he was the President. He then ordered the Rector to remove himself from the Ivory Coast and an Ivoirian was named in his place.

Nonetheless, it was usually government policy that Ivoirians should regard most things French as indispensable models. There was a French military presence in the country, and it was understood that Ivory Coast was one of the West African governments that the French would protect against the kind of military takeovers that plagued other francophone regimes.

The prosperity of Abidjan was reflected in the five-star Hotel Ivoire which boasted tropical Africa's only ice rink, a huge swimming pool, a cinema, one of Africa's finest shops selling African traditional art and an adjacent 23 story tower. Around it was planned a spectacular "African Riviera." But most dramatic, as one arrived from the airport, was the recently built skyline of Abidjan with its modern tall buildings. When one day I picked up an American labor leader at the airport who was to lecture on the American labor movement, he was struck by that skyline and then turned to me and said: "this is not an independent country." I asked why he said that. He responded that no developing country could possibly have enough technicians to repair the elevators of all those tall buildings. He was right. Abidjan was even dependent upon French elevator repair men.

A story was told, possibly apocryphal, that Houphouet, once a Minister in the French government, had developed a great admiration for all things French. Returning one evening from the airport after a trip to France, the Ivoirian President noted that there were painted lines that separated the traffic lanes on the road from the airport into Abidjan. Upon his arrival at the palace, he was reputed to have called his Minister responsible for roads to ask if there were lines separating the lanes to the Paris airport. After some research he learned there were not. He then ordered that the lines on his road to the airport be removed. They were, resulting in a high accident rate.

A young American Yale student and Rhodes scholar, Timothy Weiskel, who was completing his doctorate came to Abidjan after Oxford University Press published his book *French Colonial Rule and the Baule Peoples: Resistance and Collaboration, 1899-1911*. The book's cover depicted the decapitation of a Baule chief by a French soldier. Given the commotion around the subject, Ivoirian television invited Weiskel for an interview. The explosive reminder of the brutality of French colonialism created an uproar among the French who had sought to paper over that aspect of their history in Ivory Coast.

Another American scholar, a PhD candidate from NYU, Susan Vogel, came to Ivory Coast to do her doctoral research on the rather spectacular art of the Baule people. Susan and her mother began their time in the country by staying with us before taking off for a village in the Baule region. After earning her doctorate Susan went on to serve as curator for African Art at New York's Metropolitan Museum of Art. My own daughter Alisa, after earning her doctorate from Columbia University, later assumed that same role. Dr. Vogel, after leaving the Met, founded the pioneering Center for African Art in New York City. She then served as Director of the Yale Art Gallery where she organized an acclaimed exhibition of Baule art accompanied by an award-winning catalogue. Susan Vogel had been married to Jerome Vogel who had served as a Fulbright scholar in Ivory Coast and later headed Operation Crossroads Africa, a major exchange program funded in large part by USIA. Crossroads arranged for American students to work on assistance projects in Africa and for Africans to travel to the U.S. Jerry, an important contributor to the relationship between the U.S. and Africa, became a close friend over many years as our paths crossed often both in Washington and in a number of African countries.

President Houphouet-Boigny was himself Baoule and as his country's founding President aspired for his hometown of Yamoussoukro to replace Abidjan as the country's capital. Airconditioning, so essential to tropical Africa, was installed at exorbitant cost to cool the vastness of its cathedral, that contrary to the wishes of the Vatican, was deliberately built to exceed the size of St. Peter's. A monumental building was constructed to house the ruling party. So was the new presidential palace. Since France had institutions of higher education known as "Grandes Ecoles" so would Yamoussoukro. Their goal was to produce a governmental and business elite, just like the French, that the country lacked. Some years after my assignment to Abidjan, I returned to visit the Grandes Ecoles. I was invited to lunch by the director of one of them. We were served the finest French champagne accompanied by agouti, or bush rat, considered by Ivoirians as a delicacy.

A story was told about a conversation in which Houphouet, revealing his strong regard for his French connection, spoke of Guinea's president, Sekou Touré at the time Sekou broke with France fearing continued French domination. The Ivoirian President reportedly noted sadly that "poor Sekou," as a result of his break with France, would never again walk down the Champs Elysée.

For the first time in Africa our children's education was a concern. We lived in the Abidjan suburb of Cocody, just a few blocks from the large French School, Jean Mermoz. Since our eldest child Alisa was just entering kindergarten, we thought we'd enroll her there so she would gain some level of fluency in French. Her teacher proved utterly inflexible and she was miserable. After a few days we decided to take her out of that environment. But then what? We found a small school for African children, the Nid de Cocody. There the Ivoirian principal was delighted we wished to enroll her, as it seemed that no non-Ivoirian student had ever been enrolled there. As a consequence, Alisa had an excellent year and a very special experience among Ivoirian children who were very kind to her. The brightest spot during our tour in Abidjan was the birth of our fourth child, Adrian.

One of our most memorable trips while in Ivory Coast was to the northern town of Korhogo. The town is known for its unique Korhogo cloth produced by the Senufo ethnic group and based on traditional designs, motifs, and symbols. We witnessed how the cotton cloth was stretched on the ground after the images of birds, lizards and other shapes were made of mud pigments and then covered with dark ink. The images derive from Senufo mythology and we were told that early in their history they were used as funeral coverings. Their creation as a decorative art form was encouraged by American Peace Corps Volunteers and Catholic nuns. We purchased several of them, and framed one which has covered our entire family room wall for decades.

Another voyage that we made from time to time was to the coastal town of Grand Bassam. A coconut palm fringed coast road ran to it from Abidjan. Along the way the beaches were strewn with huts used mainly by the French as places for weekend getaways. We often stopped along the way when we saw clusters of boys at the base of the palms. For the equivalent of a dime, they would skillfully shimmy up a tree and cut down coconuts. With several whacks of a machete, they would remove their husks and open them to their milk which we would find a refreshing drink. As an alternative to coconuts, there were women along the way holding pineapples which they too would hack away with machetes and hand to us by their stalks. We would stop along the way for a picnic and a dip in the ocean or push on to the old colonial town for a lunch of fresh shrimp. It all made for a delightful Sunday. My idyllic memories of Grande Bassam are difficult to reconcile with the news in 2016 of the massacre of 19 people for which Al Qaeda took credit.

My memories of Abidjan are filled with travels on roads dominated and made dangerous by logging trucks. Years later I met an American missionary based in the country's north who recalled flying to Abidjan often. He remembered that in the 1960s his plane traversed a continuous forested terrain. He noted that by the 1990's the same plane flew over a land made desolate by French lumber companies. That same desolation has also spread over the francophone countries of central Africa, especially the once lush rainforest of Gabon.

Toward the end of my assignment in Abidjan I was contacted by my old boss at the Voice of America in Washington. He asked if I would take on the assignment of West African correspondent for VOA. I declined since it would have left Anita and the children alone a good bit of the time as I would be expected to travel around the region. It was a tempting opportunity otherwise.

From Abidjan, it was on to Milan, Italy, but first there was the matter of home leave, a perennial issue for foreign service officers especially those with families. With our four children and at a time when I was still a relatively junior officer, the question was compounded by affordability. But then came an offer seemingly from the heavens. I learned that the Wally Bynum Foundation each year offered several foreign service officers the use of an airstream trailer and station wagon. The program was designed to acquaint U.S. communities with our work in representing the U.S. abroad during the summer months. Assuming there would be fierce competition, I worked hard on my application explaining why I should be an ideal candidate. A month went by and I was informed that due to the lack of applicants the program was suspended and the trailers would instead be given to foreign journalists during the bicentennial year. I was astonished that I seemed to have been the only applicant. To make matters worse, I was tasked with recruiting an Italian journalist to participate in the program.

# VII. Fast Moving and Sophisticated: Six Italian Years

Towards the end of my two years in Abidjan it was time to bid on my next assignment. While I still considered myself an Africanist, one potential assignment attracted my attention. Milan, Italy had a vacancy. As it was the land of my ancestors, a place about which I was ignorant but one I wished passionately to experience, I asked to be considered for the job as deputy in the USIS Milan office.

My wife Anita and I had previously overnighted in Milan during a vacation. We wandered past the great opera house, La Scala and came upon a bookstore, Feltrinelli's, where a passionate debate was raging. I was impressed by the intellectual fervor of that scene. But that fervor reminded me that Milan was the birthplace of both Italian Fascist and Communist parties. For better or worse Milan was at the cutting edge of so much that was Italian and even European. An article in the Paris *Herald Tribune* noted that Milan had more contemporary art galleries than Paris. And it was notable as one of the world's leading design centers.

Especially important for our work, the northern Italian media was the most influential in the country and Milan was also the financial center of Italy. Italy, from Roman times to the Renaissance, is well known for many things, but I would come to know Milan as perhaps the only Italian city which was never greater in the past than in the present. It was simply at the cutting edge of modern Europe at a time of European unity. I was ecstatic about the prospect of going there.

Shortly before leaving West Africa, I received a letter from my future boss, Evan Fotos. In it he warned me, presuming me to be an unsophisticated African hand, that I was coming into a situation that was, as he put it, "fast moving and sophisticated." Could I cope, I wondered? I thought back to where I spent the first 22 years of my life and concluded that New York City might qualify as fast moving and sophisticated, so maybe, if I tried hard, I could function in Milan. After all, they had a subway and so did we. They had art galleries as did New York. Milan was a financial center, New York a bigger one. Both were media centers and had great opera houses. I decided that as a New Yorker I could probably handle life in Milan.

So, when the news came to Abidjan that my wish to be assigned to Milan had been granted, I immediately recalled that I had acquired Italian language tapes discarded by my agency's training division. Rummaging through my closet, I found them and put lesson one on my recorder. The first words to be uttered were: "Come out with your hands up, you are surrounded." I realized that this was probably not the most useful phrase to utter in 1972 Italy, although it would have come in handy during World War II when the recording had been made by the U.S. Army. However, we luckily found another resource. We discovered a lady from Trieste living in Ivory Coast who agreed to introduce my wife and I to the language of Dante.

Our gateway to Italy was of course Rome. Arriving in August 1972, when the mid-summer holiday brought the country to a halt turned out to be a propitious beginning. I was briefed by my congenial USIS colleagues and later by the political section. The latter briefing was the most convoluted and dizzying description of a political system I had ever heard. To clear my head, Anita and I took our daughter Alisa on a carriage ride through scenic Rome on her 6th birthday.

After meeting the Ambassador, I then completed other newcomer formalities and rented a car that would take us through the center of Italy to Anita's immigrant parents' hometown, Guardiagrele, located in the province of Abruzzi. Being amid the family in the beauty of an ancient mountain town made us wonder why someone would have ever left. Early the next year Ambassador Martin would be replaced by John Volpe whose family had also immigrated to America from that same region as Anita's family, fleeing famine at the tail end of the 19th century. We drove to Abruzzi from Rome in a little more than two hours. It was a wonder to Anita because only a few years before an autostrada had cut through the mountains. Prior to that feat of engineering, the town had been considerably more remote. Before our marriage Anita had made the trip. It had taken her most of the day to drive to Guardiagrele from Rome by bus, on local roads, through the mountainous terrain.

While Milan was not the magnet that attracted most tourists to Italy, I came to understand that in my mind it was perhaps the most important contemporary Italian city. Upon our arrival in Milan, I was delighted to find our American Cultural Center to be in the center of town, a five-minute walk from La Scala, two blocks from the Brera Museum, and the Galleria which connected La Scala to the Cathedral. We found an apartment located within a half hour's walk or a ten-minute trolley ride through the historic downtown to my office. The Center itself was an architectural marvel of the school of Bramante with a colonnaded entrance hall giving way to a large and lovely library where concerts were held, a majestic garden populated by large tortoises, and a downstairs auditorium. It was a place in which I was proud to work.

Aside from the complexities of Italian politics, the political news of the day in the media concerned European unity, Eurocommunism, the Cold War and its implications for NATO vis-à-vis the Soviet Union and the Warsaw Pact. While the U.S. had numerous military installations in Italy, most Italians gave little thought to the importance of the western alliance. It was to be my role to work with the media to help change that.

I was assigned by our Rome office to organize NATO tours for Italian journalists. The tours were of two types. The first was a tour of major European centers where important NATO-related activities were taking place. Those were NATO headquarters in Brussels, Geneva where SALT (Strategic Arms Limitation Talks) negotiations were centered and Vienna where MBFR (Mutual and Balanced Force Reduction) talks were held. Detailed briefings were provided to the journalists at each site. On one occasion we also took the journalists to Berlin and Camp Hof, a U.S. installation on the border with East Germany.

The latter visit was especially revealing. We met with U.S. officers on the front lines of the Cold War who considered themselves "a trip wire." They knew that while they would put up a fight should Soviet tanks come roaring across the border, they would certainly be overrun in the event of a major invasion. That sense of sacrifice in putting themselves at risk was moving to the Italians.

Perhaps the most significant, if comical aspect of the trip, was the bus ride to the camp. Halfway there one of our journalists tapped me on the shoulder. "Mr. LaGamma," he asked, "we're hungry, can we stop and get something for lunch?" I responded that I would ask the army driver who came this way regularly. When asked he said we would stop at a place just five minutes away. Five minutes later we merged onto the broad medium of the autobahn. We parked in front of a small brick structure.

As we entered, I was reminded of another such place in New York a long time ago. It was a wondrous automat, the walls of which contained dozens of glittering, tiny windows. Behind each was a sandwich or a dessert or something to drink. The Italians had never seen anything like it. I explained how they could transform their dollars into quarters, insert the quarters and magically obtain whatever food or drink was beyond the window they had selected. Fifteen minutes later lunch was over, and we were back on the bus on schedule. Once on the bus one of the leaders of the group came to me with a message. He said they had all heard long, erudite, assuring briefings from leading NATO officials, but if they harbored any doubts about the ultimate outcome of the Cold War it was today's lunch that had convinced them that our side would win. The reason: it was clear that the Soviets had nothing like that automat.

In addition to the NATO European tours, I was also asked to conduct three tours for Italian journalists and editors to U.S. carriers underway on the Mediterranean. There had been some controversy over U.S. carriers, assumed to be armed with nuclear weapons, docking in Italian ports. Those complaints were obviated when Italian union leaders, many of them communist or socialist, were not ready to give up hundreds of jobs for their workers at those ports over the controversy. They made the pragmatic decision, despite the ideology of their political parties, that they would continue to welcome the carriers.

The carrier visits were intended to demonstrate that the unmatched American military might was integral to NATO in the waters of the Mediterranean. Landing on a carrier deck for the first time was awe-inspiring. The first sight of the ship from the air made it seem like a postage stamp. Upon landing on its deck though, we experienced a floating city of more than 5,000 sailors. Our flight was greeted by the ship's media. A navy television crew and representatives of the ship's daily newspaper interviewed the Italian journalists upon arrival. An hour later we were to view the coverage of our arrival both on the ship's T.V. and in its newspaper.

The first time we landed, I was asked who was in charge of our group and admitted that I was. We were all then taken to our quarters. Since the admiral was not aboard, I was assigned to his rather spacious cabin. Adjacent to that cabin was an observation platform from which the deck was visible. That evening, after dark, I sat in the admiral's chair adjacent to the cabin and witnessed the volcanic takeoff of the ship's fiery Phantom jets exploding into darkness. The majestic power of that sight was enough to convince any journalist of the seriousness of the U.S. capability to defend the Mediterranean region.

That demonstration, bolstered by excellent briefings from the captain and his officers on the tracking of Soviet subs and other ships, furthered comprehension of the issues at stake. Our visitors were also impressed by how well the complexities of managing a huge carrier were handled. They were also pleased by the excellence of the navy's food, but lamented the absence of wine, which for any Italian ought to be an intrinsic part of any meal. They were informed that unlike the British navy, all recreational alcohol had been banned from U.S. warships. It seems that early in the 20th century, the wife of the Secretary of the U.S. Navy was a Prohibitionist who convinced her husband to ban alcoholic consumption aboard our nation's ships.

Upon our return to Milan, we learned that both the visits to NATO headquarters and negotiating sites and military installations all resulted, as we had hoped, in a generous amount of favorable news coverage in the Italian media describing the importance of the NATO alliance and the U.S. commitment to it. Everything from the automat to the aircraft carriers had played their part.

Then there was that irksome issue of Eurocommunism which dominated my years in Italy. National elections were looming in 1975, and the U.S. concern was the advance of the Italian Communist party. That party unlike its French counterpart, sought to portray itself as moderate and not aligned with the Soviet Union. But the question was: would it live up to that stance if it tasted real power? Italy's leading party since World War II was that of the Christian

Democrats. But that party's reputation had declined over revelations of corruption and by most measures, the Communist Party's policies on economic issues were viewed more favorably. Under those circumstances, the U.S. fear was that the Communists might win a majority of the popular vote.

One way to test the waters was a poll being prepared by DOXA, an Italian affiliate of Gallup polling agency. We decided to buy into the poll in order to add some questions of relevance to American policy. When the votes were counted, the Communists while not a majority, gained ground that paved the way for an historic compromise allowing them to share power with the Socialists and Christian Democrats. The CD continued to hold a diminished but still a plurality in the vote. What the poll revealed was that the Communists were still highest in the esteem of voters on key economic and governance issues, but they trailed on two questions. First, Italian voters considered the rise of the Communist Party risked Italy's relations with the United States. Second, they feared that individual freedom would be curtailed should the Communists dominate.

The Cold War, Eurocommunism, NATO, and European Unity were all dominant themes of our work in Italy during my first three years in Milan. Then came Walter Wells. Walter replaced my boss who had strictly adhered to the political line established by the Rome Embassy. Walter introduced what became a new and potent dimension to our work, a cultural dimension. He had served in World War II in Italy. He came to love the country and its culture despite fighting a war against its fascist government. He claimed to have been the first American to liberate Florence. As a military policeman specializing in directing the traffic of American forces approaching Florence, he had been told, erroneously that the Germans had withdrawn from the city. He says that he drove across a bridge to enter Florence only to face German tanks which had not yet left the city. He frantically sought refuge in an Italian home until our troops eventually did force the enemy to abandon the city. After the war he returned to Italy where he taught English and perfected his Italian. Walter loved Italian literature and opera, owned an unsurpassed collection of opera recordings, and had a deep knowledge of the country's culture and history. Accordingly, the dimension he introduced to our work was a passionate love of Italy which he lectured on and for which he was awarded an honor by the Italian government during his previous work in Latin America.

That deep affection for the Italian culture affected his outlook on our diplomatic approach. It was in stark contrast to the Cold War emphasis of our Embassy in Rome. Walter's first heresy according to our boss in Rome, the Country Public Affairs Officer, was to plan an exhibition. It was to be held in our splendid school of Bramante entry hall devoted to honor early 20th century Italian tenor Giovanni Zanatello, who like Caruso, had won great acclaim and wealth in the United States.

So, Walter planned to hold an event on the one hundredth anniversary of Zanatello's birth. Few recalled the strong connection between Zanatello and America. He had made a fortune touring the U.S. and singing at the Metropolitan Opera House as well as recording for RCA Victor. With much of that fortune, Zanatello financed the restoration of the ancient Roman Verona Arena. He turned it into the world-famous opera venue that it is today. That led Walter to request that our head office in Rome arrange to obtain artifacts, recordings, and other memorabilia from RCA for our exhibit which would be inaugurated with Walter's lecture on the tenor and his life. Simple enough it seemed. But our superior in Rome would have none of it, and refused to forward the request on our behalf, which we thought would have been standard procedure. But we were not even informed of the refusal.

When several weeks had gone by and we had not been advised that our request had been forwarded to Washington, Walter hurled invective at them, then contacted his brother in Boston who proceeded to make the arrangements to acquire all that had been asked for from RCA and more. They express mailed the historic artifacts and recorded music that we arranged to grace our entrance hall and accompany Walter's planned lecture. We then sent invitations to the event to several hundred leading Milanese cultural leaders for Walter's lecture. It seemed all those invited came, including the Director of La Scala who had just returned with his company from a triumphal tour of the U.S. Walter's lecture, in impeccable Italian, accompanied by old recordings of Zanatello's arias, was a smashing success. "Americans honor Zanatello" heralded the *Corriere della Sera* on its front page the next day. The Mayor of Verona and the elderly widow of the tenor who had attended the event besieged Walter with requests to repeat his lecture in Verona to an even more rabid acclaim.

The program taught me an important lesson. It was that cultural ties when intelligently, carefully, and respectfully deployed, could powerfully cement relations between peoples. Walter Wells was a master at doing just that. He lectured on Italian opera more knowledgeably than many Italian experts. He spoke eloquently about Dante's impact on American literature. And he found that an Italian philosopher, Cesare Beccaria, was the source of the concept "cruel and unusual punishment" that found its way into our Constitution. That and other historical connections were woven into an excellent speech Walter wrote for Ambassador Volpe to deliver on our Bicentennial held at the prestigious Manzoni House in Milan. I learned that the lessons taught by Walter Wells on the importance of appreciating cultural connections and the historic links between our country and others should be a key element in our diplomacy. It drove the lesson home that a genuine admiration for the culture of an American diplomat's country of assignment, too often mistaken for 'going native," is often central to diplomatic success.

Another clash came when our USIA Director for Europe came to visit us. We learned in advance that she was in the process of closing European libraries. For several decades our library and its research facilities were important dimensions of the American presence in northern Italy. When she came to our office, she asked for a closed-door meeting with Walter, whom she knew opposed closing our lovely, well attended and highly effective library. Walter came out of his office to invite me to attend the meeting as he wanted someone to witness what was said. Our Director for Europe read Walter the riot act for his refusal to comply with the order to close the library. Walter replied simply but forcibly, "no, I won't." And then, pointing an accusatory finger at her, charged her with a crime against culture by closing so many USIS libraries in Europe. He continued to say that if she forced the closure of our library he would get his brother, the head of the Massachusetts Democratic Party, to launch an investigation of her policies. It was the last we heard of the library closing until years after we both left Milan when, for reasons of security, many USIS libraries were closed throughout the world. What remained were mostly hard to access, sterile "research centers." Their closure coincided with an age of terrorism where they were thought to be easy targets.

Milan was a major world center for music. We learned season tickets to La Scala were available at half price for diplomats. A colleague and I discussed our tastes in opera and learned he and his wife were fans of Wagner and Strauss, while we preferred Verdi and Puccini. That led us to split season tickets so that each of us got most of what we wanted. Over the course of four seasons, we were treated to among the world's best operatic performances.

We were also very fortunate to be present in Milan for the one hundredth anniversary of the inaugural performance of Giuseppe Verdi's great *Requiem Mass*. Verdi had written it to mark the passing of his good friend and great author Manzoni. It was held in the church of San Marco where it was first performed one year after Manzoni's death. To hear that magnificent work in that historic place was among the single most moving musical experiences of our lives.

While the Vietnam War raged on, Daniel Ellsberg released the *Pentagon Papers*. That led the Department of State to send out one of the most bizarre telegrams I ever remember receiving. It noted that the material in the Papers were still considered classified and so we should remove the issues of the *New York Times* that contained them from our library. By the time we received that issue of the *Times*, most of the world already had access to those documents, and we did not remove that issue.

Our proximity to Lake Como allowed us to meet numerous creative Americans bound for the Rockefeller Bellagio Center. The story of the Center's origin is an interesting one. Before it became the Rockefeller Bellagio Center it had been a hotel. One of the guests, Ella Walker, the heiress to Walker Whiskey, was checking out of the hotel at the end of her stay when she asked the clerk, "how much?" The clerk replied that he would prepare her bill immediately. She said: "no, I mean how much to buy this place?" She did, and in 1957 donated it to the Rockefeller Foundation stipulating that it be devoted to the promotion of creativity and international cultural understanding.

The Bellagio Center arranged for conferences and hosted scholars, writers, and artists for four-week periods of artistic residence to allow them to pursue their work in a paradisaic setting. One visitor we had for lunch on his way back from Bellagio was American poet Samuel Menashe who was famed for his laconic style. Menashe explained that guests would mingle during cocktails and dinner. One night he was seated for dinner next to an historian who struck up a conversation. The historian, anxious to show he was making good use of his experience said he had written one hundred pages so far. Menashe, a poet known for his conciseness replied, "I've written one line, and I think it's good."

A second writer who came our way and joined us for lunch was the redoubtable Maya Angelou. She was accompanied by her English husband. We found her to be an amiable and a brilliant raconteur; her conversation, like her writing, was replete with references to her life's many colorful, but not always pleasant experiences.

Our connection with the Bellagio Center led to a novel idea from our Consul General, Tom Fina. As that center also organized conferences, he proposed that I design a strategy for holding

USIS sponsored conferences to be held in Bellagio, based on some American ideas that might be relevant to helping Italy improve its admittedly poorly managed government institutions. I drew up a plan to do so which we shared with Bellagio. I left Milan before it could be implemented.

While in Milan I especially enjoyed my work in organizing international visitor programs that involved three or four weeks of professional contacts in the U.S. for Italians. One such visit that stands out was the one we arranged for the head of Italy's national park service. Upon his return he called me to express his thanks after what he called an extraordinarily successful visit to American national parks. He also offered to give a lecture on his findings at our cultural center. I was most intrigued by the prospect of that lecture which was to be illustrated by slides. I had expected images of spectacular mountain ranges, waterfalls, herds of wildlife and magnificent forests. Instead, his slides showed tasteful signage, set-back parking areas, well-placed campsites and areas of accommodation that were respectful by not interfering with natural beauty. What he took away from his American experience was that managing national parks should in no way clash with the transcendent wonder of the parks themselves, an idea he would borrow for Italy.

On the lighter side of our work, we arranged for a successful exhibition of American crafts organized by the Johnson Wax company. This was an especially appropriate exhibition for Milan since it is a major center for design. While the array of crafts was imaginative, we had to work hard to keep the focus as agreed upon, on the artifacts instead of the promotion of Johnson Wax.

We also used our library as the venue for a series of concerts by visiting Americans. Many came to enhance their resumes by performing in Italy and hoped they might attract some press coverage. Occasionally we would host an organist. But when it came to organists, we had to research churches that had functioning instruments. One discovery was in the hill town of Bergamo. In exchange for arranging to tune their organ the church pastor agreed to find an audience for a concert. The hilltop section of Bergamo has been described by Frank Lloyd Wright as the most perfectly preserved medieval town in the world. Its culture in many ways recalled earlier eras.

When our organist explained to our host pastor that he would play a John Cage piece that would last more than an hour and a half without a break, the pastor informed him that there had to be an intermission halfway through the piece. The musician tried to insist that the work was designed to be played with no break. The pastor explained that Bergamo still observed what had been part of a Napoleonic decision to announce an evening curfew. They had retained the early 19th century tradition of the ringing of a church bell, immediately above the organ, at 10 pm every night. Accordingly, our organist was obliged to stop playing at ten.

One aspect of the Italian Renaissance that was kept alive in Milan was the casting of bronze sculpture. I was asked to escort the Mayor of San Francisco, Joseph Alioto, to the famed Foundry Battaglia where he came to check on the progress of the forging of the bronze doors for his city's Cathedral. I asked the director of one of the oldest artistic bronze foundries in the world, what techniques were used in the making of bronze art works. He responded by saying they used the same lost wax techniques deployed by Benvenuto Cellini during the Renaissance. After his inspection of the work on the doors, I accompanied Alioto to an international conference of mayors held in Milan. He said the first day of the conference had put the audience to sleep and promised his intervention would wake everyone up. When we parted Mayor Alioto flattered me by asking if I might be interested in working for him and if so, I should call on him if I expected to visit California in the near future.

In May of 1976 the earth shook in Northern Italy causing hundreds of fatalities and leaving thousands homeless. Churches and homes that had survived for centuries crumbled. The U.S. response was to help. President Ford called on the Congress to provide funding and had Vice President Rockefeller fly out to assess the need.

Since Milan was our closest USIS post, we were asked to provide public affairs support for the visit. Rome called me at 9 am and told me they had arranged for me to fly to our base in Aviano. They said I had only an hour and a half to catch an Italian airforce flight. So off I went home to pack an overnight bag and have our car take me to the airport. Once there I met with the Italian pilot and crew who were in no hurry to take off. After all, the pilot announced, it's almost lunch time. So, I waited two more hours and was invited to join them for an ample several course Italian lunch, after which they found some other things to do. We finally took off at 4:30 p.m. and landed at Aviano airbase at almost five.

Once there I was barely in time for Rockefeller, but he arrived too late to visit the affected area until the next morning. After breakfast we helicoptered over the disaster area. We witnessed devastated towns and great human suffering., The Vice President had been told that the Italians might need heavy earth moving equipment to deal with the situation, but once in the air Rockefeller saw that Italy was fully equipped with the heavy machinery needed and decided instead to recommend assistance to the homeless.

Our fifth and final child, Florence, was born towards the end of our time in Milan. The celebration of Florence Catherine Renata LaGamma's birth coincided with my being assigned to the city I said was named after her. When deputy director of USIS Rome, Stan Burnett, called to congratulate me, he said he had learned we had named our daughter after the place of our next assignment. He wondered if Ouagadougou wasn't an odd name for a child. It took a moment to realize it was his attempt at a joke.

When the time came, we sought to have Florence baptized. Our apartment was located a few short blocks from one of Milan's oldest and most venerable churches, the tenth century Basilica di Sant'Ambrogio. We had often gone to mass at that church but when we asked to arrange the baptism there, we were informed that we technically "belonged" to an adjacent parish. When we inquired about permission to hold the baptism at Sant' Ambrogio, the local parish denied that permission. I then called the pastor and told him my wife was a good Catholic, but I could await our return to the United States if permission was not granted to hold the baptism at St. Ambrogio. The pastor gave his permission, and the ceremony was held before the original nineth century octagonal stone baptismal font and Sant' Ambrogio's magnificent Golden Altar composed of gold and silver repousse, semiprecious stones and enamel plaques. Depicting scenes of the life of Christ on one side and episodes from the life of Saint Ambrogio on the other, it is the single surviving example of the luxury altars commissioned by popes beginning in the 8th century. Another neighboring religious monument in Milan was Santa Maria delle Gracie, home to one of the world's greatest artistic creations, Leonardo da Vinci's "Last Supper." That masterpiece was preserved in a church bombed by the Allies during World War II. Protected by sandbags and the monks prayers, it was believed to have been miraculously saved despite the destruction all around it.

I became aware in Milan, as I was to experience in other assignments elsewhere, of the importance of the work of foreign service nationals. They are often the critical connections between their country and ours and are key to our having effective contacts with the academic, media, civil society, and cultural figures with whom we work. Their advice and guidance was often fundamental to the success of our operations. An example of how significant their reputation can be occurred when our Italian cultural officer, Luciano Mercatali, received a call from the Nobel Prize Foundation. It seemed that author Eugenio Montale had won the Prize for literature. As Montale lacked a telephone, the Foundation called Mercatali at our office and asked that he contact the author to inform him of the prize. As Montale's office was next door to our cultural center Luciano was easily able to convey the happy news. The next week Mercatali arranged for me to join him when Italy's most important newspaper, the *Corriere della Sera,* held a reception for Montale who in addition to being a poet, was also a columnist for the paper. That event was an extraordinary opportunity for me to meet one of the world's greatest poets.

The importance of our local employees led me on occasion to be at odds with my first boss in Milan who I felt was insensitive to the good judgment of the Italian staff when it clashed with his on both important and mundane issues. I often felt compelled, at great risk, to side with them. His management style was straight by the book, whereas Italian practices tended to be, in the view of our Italian colleagues, commonsensical and less bureaucratic. When Walter Wells took over he thoroughly respected and absorbed the views of our Italian staff.

Towards the end of my time in Milan, we arranged for the visit of one of America's outstanding economists, Professor Franco Modigliani of MIT. Modigliani had been born and educated in Italy before immigrating to the United States. He was an economic analyst who knew Italy well and understood its economic problems. A decade later his analysis of savings and finance would earn him the Nobel Prize in economics. His reputation drew a full house of Milan's major financial and industrial leaders at the headquarters of Italy's association of industrialists. Invited to preside was Gianni Agnelli known as "the king of Italian industry" and head of Fiat, probably Italy's most successful enterprise. He was also head of the Industrialist Society. We awaited his arrival until the appointed hour when I called his office. His secretary informed me that he had just left Turin for Milan. She said he would arrive in 40 minutes, which was difficult to believe since for ordinary mortals it was a two-hour drive. Nonetheless he arrived in 40 minutes in his Ferrari. Modigliani's lecture addressed fundamental policy that led to heavy press coverage. His recommendations and the comments by a number of those present indicated that his ideas would likely impact favorably on Italian government policies.

Another remarkable Italian-born celebrity, Paolo Soleri, returned to Italy under our auspices to lecture on his utopian ideas on architecture and urban planning. His vision, developed in the desert of New Mexico, involved concentrating population in order to free the land around unique urban centers. His ideas received wide dissemination in the Italian press and through the lectures we arranged.

Stan Burnett, who I considered a friend, later went on to the top job in Italy. His time in Rome was characterized by the good advice he regularly provided to our ambassadors on sensitive matters, especially about Italy's role in NATO and our security concerns following the terrorist killing by the Red Brigades of former Prime Minister Aldo Moro. Later still, he became the senior career officer in USIA Washington. He, like Walter Wells, had a deep if vastly different kind of understanding of Italy, especially the intricacies of its politics. He held a doctorate in political science having written his thesis on Nicolo Machiavelli. Burnett had also co-authored a book, entitled *the Italian Guillotine*, after retiring from USIA. Stan, in my estimation, is the model of a superior diplomat, one we need more of in the Foreign Service, especially given his mastery of public diplomacy.

During our time in Italy, our family reveled in visits to Assisi, the town of St. Francis. Most of our visits there were during the Christmas holidays. The pink glow of the city's dwellings shone brilliantly as in a fairy tale, as we drove toward it. Anita had discovered in the book *Bed and Blessings*, a compendium of monasteries and convents that had been partially or fully converted into comfortable, reasonably priced guest houses throughout Italy. We arranged to stay at a lovely Assisi convent run by American Franciscan nuns. The convent was a brisk fifteen-minute walk from the stupendous San Francisco Basilica.

We had visited countless medieval and renaissance churches during our time in Italy but none matched Assisi's grand Basilica. Unlike most of the great churches of Italy that had been built over centuries, Assisi's Basilica had been constructed and decorated in little more than sixty years. At the death of St. Francis, his religious brothers disputed how best to commemorate him. Some, recalling his life of the utmost simplicity opposed the construction of a great church. Others prevailed and called upon the greatest artists of their time to contribute their works. Hence the frescos painted by Giotto, Cimabue, Simone Martini, Pietro Lorenzetti, and Pietro Cavallini illustrating the life of Christ as paralleled to that of Francis.

During the Christmas season many Assisi inhabitants replace their vehicles in their garages to carry on a tradition begun by St. Francis. Those garages are transformed with imaginative versions of one of the delightful innovations of St. Francis, the Christmas creche. Throughout the town many local residents compete to design their interpretations of the scene of Christ's birth in the manger. The best of them win prizes. Our children were enthralled perhaps more by their highly inventive garage creations than by the great frescos that adorn the town's wondrous churches.

Our children were also enchanted by the many stories attributed to St. Francis: his casting off of his father's wealth, how he tamed the wolf of Gubbio, how the birds flocked to him and perhaps the best story of all. It was said that the young Francis had a crucifix speak to him. It asked "Francis, build my church." Francis gathered his friends and they repaired a run-down neighborhood church. But later followers took the message to be that Francis, through his creation of the Franciscan order, should reform a church that was riddled with corruption as he subsequently did.

Our final visit to Assisi took place after a tragic earthquake that severely damaged some of the Basilica's precious frescos: Anita's poem reflected our thoughts about Assisi:

**Giotto's Fragments**

The sun rises with Assisi stone to tint the town in rosé
On cobbled streets the worm crawls undisturbed where
St. Francis preaches to the birds. Giotto's frescoed quail,
Goldfinch, sparrow and pigeon listen docilely. Cowled larks
Swell the sky above stone prayer cells on Mount Subasio.
And despite the prowling hawk not a sparrow falls..

We feel snug in our fleece-lined parkas when frigid winds
Attack the valley where Francis gives his cloak to a
poor knight.
Renouncing his father's goods and earthly riches he
stands naked
Before the bishop in Piazza Santa Maria Maggiore,
then exchanges
Embroidered silk for a beggar's rags. Let us cover him
With the finest wool combed from the sacrificial lamb.

*Francis repair my house which is falling into ruin.* He begs for
stone

to rebuild San Damiano that will shelter cloistered women
in prayer,
stone from Mount Subasio that will simmer in Assisi sun
and cool
in its moon. For eight hundred years the Saint lies within
the great Basilica.
Now moving earth has toppled walls whose fragments are
sent round
the world. We sift through frescoes to rescue an eye
or smile.

As 1975 progressed I awaited a new assignment assuming that after four years in Milan we would be leaving Italy. My dozen years in the Foreign Service up to then had been a bewildering succession of posts totally lacking any sense of continuity. Then came the most momentous phone call of my career. Stanton Burnett, deputy director of USIS in Rome called to tell me I would be assigned to Bologna. However, my next assignment was not to be Bologna, and I was in for a big surprise!

# VIII. Florence (1976-78)

LaGamma family at home in Florence

We had named our newborn Florence after the city that had utterly captured our imagination. The news that we probably would be assigned to Bologna was joyously welcomed. Bologna was dynamic, fascinating and would allow us not to be far from Florence. The reason, for Bologna, I was told, was that our government, obsessed with the threat of Eurocommunism in Italy, felt the need to show the American flag in Bologna, an important intellectual center long dominated by the Italian Communist Party. But the 1975 Italian election, resulted an historic event. For the first time the Communist Party had won the local election in Florence. That led to a second call from Rome, this one advising me that instead of basing me in Bologna, I would be going instead to Florence and to cap it off, going there during the bicentennial year of U.S. independence. The fact that we had a Consulate in Florence would provide me with the administrative support not available in Bologna.

The dream assignment conjured illusions of grandeur. I would be heading into the Renaissance where I would be representing the world's most powerful nation and its cultural agency to the Court of the Medici. The city of Florence and its surrounding territory was alive for us with visions of Dante, Michelangelo, and da Vinci, the great cathedral dome of Brunelleschi, the frescos of Giotto, the sculptures of Donatello, and the golden doors of Ghiberti, among countless inspired signs of creativity that had transformed the world as it had been known.

More pragmatically I expected instructions from our Rome office in order to fully comply with what would be expected of me in Florence. My new boss in Rome for most of my time in Florence was one of USIA's most senior officers, Jock Shirley. He was a tough, skillful, sophisticated manager of Cold War politics. He summarized my instructions in three words. My relations with the governing Communists in Florence were to be: "cool and correct."

The ambassador when I arrived in Italy was Graham Martin who left Italy to serve as Ambassador to Vietnam and tragically preside over the fall of Saigon. He was replaced as ambassador to Italy by John Volpe, former Governor of Massachusetts, and more recently in the Cabinet of Richard Nixon as Secretary of Transportation. Volpe was delighted to be in the ancestral country of his parents' birth. His parents had come from the province of Abruzzi as had my wife Anita's parents. Volpe made much of his parent's ancestry and how they had escaped starvation to immigrate to America. He also often publicly expounded on the rags to riches tale of how he became a wealthy man in our country and went on to his highly successful political career. While he was thrilled in his role as ambassador, Volpe ran into problems. His successor, Richard N. Gardner accurately captured those problems in this way:

> The Italian elite both political and intellectual, is well known for looking down on Italian Americans from Italy's South, and many of its members made fun of John and his Abruzzese accent. His genuine love of the Italian people and the country of his ancestry seemed to count for little, nor did his tireless efforts to visit Italian regions to contact the common people.

This was especially evident in Milan with its snobbish elite. And it was painful to me as an Italian American diplomat whose family came from Calabria in the south to witness this disrespect for an honorable, decent man who had risen so high in American life.

Richard N. Gardner, Volpe's replacement as ambassador could not have been more different. Volpe as a politician sought to appeal to the common man. He had been sent by Nixon to Italy to rid him from his cabinet. In contrast, Gardner was close to President Carter who had served with him on the Trilateral Commission. It followed that Gardner was only the second ambassadorial appointment made by Carter after the nomination of his good friend Andrew Young, who was named ambassador to the United Nations. Gardner was also a member of an international academic elite, as a respected professor of law and international organizations at Columbia University. He too was related to Italy, by marriage to his wife who was from Venice. That had led him to frequently visit Italy throughout his career and closely follow Italian politics. Those qualifications meant he was an envoy who could reach out to the White House when needed, something Volpe lacked the ability to do.

Gardner also sought to lend his support to my own profession, public diplomacy. He advocated for a great expansion of our Fulbright graduate scholarships program for Italy, as well as for bringing young professionals to the U.S. under the international visitors program. He also sought to promote exchanges in key fields such as energy, health, the environment, and law enforcement. Another notable effort, if doomed to failure, was that of trying to help Italians collect taxes. I recall accompanying Ambassador Volpe to the city of Brescia where he met with the mayor. Volpe sought to define something as certainty. He told the mayor: "as we say in America: it's as sure as death and taxes." The mayor responded, "we have death here too."

Upon arrival in Florence, I found myself in a unique but often perplexing situation. The new mayor of Florence, Elio Gabbuggiani, claimed to be the epitome of a new brand of Eurocommunism, one that seemed to distance itself from Russia and be open to Western democracy. It seemed he wished to go to great lengths to demonstrate that communism Italian style would not be incompatible with either Western values or good relations with the United States. Already, prior to my arrival, the city of Florence had sponsored a series of events to mark the American bicentennial. Featured were jazz concerts by American musicians and theatrical performances by American groups all funded by the Communist government of Florence.

Now that I had arrived, the local government sought my attendance in other activities to showcase American culture. Featured and highly publicized was a show of the works of noted American photographer Paul Strand organized by the city. Strand had spent part of his career in Italy some fifty years earlier. Featured in his show was a portrait of a young women from a village near Bologna. To enliven the event that woman, then in her sixties, was found and brought to Florence for the exhibition's opening.

Artist Robert Rauschenberg, who had come to Florence for inspiration at the beginning of his career, was invited to Florence for a show of his brilliant illustrations of Dante's *Divine Comedy*. At the vernissage of that exhibition, he explained that his visit to Florence when he was young had almost prematurely marked the end of his career as an artist. He said he had been so overwhelmed by the brilliance of Renaissance art that he threw what he considered his own inadequate paintings in the river Arno.

The 25th anniversary of the Syracuse University study abroad program in Florence was celebrated in the magnificence of the Palazzo Vecchio. To mark these and numerous other events the mayor hosted lavish dinners to which I was invited. I was unsure how to be "cool and correct" under the circumstances.

The sum of cultural activities devoted to the wonders of American culture sponsored by the city of Florence during the bicentennial exceeded those of any other foreign city in the world. I was advised years later by a former intelligence official that after the collapse of the Soviet Union, the opening of Soviet archives showed that Moscow had covered the extensive costs of Mayor Gabbuggiani's cultural offensive. That initiative was, as we suspected, part of an effort to legitimize Eurocommunism and to show how it was compatible with friendly relations with the United States. By so doing, the Communist Party could show the Italian people that a Communist Italy could still be democratic and share values with the United States.

Florence lived up to and even exceeded our dream of it. We arrived at a time when the dollar was strong, and housing and restaurants made life affordable even for those, like us, of modest means. Our search for housing was an adventure. With five children, we decided we needed a house. We made an advance trip from Milan and with the help of a real estate agent we began the search. One rather palatial house a couple of miles from the city center was rather grand but affordable and came with a vineyard. I suggested to my wife Anita that we consider it. She rejected it out of hand, pointing to the high ceilings and asking, "who would we get to clean it?" After several rejections, the agent called and said there was one other possibility, but she thought it might be too difficult for a family with young children. I said I'd be happy to see it alone since our infant had a fever and Anita had to stay in the hotel with her.

**The author's villa in Florence**

When I arrived at via Monterinaldi # 3 the house took my breath away. It stood on a hill amid a dozen other similar houses that had been designed by Leonardo Ricci, one of Italy's leading architects. He built them all with local stone quarried from the hill. Each house had an expanse of windows looking down at the city of Florence.

The house I came to look at required eighty-one steps to reach its first level and two winding wooden staircases of eighteen steps each after that. From its facade's shimmering windows, one could see not only the city below, but the lovely hillside of Fiesole and the countryside dominated by olive groves and stately cypresses. The rest of the house, constructed of the hill's native stone included interior walls built into the hill itself. A garage stood at the bottom of the hill that could house my Vespa and our Volkswagen bus. Beside the five bedrooms, it contained an adjacent annex where we could house our guests with its own bedroom, bath, kitchen and living room.

Outside the upper level of the house, adjacent to the kitchen, was a garden graced with a dozen olive trees. We later discovered that pictures of the house took up four pages in a volume entitled *Great Villas of the World.* Thinking I knew my wife, I told her of the find and suggested it might be too difficult for our young children because of the need to ascend over one hundred steps. She asked to see it and contrary to my assumption, the poet in Anita immediately fell in love with the house we would come to live in for the next two years. It was the grandest place we ever called home, and its rent was less than our three-bedroom apartment in Milan.

I decided that our arrival called for me to host a dinner for a gathering of the Florentines I would be working with, so we developed an invitation list of some key 50 individuals: editors, academics, cultural figures, and a few politicians. We wondered if they would be daunted by having to climb all the steps to arrive at our clifftop. To our astonishment every invitee came, some out of curiosity about our astonishing house. Anita was up to the challenge and unaided, prepared the feast. The next day one of our guests, the wife of the newly arrived President of the European University Institute, showed up in her limo and called on Anita to ask who the marvelous caterer of the previous evening had been. Anita had to admit she had done it all herself.

It was a tradition of that time that Foreign Service spouses were expected to play an important role in what we called representational activities. My wife Anita assumed that role without question when it concerned my work. She believed it to be an integral part of a life we both took pleasure in, a life that supported us in many ways including living in a fine house in one of the world's greatest cities. That did not interfere with her love of writing poetry, raising our children, or continuing her profession as a teacher when it was feasible, as she did in a number of African posts. In more recent times, a majority of Foreign Service spouses feel exploited, perhaps rightly, if such chores are asked of them. It is imperative that the Department of State study this change and seek to provide support to officers whose spouses are otherwise engaged.

One of the high points of our time in Florence was the establishment in 1976 of the European University Institute, located on a hill overlooking Florence adjacent to the hill on which our own house stood. The Institute was a post graduate school established by the European Union to "foster the advancement of learning in fields which are of particular interest for the development of Europe." It was inaugurated shortly before our arrival. One of the first official visitors I received was its newly named president, Max Kohnstamm of the Netherlands. He along with Jean Monnet had been one of the founders of the European Union.

Kohnstamm called on me to help him solve a dilemma. The Institute, which comprised 70 scholars at its establishment was composed of professors and graduate students exclusively from the member countries of the EU. He explained that accordingly, no Americans were on the faculty despite the fact that faculty members felt the absence of Americans was a major issue, especially in the leading fields of political and social sciences. He told me that he would be able to fund all but the travel to Europe of American scholars. What was lacking, and what he was asking me to arrange, was a partnership in which we paid their international travel from the U.S. to Florence. He then produced a list of American academics provided to him by his faculty. It was a veritable Who's Who of political, economic, and social science in America. I expressed an admiration for the list but wondered if such elite academics could free themselves to come to Florence for several weeks during the coming academic year even if we could fly them there.

Nevertheless, I said I would make the case to USIA Washington that this could be a grand opportunity to get a foot in the door of a leading European institution at its inception. Our Agency agreed and said they would fund travel for anyone on the list if the Institute would pay an honorarium and cover living expenses. My doubts were erased when I realized that the lure of coming to Florence and to the new Institute was irresistible and most of those invited did come, providing several weeks of an American perspective on the scholarship in their fields.

I learned about one interesting dimension that characterized the European Institute when I asked what the language of instruction was. It turned out that this was a sensitive issue. I was told the common language of instruction was English, which therefore was the working language of professors and students. All documents produced by the Institute, in principle, had to be published in all the languages of the member states. However, because of the extreme sensitivity of the French government, usually that meant in practice, most documents had to be available in French but not necessarily in the other languages.

At the same time, University of Florence like most Italian universities, was in turmoil for political reasons. A good friend, Luigi Lotti, recently named Dean of the University of Florence's prestigious Cesare Alfieri faculty of political and social sciences, had a problem. The walls of his faculty building were defaced by students who covered them with graffiti. The new Dean asked the Rector to have the building painted. In response, the Rector sent him a can of paint which he was told he could use to cover the most offensive writing.

Of course, our everyday experience of Florence was characterized by the vast river of tourists that incessantly flooded through its streets, cafes, and museums. Another kind of tourism, a continuation of the 19th century "Grand Tour" was represented by several dozen American university study abroad programs located in Florence. It was our task every September to welcome newly arrived students and to brief them on the rigorous enforcement and severe consequences of violations of Italian drug laws that could result in having them spend their year abroad in an Italian prison.

This was my first experience with study abroad programs. Florence was home to an incredible number of them. I found several of them highly serious in their teaching of the Renaissance, art history and the Italian language. Perhaps best among them was Stanford in Florence, founded by Italian scholar Guisseppe Mammarella and housed in a lovely villa on the outskirts of town. However, the majority of the students in many of the others were there for the glamour and beauty of Florence, the good food and the opportunity to travel through Italy and elsewhere in Europe.

We had a number of family and friends visit us in Florence. Perhaps the most special of all for us was that of Father William F. Lynch, an extraordinary scholar and great friend. Lynch was a Jesuit who began professional life as a *New York Times* journalist before his teaching career at Fordham and Georgetown universities. He was the author of nine books on faith and the imagination. My wife Anita met him quite accidentally as she began her enrollment as a student at Fordham. At that time Lynch, a classicist, ran a much-heralded Greek Theater at Fordham as well as editing a prestigious journal, *Thought* magazine. During his stay we helped organize his visit to Florence, the place where ancient Greek civilization was rediscovered and inspired the Renaissance. Among those appointments was a very special visit arranged to the Villa I Tatti, the Harvard Renaissance library and study center founded by the renowned Renaissance scholar Bernard Berenson.

After leaving Milan to be posted in Florence, I learned that leading U.S. international affairs experts with special expertise on Italy had been invited to Turin to speak at a conference on the political situation in light of impending historic elections. Accordingly, I contacted them and arranged an evening dinner-debate at my residence entitled: "Whither Italy?" to which I Invited Italian politicians, academics, and journalists. One of the U.S. scholars, Kenneth

Organski, had been my own college professor of international relations. As the contentious debate, which focused on the implications of Eurocommunism for the U.S. heated up, I decided to call a time-out for coffee. During the break Organski came over to me with a broad smile on his face and said, "Bob, calm down. Italy, she is going nowhere." I asked why he thought so, and he gave me two reasons, ties of blood and culture. He explained that Italians prized their relations with America especially since we had welcomed so many of them as immigrants. He added that Italians also shared a commitment to individual freedom.

The heart of Florence is the glorious Piazza della Signoria and its grand Palazzo Vecchio. In 1977, to that center of the Renaissance universe came Maurizio Seracini, an Italian who had spent some time at the University of California and who was obsessed with the goal of finding a lost Leonardo. He and an American art historian told the tale of the "school of the world," a moment in time when both Leonardo da Vinci and Michelangelo were commissioned to fresco facing walls of the Palazzo Vecchio with vast scenes of battles won by Florence. According to the father of art history, Giorgio Vasari, artists descended upon Florence from all over Europe to observe the two great masters at work.

As the story goes Michelangelo's fresco technique was unsuccessful and so was abandoned. On the other hand, some believe that Leonardo, while also having technical problems, completed a masterpiece, the "Battle of Anghiari." And the tale told is that either for political reasons having to do with the then ruling faction losing the battle depicted, or because the fresco was deteriorating, it was subsequently covered with a fresco by the artist Vasari.

If that were the case, thought Seracini, the Leonardo masterpiece would still be underneath the Vasari fresco, and with the proper 20th century technology it could be found and uncovered. To acquire that technology the two scholars returned to California where they called on Armand Hammer, CEO of Occidental Petroleum. Arguing that he would gain immortality if he helped find the lost Leonardo, Hammer agreed to arrange and provide the technology they said they needed. Decades have gone by and the quest and search, while still alive, has not yielded results. In fact, in recent years some art historians have even expressed doubt that Leonardo ever worked on or finished the fresco. Those responsible for the Palazzo have adamantly refused to let the Vasari work be compromised in the process of the search. So, the battle over the "Battle of Anghiari" goes on.

Because of glorious museums and architecture, Florence was a magnet for artists from around the world seeking inspiration from the Renaissance. The contemporary art scene too reflected the desire of Italians to attempt to live up to their past. In visiting galleries, we came across a painting we especially liked and could afford. It depicted a wall of an historic building on which was painted graffiti that said "*La Poesia e nella la strada*" (poetry is in the street). Next to that text was the image of one of those foot high sculptures of a Madonna inserted in a niche on the wall reflecting an age-old art form commonly found in the streets of Florence. Some months later, our friends Carol and Giovanni Latini, who knew of our fondness for the painting, bought us another work by the same artist. It was of a group of children being escorted up a long flight of stone steps by some nuns, similar to the staircase we mounted with our five children each day.

One of our very favorite places in Florence was the monastery of San Marco. It had been a Dominican monastery since the 15th century when it served as a refuge for the Medicis and as the base for the charismatic Dominican monk, Savonarola, the powerful prelate who had denounced the vanities and was responsible for the public burning of many paintings and other luxuries. The monastery itself had been intensely decorated by the Renaissance monk, Fra Angelico, who among other places painted striking religious frescos in each of the monks' cells. The story is told that upon the death of the bishop of Florence, the Pope thought to name Angelico in his place. When Angelico learned of this, he demurred and asked that his friend be named instead. Then upon his death, a cardinal suggested he be nominated for sainthood. Another challenged that proposal asking what his miracles were. The Pope, who knew him well declared his paintings were his miracles. Thus began a process that ended with him being declared "beato Angelico" or blessed Angelico, a step short of sainthood. But in the annals of art history, he clearly earned the equivalent of sainthood.

Being based in Florence also meant I was the USIS officer responsible for the territory that included Bologna, Pisa, Lucca, and other cities in the regions of Tuscany and Emilia Romagna. While that vast territory was too much for one person to handle more than superficially, we could at least "show the flag." One opportunity to do so was afforded when I was invited to deliver a lecture on Robert F. Kennedy at a school in the coastal town of Viareggio. Not having great confidence in my ability as a public speaker in Italian, I worked hard on a lecture about a politician I had fervently supported for President before his cruel assassination.

As the day approached for me to speak to the students, I felt reasonably prepared. But the day before the talk, I received a call that the venue had been changed from the high school to the town hall. I was further advised that instead of just students, the townspeople had been invited and I was to be part of a two-person panel. Then I was told that the second speaker was to be Ruggero Orlando, a member of Italy's Senate and a famed former U.S. correspondent of Italy's leading daily newspaper, the *Corriere della Sera*. The news of the changes hit like a ton of bricks, but even more stunning was what I saw upon arrival at the town hall. National Television (RAI) had sent a crew to broadcast our debate. My heart palpitated on the way into the town hall. I was ushered into a room off the main auditorium in which was seated what seemed to be the entire town.

Once in that room I was introduced to the great Senator Orlando. He greeted me warmly, but I noticed he was utterly intoxicated. So, I thought, perhaps I would come out of this alive. When asked who would speak first Orlando deferred to me, Console LaGamma. My preparation stood up and I delivered my remarks without disaster. I spoke of Robert Kennedy's passionate commitment to civil rights and his experience as a member of the Cabinet as advisor to his brother, the President, and his opposition to the Vietnam War.

Then came Orlando. He began with: "I agree with everything said by Console LaGamma," then proceeded to elaborate on what I had said while appearing quite sober in doing so. The program was broadcast in its entirety on Sunday evening by RAI national television, and while I was too frightened to watch, I was told I acquitted myself well as confirmed in a judgment from my Rome headquarters the next morning.

A rather unique aspect of our U.S. diplomatic presence in Florence was the responsibility of being accredited to the Republic of San Marino, a tiny hill-top nation with a population of thirty thousand that expanded to close to a hundred thousand during the tourist season. It was a country completely surrounded by the Italian provinces. Our embassy in Rome preferred not to involve itself in the time-consuming affairs of that self-important country.

At the time of our presence in Florence there occurred what I came to call "the T.V. wars." Italian T.V. at the time was entirely government controlled. The government of San Marino, situated on a high hill launched its own competitive T.V. station which reached half of Italy. The Italian government protested its loss of revenue caused by the competition. San Marino responded it had a sovereign right to broadcast. Italy responded that it had a right to close all roads in and out of the Republic. The feud was resolved when Italy agreed to pay a modest fee if San Marino shut down its broadcasts. If Rome wished that the Florence Consulate cover San Marino, the Consul General, Robert Gordon decided that our main relationship with the minuscule nation would be cultural. Therefore, I was sent, accompanied by my wife and children to see what cultural activities we could arrange for San Marino. I was able to do a couple of lectures and include them in a cultural event.

When we arrived back in Florence though, the next day found my wife Anita had somehow contracted a fearsome case of meningitis. As our medical crisis occurred during the annual Ferragosto vacation period, we feared we might not find a doctor to deal with the illness. By a great stroke of luck, our next-door neighbor knew a doctor on our street who diagnosed the illness and arranged for her hospitalization. Luckily, she recovered in a week. In all our time in Africa, we had never had such a serious health problem. Three days in San Marino was enough to disastrously change that.

Since its inception, television in Italy had been controlled by government. In the 1970s both the Christian Democrats and the Socialist Party each controlled one channel of RAI with the Communists clamoring for control of a third channel. Then one day it all changed. The Supreme Court of Italy, in a landmark decision, determined that while the government could continue to broadcast on its part of the spectrum, the unused portion could be given to private companies. Those companies would be allowed to broadcast locally but not form national networks according to the Court. If it is true, that "all politics is local" then the creation of local television stations had a profound impact on Italian politics. Accordingly, the political landscape of Italy was soon transformed by political entrepreneurs like Silvio Berlusconi who used the new media opportunity to sway Italian voters to bring his party to power. Sensing the new political winds, I did my best to contact and work with the owners of local T.V. stations in my region. Notably, I developed a relationship with broadcasters in Florence, Lucca and Barga in my final year in Italy to provide them with USIS produced T.V. programming.

While much of Tuscany and Emilia Romagna was dominated by the Communists, sometimes in alliances with the Socialists and other parties, one place stood out as different. The historic town of Lucca defied the politics of the surrounding region. Solidly Christian Democrat, it was surrounded by a proud agricultural area with a town built inside a great wall. In fact, at one time Lucca had a museum of walled cities embedded in its walls. Economic hardship had caused it to be the major source of immigrants to the United States. Its people had not supported Mussolini's Fascist party and in contrast to other resistance groups, the population of Lucca, opponents of the fascist regime, was heavily made up of Christian farmers. For those reasons, showing an active American presence in Lucca was uniquely welcomed. While Lucca might have lacked great Renaissance art, its cultural contribution to Italy was one of opera's leading composers, Giacomo Puccini.

Toward the end of our six years in Italy, a tragedy shook the sensibilities of the country and would impact the future for an array of people in governments everywhere including diplomats. It was the March 16, 1978, kidnapping of former Prime Minister Aldo Moro by the Red Brigades and his subsequent assassination. The Red Brigades terrorist attack coupled with their assumed hatred of the United States was a preview of the massive security threats that would soon impact Italy as well as American diplomatic missions around the world. Two years after our departure from Italy, the Red Brigades struck again when they kidnapped American General James Dozier in Verona. Unlike the kidnapping of Moro, Dozier was rescued but the ability of a terrorist group to accomplish the taking of a high level American military officer led to the adoption of stringent security measures. At the same time, all of us overseas felt vulnerable. Accordingly, most of our operations had to be adapted to take security into account.

The vulnerability of American embassies was of course exemplified by the seizure of our embassy in Tehran and the taking hostage of our diplomats. In 1998 the bombing by Al Qaeda of our embassies in Nairobi and Dar es Salaam led to security measures that fundamentally changed the nature of our embassies, but most especially our USIS offices. That meant that our libraires, especially in places where they were most needed, could no longer be wide open to the public but had to be located behind protective embassy walls and reduced to reference services. No longer could an African student wander into an American library in Africa and borrow *Moby Dick*. Since the targeting of American diplomatic buildings, the fundamental nature of the American cultural presence in Africa and elsewhere around the world has been placed behind concrete barriers and metal detectors.

The Renaissance that flourished in Florence is alive in its art, scientific discovery, the ideas of its philosophers, in its churches, buildings and institutions. That staggering accumulation of creativity is literally a rebirth of classical Greece and Rome after centuries of the Middle Ages. Together that history conspires to leave anyone living in that city in a persistent state of wonder not unlike what one would experience after attending a great concert or theatrical performance. Many historians have sought to unravel how this miracle came about. It caused us to wonder what might be necessary to replicate it, and how the example of Renaissance Florence, or for that matter, ancient Athens from which it drew inspiration, might produce a similar age of creativity.

# IX. Back to Africa: Togo (1978-81)

After six years of Italy, we found we were invigorated to be heading back to Africa in 1978 but were concerned about our new destination, Lomé, Togo. Togo was an egregiously bad example of a country that betrayed the hopes so many of us had for newly independent African countries. That country had been a German colony until World War I after which it was transferred under League of Nations mandate to France. As colonialism expired, African soldiers who had served in the armies of France in places like Algeria and Vietnam returned home. In the case of Togo one of those soldiers, Gnassingbe Eyadema, a sergeant in the French army, returned expecting to be made a high-ranking officer in the Togolese military. Togolese President, Sylvanus Olympio, a distinguished African leader, and graduate of the London School of Economics, who was honored during a visit to the United States, met with members of the returned military. He reportedly thanked them for their service and told them they would no longer be needed as Togo had no military adversaries. He wished them luck in returning to their villages.

This led to the first military coup d'état and the first assassination of an African president, President Olympio, in the post-independence period. Noteworthy was the fact that the residence of Togo's president was across a wall from the U.S. Embassy compound. When the coup plotters forced their way into his home, he tried to escape by climbing the wall and seeking refuge in the embassy. He was shot as he reached its back door The bullet holes remained in that door while I was in Togo. That military takeover resulted in a failed effort by Guinea's President, Sekou Touré, to exclude Togo from the newly established Organization of African Unity. His argument, which proved prophetic, was that if a military takeover was allowed to be considered legitimate in Togo it would encourage coups elsewhere in Africa. Coups subsequently became a chronic issue resulting in the overthrow of democratically elected leaders in many African nations.

Eyadema eventually seized power formally in 1967 and remained President until his death, thirty-eight years later. Togo under Eyadema was an authoritarian tyranny which practiced a cult of personality for its leader who controlled the courts, the parliament, the single party, and the media as well as the security forces. Opposition leaders were either exiled or imprisoned. The young acting editor of Togo's only daily newspaper was jailed because the paper carried a wire service item on Amnesty International which had nothing to do with Togo. Eyadema's rule left Togo according to one study, as the world's most unhappy country.

When I first had the opportunity to visit the headquarters of the Ministry of Information, I recall walking into a courtyard. Looking up at the building's two balconies, the sight I saw was right out of Orwell's 1984. Starring down at me were dozens of eight-foot-tall posters of Eyadema. I learned most of the Ministry's budget went for images of the *guide bien aime* (the well-loved guide), as the President was known. The two major Lomé hotels, the Sarakawa and the Second of February, were both named for events in the life of the dictator. A ten-dollar wristwatch, made in North Korea, became a favorite among Peace Corps volunteers. It showed the apparition of Eyadema every twenty seconds. Inevitably, his authoritarian rule did not last eternally. As in Shelly's poem, "Ozymandias"

> *look upon my Works ye Mighty and despair! Nothing beside remains.*

His thuggish legacy was nothing but a Presidential palace and some vanity projects that soon deteriorated.

The good news for an American diplomat was that the Togolese people were warm and welcoming, and the dictator had chosen to be pro-Western when it came to Cold War politics, voting regularly with the U.S. at the U.N. Unlike my experience in the Congo, I found the Togolese in Lomé, the capital, to be relatively well-educated and most friendly.

I was to oversee the USIS Togo operation as the only American officer for what USIA called "a one-man post;" although I was also responsible for several junior officers during their first overseas training tours. Under the right circumstances, a stable situation and a good ambassador, there was no better job in the USIS foreign service for a young officer than to serve as the cultural, educational and press officer representing the government of the United States in a U.S. diplomatic mission. As long as there are no crises and the post is normally running, the Public Affairs Officer has "a bully pulpit" and a great deal of autonomy. The American Cultural Center, with a dozen competent Togolese employees was located across the street from the American Embassy.

U.S Ambassador to Togo, Marilyn Johnson at inauguration of Peace Corps School

I learned, while still in Italy, that a newly appointed U.S. Ambassador to Togo was to follow our own arrival in Lomé. I knew that this would be critical to my three-year tour there. So, it was a time of heightened anxiety. When I first met Ambassador Marilyn Johnson, I immediately took a liking to her. The encounter marked the beginning of a lifelong professional and personal friendship between Ambassador Johnson and my family. My initial impression was that she was warm, friendly, and intelligent and most significantly, a Chief of Mission who had come from USIA as I did. Furthermore, she had a background in francophone Africa and unlike some other American ambassadors in Africa, she had a strong affinity for the African people and their aspirations. Also, I soon learned that Marilyn, was someone who knew public diplomacy and would not seek to micromanage what I saw as my responsibilities. Oh, happy day! What more could I have wished for in a boss?

Early in my time there, I decided to take a risk that might have had me removed from my job. In assessing the resources available to carry out what I hoped to do, I found that they were meager. I discovered a copy of a document written by my predecessor who had been a European hand. In it he told Washington headquarters that the American cultural presence in Lomé was a waste of taxpayers' money. Furthermore, I had heard stories told about how much he disliked being in Africa and that he was not particularly well disposed toward Africans. As a result, the activities of the American Cultural Center during his tenure were at a low ebb. To turn things around, I wrote a somewhat different message to headquarters. In my message I agreed that the cost of being in Lomé would be a waste if we failed to have resources to conduct an active program and lamented the lack of budget to do so. I said in effect, "give me money or close the Togo office."

In response, the head of our Office of African Affairs, Arthur Lewis, dispatched our regional administrative officer, Stedman Howard, to determine whether I should be removed from the post or provided budgetary support that I had requested. He recommended the latter and I was given what I needed. We were open for business! Sted, a fellow Africanist, was to remain a close friend throughout the years.

The new resources allowed me to open lines of communication with many Togolese audiences. Despite its dictatorship, we were able to speak of human rights and democracy. We sponsored a spectrum of lecturers, sent more Togolese to the U.S. than ever before, arranged for several Fulbright scholarships, and ran an active library and film program. But above all three initiatives stand out.

The first involved a brief newsletter that we disseminated weekly to our Togolese subscribers that included a story about a UCLA archeologist, Merrick Posnansky's work in neighboring Ghana. The Togolese head of research at the Education Ministry, Dovi Kuevi, after reading about the project, called me to ask if Posnansky could come to Togo. His objective was to have a respected archeologist conduct a survey of Togolese historic sites to establish priorities for archeological digs. His reason was the absence of the country's knowledge of its historic significance. The French had dismissed Togo and neighboring Benin to be what they called West Africa's "path between the forests," believing the region lacked any significant kingdoms or other significant historic remnants.

Our invitation to Professor Posnansky received a positive response. He offered to make a preliminary visit in conjunction with his project in Ghana. When he arrived, he presented a plan to conduct a survey to explore a number of promising sites the following year. He returned to travel throughout the country and prepared a hundred-page report for the Togolese Ministry of Education identifying potential archeological sites. As his priority, he identified Notsé, a town some sixty miles from the capital, Lomé, where he proposed to conduct an excavation the following year.

When he returned the next year the Posnansky expedition was launched. Lacking a car, he bargained with the Ghanaian university to use its Land Rover in exchange for providing it with new tires that while not available in Ghana, could be had in Togo. He was accompanied by a UCLA PhD candidate Phil de Barros. Phillip, a former Peace Corps volunteer in Togo, had a Togolese wife. Along with him and rounding out the expedition were Ghanaian professors, and several UCLA students on their junior year abroad.

When Posnansky began the dig, he found it required significantly more manpower than his group could provide. His solution was to contact a local prison and arrange for some of its inmates to join in clearing the site. The result was the unearthing of the Great Wall of Notsé built by a 17th and 18th century Ewe kingdom. It proved to be the ancestral site of the Ewe people. The excavation revealed a wall extending to two and a half miles and a highly developed town. The discovery typified a phrase coined by Professor Posnansky in a lecture given at our cultural center: "towards a new past." It was to be his great gift, a gift of heritage, to the Togolese people, and opened up the potential for further explorations of their past.

Building on Posnansky's initial work, the archeological project developed numerous dimensions. Historians and other faculty members from Togo, Benin and Ghana worked together and eventually took over the archeological explorations. Posnansky organized two international conferences on the discoveries. It also led to the UCLA study abroad program in Togo which lasted eleven years, perhaps among the most successful study abroad programs ever to have taken place in Africa. Later it developed into a linkage program between UCLA and Togo's university which resulted in an exchange of faculty members. As a result, UCLA became the major U.S. university involved in Togolese studies.

A second initiative involved the sending of African francophone university students to the U.S. where they would serve as summer camp counselors. The idea was borrowed from an initiative I had known about and supported in Abidjan. The New York based International Camp Counselors Program (ICCP) managed by the YMCA in New York, was prepared to support, and place African college students as counselors in American summer camps provided that they could cover their international airfare to the U.S. and reasonably command the English language. To meet those requirements, we entered into a partnership with the University of Togo's English department. We publicized the program, arranged to conduct interviews, and let the students know they would have to devote their summer scholarship money to cover travel.

We aimed at finding some 16 candidates. More than 40 applied. The results were impressive. Our students were mature, highly motivated and had certain skills relevant to summer camp requirements. They could make campfires, hike great distances on forest trails, arrange to sleep out in the woods, and relate to nature, all skills they had acquired as boys in their villages. As part of the program, the ICCP also arranged to send the African students on a ten-day trip of the U.S. region they worked in at the end of the season. The success of the experience was apparent when the following year we had huge numbers of candidates for the program which we continued for the next three years I was in Lomé.

The program was an ideal exchange mechanism. In exchange for their work, the African students had opportunity to experience American culture at the grassroots level, perfect their English language skills, including choice profanities, and end the season with a two-week tour of an American region. Their American experiences led to their close relationship with our Cultural Center and me personally. During my three years in Togo, we built a group of almost one hundred students who had participated in the program. One anecdote recounted to me by one of the students was that American campers occasionally sought to play tricks on their counselors. A Togolese awoke one morning in terror to find a snake in his bed. While most snakes in the U.S. are harmless as was this one, most African snakes tend to be poisonous, hence the terror experienced by our counselor.

The third initiative built on our contacts with UCLA. While Togo was an authoritarian country it had a reputation for internal stability unique in the region. It was also quite friendly toward Americans. As a small and rather poor African country, it also sought greater international acceptability as a welcoming country. To enhance its reputation, its leaders had directed the university to establish a language center for the teaching of French. Knowing that American colleges generally found African countries to be inhospitable for their study abroad programs programs, we worked with the University of California to entice its students to come to Lomé to study French and pursue African studies.

That project evolved into a junior year abroad with a semester in France, at Bordeaux University to initiate California students by taking courses on Africa and the French language. That was followed by a second semester in Togo at that special language center where they were housed in a new facility and where they would continue their studies in Africa and French. An incident occurred that greatly influenced my attitude toward study abroad programs and how important it is to have support on the scene to help and advise students when they encounter problems. One of the American students decided to fulfill the program's requirement that he do a research project on local customs. He decided, despite a strong warning against getting involved in the project he selected, that he would observe religious ceremonies related to a local variety of Vodou. That evening after the ceremony he attended, his colleagues brought the student to my house. He was having delusions and was feverish apparently because of his reaction to the ceremonies. I decided to tell him we had a powerful substance that would help him recover. I didn't specify what it was, but we had him drink a bowl of my wife's delicious chicken soup and put him to bed. In the morning, he woke up grateful, feeling fine and freed from whatever spirit had possessed him.

In helping design and set up the program, I had extensive contact with the UC Study Abroad staff. The success of that program resulted in an invitation that I join their staff. As I was not prepared to leave the Foreign Service, I offered to apply for a year off at the end of my Togo tour. My request was granted by USIA under a program that allowed for professional development outside of government in a field related to foreign affairs. Accordingly, I was assigned to the University of California at Santa Barbara, the headquarters of the

UC systemwide study abroad program's ten University of California campuses. I was given the title of Deputy Director of the largest study abroad program of any American college and was blessed by spending the next year with my family in beautiful Santa Barbara where I learned a good deal about overseas study programs. I also was immersed in the negotiated tradeoffs needed for American universities to develop partnerships with foreign counterparts.

One memorable incident from my time in Togo involved the visit of a Peace Corps volunteer from Niger. He came to Togo to vacation with his parents, as he considered it more congenial than remaining in the heat and dust of Niger. While getting to know him, he brought his parents to my office. His father asked lots of questions. He was especially curious about traditional medicine. He asked where it was sold. I told him there was a marketplace just around the corner and offered to take him there. At the market we saw several stands that sold spices and had various uses. Some were simply herbs used to make soup. But others had decidedly different objectives. Herbs were sold to relieve aches and pains, including stomachaches and headaches. Parts of animals, including monkey paws, were sold at the same stands and we were told they could be mixed with other substances to cast spells, ease pregnancy, and even injure or poison enemies.

We would later meet again with our friend's parents, but the father's probing questions sent me to our USIS library to consult *Who's Who in America*. A quick check revealed the man I had taken to the market was a senior professor at the University of Virginia. He was both a famed doctor and head of its School of Pharmacy. That information led me to introduce him to officials at Togo's Ministry of Education and Togo's university. Subsequently, we identified a candidate for a Fulbright scholarship from the medical school who would go on to earn a PhD at the University of Virginia and conduct research with the professor which led to identifying traditional African medicine that could be effectively used to treat heart disease. I found this kind of serendipitous encounter to be the natural outgrowth of relations between Americans and Africans if given the proper stimulus.

One day when we were concluding our interviews of Fulbright graduate scholarship candidates, I was told by a Togolese staff member that there was one more candidate to be interviewed. It seemed that the candidate had been a victim of polio as a child and had no use of his legs. I wondered whether such a disability could be overcome, enabling him to study in the U.S., but decided he should be allowed to compete. I sent word that he should come for an interview. The next day I was told he was available that afternoon and I explained that I would come downstairs to conduct the interview. When he was informed that I would meet him downstairs he said no, he wanted to climb the stairs to meet me in my office. Later that day I met him. His knees were bound in a portion of an auto tire. Nevertheless, he climbed the steep staircase on his own. He impressed me in the interview and signed up for his English language exam. We later learned that he was successful in that and other examinations. We recommended him for a scholarship. He was approved.

The final step was to place him in a university graduate program that would accept him. Ordinarily that was a routine process but months went by without our hearing about his admission. Finally, I contacted the program agency and learned that they had given up on placement without informing us. I rebuked them, then contacted Professor Haig der Houssikian, the Fulbright professor who had conducted research the previous year in Lomé. He was at the University of Florida, which I thought would be appropriate given the climate. Haig, a professor of linguistics, was able to secure his admission. Months later I was informed that the student had been a success not only academically, but also was an inspiration at the university for his ability to navigate the campus, especially after a wheelchair had been provided. The miracle of the story was that he attained a Master's in Economics and returned to serve in Togo's economic ministry.

Professor der Houssikian research in Togo was to develop a dictionary for a Togolese spoken language that had no written language. Upon its completion he discussed it with me and by a stroke of serendipity, a captain in the Togolese army who spoke the language Haig had devised a written form of, called on me. I showed him Haig's work and it astonished him to see a written document in Kotacoli, the language of his people.

Our promotion of educational ties also led to a relationship with the University of South Carolina's School of Education. The Dean of that school together with three senior professors came to Togo to discuss how mutual interests could be developed that would benefit both sides. Their first initiative was to do a survey of Togolese education from elementary school to university on behalf of the Ministry of Education. After ten days of visiting schools at all levels, the Americans prepared a preliminary report which they shared with me and asked that I react to before presenting it to the authorities.

After reading the report, I met with the group to discuss their findings. They had found students often had to walk great distances to attend school. The report noted the schools lacked books, classrooms were woefully overcrowded, teachers often were not well trained, schools lacked desks and school buildings were in poor shape. I reminded them that Togo was a poor country and the problems they wrote about were therefore endemic. But I also challenged them when I noted that despite all the shortcomings, many Togolese students seemed to have a passion and motivation for learning, and some successfully overcame all adversities and completed school. I advised them that their study should note the high degree of motivation children had since their parents imbued them with the notion that success in school would determine success in life. That reality awakened them to just how much was at stake. The Americans revised their study to include those considerations. It was important too that they realize that Peace Corps' highest priority was the construction of three-room schoolhouses. Over the previous years, more than one hundred of these schools had been built in Togo.

One day at the Embassy, a colleague asked me if I was going to the piano concert to be held later in the week at the Soviet cultural center. I admitted I was unaware of the concert and asked why I might be interested. He informed me that while the winner of the famed Tchaikovsky piano competition would tour London, Paris and New York, the runner-up would have the privilege of performing in Togo. I went and was impressed but found that most of the audience consisted of foreign diplomats and only few Togolese were present.

The happiest of visits for me in all our times abroad was that of my father, Frank LaGamma who took great joy, especially in getting to know the children better. Besides Togo he had been with us in Italy as well and later in Senegal. He was the family member I missed most deeply as I had been very close to him throughout my youth and appreciated him for his goodness and integrity.

The education of Foreign Service children, especially in Africa is always an important issue. In Togo, the American school where Anita taught stopped at sixth grade and our eldest daughter Alisa was beyond that. We felt Alisa was exceptionally bright and flexible so we sought to enroll her in the French school. They told us they would have to test her first and when they did, they determined her French was not adequate to place her in the expected grade. More than that, they clearly questioned her academic ability and hinted that her intelligence might not be up to par. We understood that French educators seemed to judge intelligence by the command of their language. The compromise was to put her in a grade lower than her age would suggest with the hope she could do well enough so that the next year she would advance to her proper grade level. While it was trying on her, she made it through the year. The next year, she was placed at her proper age level. At the end of the year, the school principal was somewhat embarrassed to learn she had finished near the head of her class.

Respect for Human Rights was a persistent concern for us in Togo. Our residence was located across the street from a children's detention center. For weeks after arrival, we regularly heard the cry of children from punishment in the form of beatings. I raised the matter with Ambassador Johnson and our political officer and it was suggested we add the issue of corporal punishment of children to our annual State Department Human Rights Report as required by Congress. I did so and several weeks after the report was submitted to Congress, the sounds of what I considered torture were no longer heard. We attributed that to our report.

The rivalry of the United States and China, the outgrowth of the Cold War, had long complicated our work in Africa. While we were in Togo, Kissinger, then Nixon opened the floodgates of our relations with China. Our USIA film unit acquired footage of the February 1972 walk on the Great Wall, and the lavish banquets and sundry ceremonies marking the new relationship. Togo had recently abandoned its recognition of Taiwan and replaced its embassy with that of the People's Republic. What this meant for our diplomatic work was not immediately clear, but I explored the possible public affairs consequences of the new relationship in a long telegram to Washington.

One of those consequences began to emerge when soon after the Nixon visit, I received a call from the Chinese embassy. The caller asked if, what he termed my "counterparts," could call on me. I said, "yes, of course" and asked how many counterparts would be coming. He responded there were six of them from the press and cultural offices. I was pleased to learn it took six Chinese to do my job and invited them to come the next day.

To prepare for the visit, I thought it appropriate to queue the video I had received from Washington just a few days after the Nixon-Kissinger visit of Beijing. They would be impressed, I thought, at the timeliness of the video. When they arrived the next day, we exchanged pleasantries, especially since U.S.-Chinese relations in Africa had been so adversarial. I then told them I would like to crown the visit with some images and pressed the video's start button to reveal the Great Wall, the banquet hall, and the interaction of our leaders. One of them seemed fascinated. He rose from his chair and slowly walked over to look very closely at the T.V., then returned and solemnly announced to his colleagues: "IT'S A SONY." The fact that we Americans were using Japanese technology obviously impressed him more that the historic opening of our relationship.

The visit of my counterparts was followed by an invitation to a banquet at the new Chinese Embassy. It featured a film of the story of a young Chinese girl who became an Olympic diver. The two-hour long film took the athlete from having an enormous ego to realizing she was merely a product of the great socialist revolution. While we appreciated the hospitality, the film was a ghastly example of Communist propaganda. Aside from the awful, interminable film, we unfairly left the Embassy with quite another critique of the People Republic's hospitality. We lamented that their cuisine had been decidedly less good than that of the Taiwanese who had been expelled.

Our nearest neighbor was a congenial British businessman. He told us that while he was preparing for work one morning, he could not find his favorite tie. He concluded that one of his servants must have taken it. But how could he possibly recover it? He called his several servants together and explained that if the tie was not returned by the next day, he would call the police to investigate. Since Togolese police methods were known to be brutal, the servants knew they were in serious trouble. The next day, he told us, as he left the house, he found a dozen of his ties festooned from a tree in the garden. Clearly, he only missed his favorite tie and the thief, not knowing which tie was the one he missed, had returned that one and twelve others taken over a period of weeks.

The arrest of a young journalist for allowing the publication of an article in the daily newspaper that briefly mentioned Amnesty International's perspective on human rights had infuriated President Eyadema who ordered his arrest. This posed a quandary. This was an egregious violation of human rights that our government opposed. We had worked with the young man and both we and his colleagues respected him. I was determined to try to help him. It happened that at that time the Cameroonian editor of the Paris-based African weekly magazine, *Bingo*, was visiting Togo. I decided to invite him to lunch and raise the issue of the arrest, noting that once the news was known, Togo's reputation in the international community could be damaged. The Cameroonian nodded his assent. I asked if he could make that point to the President's Chief of Staff with whom he had an appointment. He agreed.

The next day I was called by Ambassador Johnson who said that President Eyadema was furious at my interference in the internal affairs of Togo and wished to expel me from the country. In response, Ambassador Johnson told the President she agreed with what I had attempted to do. Further, she felt that freeing the journalist would be in Togo's interest. She urged that no action be taken against my staying in Togo. When I learned that the Cameroonian had not supported my call for a release of the journalist, I felt betrayed. I later learned that the reason he had come to Togo was to collect his "envelope" containing a periodic bribe designed to assure favorable coverage of Togo in his magazine.

I discovered that it was a standard practice for editors of his and other Paris-based African news magazines to take similar bribes. Despite my initial failure, I thought of a plan B which would be more effective than my first failed effort to help free our journalist friend. It happened that the young journalist, son of then French President Mitterrand, was the resident Agence France Presse correspondent in Lomé. If I could convince him to intervene, I thought, it would have greater impact than my earlier effort. I met with him, explained the situation and he acted immediately. Our friend was freed a couple of days later. That young man went on to become a highly respected editor of an African journal in Paris several years later.

In September 1979 I received two unusual visitors. They were a professional boxer and his manager. John Mensah Kpolongo was African bantamweight champion of Togolese nationality, who had been trained in Ghana. He was returning home to Lomé to prepare to challenge world champion Carlos Zarate of Mexico in a bout to take place in Los Angeles. They asked if we could provide any assistance. I pondered how we might help and came up with the following request for Washington. I asked if Kpolongo could be afforded support while in Los Angeles to cover a few days living expenses. I requested that a photographer cover his Los Angeles visit and that the Voice of America cover the build up to the fight and the match itself. Washington agreed. When the championship bout took place, the arena was packed with Mexican American fans of Zarate. The champion had been undefeated and had a reputation as a ferocious knock-out artist. He lived up to that reputation, knocking out our Togolese boxer in three rounds. After a journey of over seven thousand miles, Kpolongo lasted ten minutes. While I was saddened by his defeat, he and his manager returned to my office satisfied by a decent, if not generous payday. I was able to give them scores of photos of their Los Angeles visit about which they were delighted.

My work in Togo led me to develop ideas for two important initiatives that were well received in Washington. The first involved our Fulbright scholarship program. While I acknowledged that it was a superlative flagship program, I argued that poor countries like Togo that needed educational opportunities were disadvantaged by its high academic standards. I suggested that we develop a program for such countries designed to assist young government officials by providing them with a year of academic training coupled with a professional internship related to their professional needs. Our office of academic exchange programs for Africa welcomed the concept and set to work creating what came to be known as the Hubert Humphrey program. Initially, that program was designed for Africa but after a year its success was replicated for all other world regions.

The second initiative involved linking American universities with African counterparts. Our initial success in matching UCLA with Togo's university demonstrated that both institutions stood to gain; the U.S. students in gaining fluency in French and African studies, and the Togolese in developing an important archeological project. I was delighted that the initiative was developed by USIA as a university linkage program. It provided up to one hundred thousand dollars for exchanges over each of three years based on a project proposal developed jointly by both sides. Its success led to its becoming a worldwide USIA program in the following years.

On the cultural front, I was impressed by the creativity of Togo's leading artist, Paul Ahyi. Initially, I got to know Paul through his massive public works. Lomé's one supermarket was adorned with his large sculpture on its façade. Furthermore, he had designed the Togolese flag, provided the sculpture for its independence monument, and one for the façade of its newest, grandest hotel. His monumental works were prominently displayed in the capitals of other African countries and could be found as well in Canada, and his smaller sculpture in the Vatican Museum. I made an early effort to meet this creative genius. I called on him at his home studio which consisted of an expansive workshop manned by six assistants. Paul was amiable, and especially friendly to an American. His great talent allowed him to frankly express his opposition to President Eyadema's dictatorship with no negative affect.

Paul's outdoor monuments led me to imagine what it would be like if I commissioned him to provide a sculpture for the exterior of our American cultural center. I explored the idea with him, and he found the idea appealing. He offered to do it for us for the cost of the materials only. I asked if he could provide us with sketches of his proposed sculpture. Several weeks later, he called on me with the proposed drawings. If it had been Picasso himself, I could not have been more frustrated or found it more difficult to say no to him. The drawings might have been artistically excellent, but it would have been embarrassing to have images of couples making love on a U.S. government building.

When I asked if he could choose a different design, he asked that I suggest a subject. One leapt to mind. "How about jazz?" I rejoined. Two months later the American Cultural Center was adorned by a thirty-foot long, six foot high, image of a jazz band with trumpets soaring from its top, and lights installed behind it to illuminate it at night. Our building was on the must-see circuit for visitors to Lomé, in stark contrast to the building across the street, the brown-with-dust American Embassy.

Our Paris office that provided lecturers and other services to francophone Africa offered an American lecturer on literature. Pat Samway, a Jesuit scholar, was a professor of American literature serving as a Fulbright professor in France. His specialty was the literature of the American South. He stayed with us in Lomé. His program was to deliver a series of lectures on Faulkner at the university. Returning to our home after the initial lecture, he admitted that his talk had fallen on deaf ears since the Togolese students had never read Faulkner nor had they understood the context for his writing. Samway therefore made the decision to revise his lectures to explain why Faulkner was so important and provide the students with keys to understanding his work. He stayed up until late at night doing the revisions. Amazingly, his lecture series, after the initial problem, turned out to get rave reviews. Our library two weeks later had a run on the novels of Faulkner, books that had never circulated before.

My Togo tour concluded with ambivalence. On a positive note, I had a sense of professional satisfaction in having developed several highly successful initiatives, among them: the university partnership program and what was to become the Hubert H. Humphrey exchange, adopted for use throughout Africa and world-wide. Our family had thrived. On the other hand, there was the sadness of leaving behind Togolese friends who continued to suffer under a tyrannical regime. I continued following events in Togo for some years. After yet another rigged election following the death of Eyadema, his son benefitted from fraudulent election results in 2005. I published an op-ed in the *International Herald Tribune* entitled "Why Togo Matters?" in which I called for the African Union not to recognize the illegitimate government produced by what was clearly a fraudulent election. My later work after my retirement did see the African Union act to sanction the seizure of power by authoritarian leaders.

Toward the end of our Togo years, we went to sleep one night, only to be awakened early in the morning with an outcry from our daughter Thérèse. I got up drowsily only to discover my shoes were gone, replaced by plastic flip flops. At that everyone was up and assessing what had happened. We soon realized that we had been robbed. The children's piggy banks had been taken as had my wife's wallet with her teacher's salary. The door to the balcony was open and several of our suitcases were outside with their contents strewn open. It was the one and only time in all our years in Africa that we were victims of theft. We suspected it was an inside job with the aid of one of our servants, but we never solved the mystery of who done it. Eventually, we were reimbursed by the State Department for our loss but only after a bureaucratic hassle.

As a result of my work in Togo, Ambassador Johnson nominated me for USIA's Superior Honor Award which gave me a needed career boost. I ended my time in Togo and went on to spend the following year at the University of California at Santa Barbara (UCSB) where I served as Deputy Director of the largest university study abroad program in the United States, the study abroad program of the entire University of California system. Arriving in Santa Barbara, an astonishingly lovely town, with very great luck, we found a house in Montecito, just a few miles from the campus across the street from an elementary school for two of our children.

While at UCSB, I traveled extensively to those other campuses and helped develop reciprocity to enable foreign students to conduct graduate study in California. I recall visiting UCLA's Russian department head. It was to have been time for the preparation of Olympic athletes and the professor spoke of offering a course in what he called: "Russian for athletes." I asked how the student athletes were doing and he said he considered the term, "student athletes" an oxymoron. In any event, the Russian invasion of Afghanistan canceled our participation in those games. Once at UCLA we sought that university's participation in alumni travel to Germany to celebrate the 25th anniversary of an exchange program. We were categorically told that was impossible since the date coincided with the homecoming day football game which was a priority for alumni.

The lovely woods and nearby ocean of Santa Cruz left me wondering how any studying ever took place there. Berkeley was the jewel in crown of the system, the most politically active and dynamic. Our travel most often involved discussions with geographic and linguistic department heads, former and future directors of our country programs and other faculty members who were supportive of study abroad. I recall a pleasant picnic on the Santa Barbara beach with Malcohm Kerr, a truly great scholar of the Arab world. He had been our recently returned director of our Cairo program. Professor Kerr had just been named President of the American University of Beirut. Shortly after his arrival there he was tragically assassinated by Islamic Jihad in his office.

One of our tasks was the selection of faculty to direct our overseas programs. I recall one instance when we had to choose the director of our U.K. programs. We had a dozen candidates. I was in favor of a young political science professor. The decision was in favor of a much older professor of English literature with an impressive list of publications. When he got to the main office in London his girth did not allow him to fit through the office door. Further, he let us know he was reluctant to travel to our programs for which he was responsible in Ireland, Scotland, and Wales. Soon after arrival he resigned and we appointed the young political scientist. I found that too often there was a strong bias in the selection of our overseas directors. They were chosen based on their academic achievements and not on their ability to handle solving the problems and managing the complex lives and academic programs of our students.

The year provided me with the opportunity to learn a great deal about the relationship between the academic world and the U.S. government. My work there was especially useful in my next job as Educational and Cultural Coordinator for the USIA Office of African Affairs, before moving back to Africa as Public Affairs Officer in Dakar, Senegal.

# X. A Washington Tour

Prior to returning to Washington to take on my new assignment, an event all Foreign Service officers look forward to but some consider a highly stressful and complex reentry came to pass. It was home leave. After years overseas most of us lacked a U.S. home to come back to for the month or six weeks leave we had earned in the U.S. Anita and I both had called New York City home, but with five children, our apartment-living families, much as they wanted to see us, had difficulty accommodating all seven of us for an extended period. Luckily, we were warmly welcomed by Anita's sister's family in Los Angeles which was our home leave address. Over the course of my overseas career, we regularly took advantage of their hospitality. It also served as a launching pad for our favorite vacation activity, visits to California national parks, especially our favorite, Sequoia. At the time, we were able to rent lovely log cabins in Giant Forest amid ancient, massive sequoia trees. And while our stay was in summer, the mile-high altitude kept the temperature mild and pleasant. We spent a couple of weeks there each time, hiking in a wonderland of forests, flowers, birds, and animal life, and attending lectures from the god-like rangers who provided insights into the natural world, and whose profound and knowledgeable respect for the environment afforded thrilling lifelong role models for our children.

**LaGamma family vacation in Sequoia National Park**

After six Italian years, three in Togo and a year at the University of California at Santa Barbara I returned to the Washington office in which I felt most comfortable, and where my career began; the Office of African Affairs. The job as Educational and Cultural Coordinator involved working on behalf of our more than 50 African posts with what I considered the Bureau that had the most valued resources for those posts. Those resources included exchange programs such as: the Fulbright and Humphrey academic exchange programs, our International Visitors Program, our university and other linkage programs, and the Arts America Program among others. While I lacked control of the funding and management of those programs in Washington, we were able to negotiate with the Educational and Cultural Bureau and to speak with authority about the needs of our African posts, and our implementation of those programs.

One struggle I felt we needed to wage within the bureaucracy concerned the traditional imbalance between the meager resources provided to Africa compared with those provided to other world regions. I most frequently made the point that the impact made by the resources allocated to Africa tended to have a greater and more positive impact than those afforded to any other part of the world. I argued that those resources most often related to the fundamental needs of African nations which lacked educational and professional training. These programs had a decided and formative influence on our relations with those countries. Our programs affected young government officials with potential, and African civil society and its publics who were becoming dynamic factors in shaping the politics of many African countries. When challenged that my demands for resources were too great, I was asked "LaGamma, what do you want?" I answered with the famed one-word response that labor leader Samuel Gompers uttered to that same question: "MORE." The challenge then was to find ways to elaborate on why spending more for Africa resulted in a positive impact for American interests in that part of the world.

A major cultural accomplishment based on the request of our PAO in Bamako, Mali was a response to the problem of illicit exportation of precious archeological objects to the United States, Europe, and other developed countries. The government of Mali found it impossible to protect its many geographically scattered archeological sites that were regularly looted. While Bamako had one of Africa's best museums, its problems were typical of those of most African countries' efforts to preserve cultural artifacts throughout the continent. In an article I published in a volume entitled *Plundering Africa's Past*, I sought to identify five problems common to most African countries. They were:

- First and foremost, there is a laxity of security at museums charged with protecting art treasures.
- Second, priceless works in insecure environments are vulnerable because they can fetch a king's ransom in Western markets. In fact, only the scrupulousness and integrity of a potential buyer keep works from disappearing without a trace.
- Third, there is the matter of poor channels of communication between African countries, the art markets where the works are sold, and potential allies in the United States and Europe.
- Fourth, the bureaucratic tangles in African governments can be daunting.
- Fifth, there is a dearth of political will, the absence of resources and the relatively low priority given to cultural matters.

We were encouraged to take action to prevent the importation of the looted work to the United States. We did so by appealing to the Department of State which resulted in a ban of archeological objects to the United States from Mali in line with UNESCO policy. Not long after the ban, custom officers seized a number of such works and returned them to Mali. It was the first ban of its kind to protect Africa's artistic heritage. Years later, it resulted in France adopting a similar ban. When I next visited Mali, I called on the Director of its National Museum. He took me to see several works that had been returned to Mali by U.S. Customs since the adoption of the ban.

As cultural coordinator for Africa, many unorthodox ideas crossed my desk. One of the strangest was a call from the Rockefeller Foundation. One of their senior program officers asked for my help in arranging a voyage to the Congo, specifically to the Ituri Forest. The objective was to recruit a group of pygmies famed for their traditional music. Andre Gide once reflected that their polyphonic music resembled that of J.S. Bach. Their project involved having the pygmies interact with a variety of musicians from different cultural traditions, including Native American, and developing a program of concerts to be held across the United States. Their request to me was to provide vehicles to take them from Kinshasa to the forest. My answer was "no." When asked why, I referred them to the map and explained that what they were asking was to travel about a thousand miles on impassable roads. They then asked what I suggested instead. Again, I referred them to the map. I noted that we might suggest flying to Bangui in the Central African Republic and determining if our Embassy there might provide a vehicle to drive them to the nearby forest in the south. I then contacted our Embassy in Bangui and they were willing to help.

Well, it turned out that the group successfully made the trip, contacted the pygmies and had them give a concert at the ambassador's residence on the condition that they wear appropriate clothing.

From there they flew to the U.S. and met and made music with the other ethnic groups, and successfully performed in American cities. I later learned that beside the Rockefeller Foundation, the project was funded by *ABC's Wild World of Sports* and accompanied by an American supermodel for good measure.

The role of France in Africa was unique among former colonial powers. That role had been shaped by the policies of Charles de Gaulle who decided to continue French policy by providing technical assistance and a vast number of French technical experts to the newly independent former French colonies. To better understand French policy in Africa, I invited a good friend who had the job of the State Department's" Africa watcher" at our Paris Embassy to brief USIA's Africa Bureau on that policy. His briefing began by defining that role in one short word. That word was: "oil." Noting that France had no petroleum resources of its own, he told us that Africa was to France as the Middle East was to the United States. He further observed that French involvement in its former colonial African empire had evolved to focusing on Gabon and Cameroon for their oil resources. Furthermore, it had focused increasingly on developing relations with Nigeria and Angola, also for reasons of their petroleum, rather than its past colonial territories of Senegal, Ivory Coast, Mali, Burkina Faso, Togo, and Benin.

Paris also was the location of our African Resource Service office headed by an American officer and a dozen highly skilled French employees. That office provided francophone African posts with artists and lecturers as well as a weekly press journal that could be adapted by local African offices to their needs and distributed to our key contacts. It also produced French language translations of American books; everything from paperback economic texts to literary works that were widely distributed by our cultural centers and featured in our libraries. The Paris office made all our francophone African cultural centers highly effective.

During a lunchtime conference with colleagues, an idea was born about how to enhance relations with African diplomats in our own capital. Desk officer Mary Ellen Connell raised the issue of the fate of African ambassadors to the United States. It seemed to those of us with experience on the continent, that diplomacy between the U.S. and Africa was conducted almost exclusively through U.S. embassies with the African foreign ministries, rather than in consultations with the African embassies in Washington which had almost no role at all. One of us noted that the African ambassadors usually came to America with high hopes of having access to the President and other key officials, only to learn that their main contact would be a low-level State Department desk officer and occasionally an Assistant Secretary. Most of our contact was with the ambassadors and their staff members that took place when we attended their annual national day receptions. Most of their meager budgets, aside from paying salaries and rent, went to caterers to mark those celebrations. Furthermore, while most were senior officials in their own governments and were highly educated, in general, they knew little of how the United States government functioned with respect to their own national interests.

Their lack of knowledge extended to a failure to understand that decisions affecting their countries would be a product of numerous governmental agencies and institutions of civil society. This included some key elements of American government and society that required a fundamental understanding if they were to be effective.

Out of this conversation grew an innovative idea on how to assist them to understand the country in which they were accredited. We designed a four-week program that would begin with a week of Washington briefings, followed by three weeks of travel to the U.S. hinterland. In Washington we would provide them with briefings on the Congress, the State, Treasury, Agriculture, and Commerce Departments, the national media, and universities; all of which impacted on the way their countries were perceived and how our policy toward Africa was influenced. We would attempt to illustrate how those organs of government might relate to shaping the policies that affected their countries. The briefings would provide them with suggestions on how best, and at what levels, to interact with those institutions. The travel dimension would put them in touch with some of the places outside of Washington that influenced our relations with African countries.

After providing that input to a program agency, that agency would arrange travel, hotels, and appointments. It was decided that our office would handle the Washington briefings while the program agency would arrange for visits to Boston, Little Rock Arkansas and a place called Pritchard, Alabama. I would lead the two southern stops, while my assistant would take them to Boston.

We extended the invitation to all Washington based African ambassadors. Twenty-three accepted and five others asked if they could send their deputies, making a total of twenty-eight in all. The first Washington week went smoothly with the active participation of all the attendees. They clearly wanted to learn how to be more effective in dealing with one of the most complex diplomatic jobs in the world. One blip in the program elicited their anger, but at the same time illustrated a problem in their relationship with the American media.

Veteran NPR journalist and former Africa correspondent, Sanford Unger, launched a discussion on how best African ambassadors might relate to the press. Had he framed it positively, there would have been no problem. Instead, he told them how not to do it. He recounted an experience in which he had arranged a Washington interview with one of their colleagues. On that occasion, he had been ushered into the ambassador's office only to find him engrossed in a T.V. soap opera. Nevertheless, they began the interview. Clearly the two things were incompatible, so the ambassador got up and raised the volume on the soap opera. Hearing this, the African ambassadors understandably found it an insulting tale about an incompetent diplomat that reflected badly on them. While agreeing that this was an undiplomatic story to tell diplomats, we knew it held a grain of truth for at least some part of the African diplomatic community.

Boston had been chosen for our first visit outside of Washington for its influential and prestigious universities, several of which had important African studies programs. The regional Boston Globe provided insight into foreign news coverage. And importantly, Boston's racial climate was not always pacific. Little Rock and Prichard were profound opportunities to observe the changing American South and instances of very dramatic historic connections with Africa.

Little Rock Arkansas had been on the front line of the struggle for school integration. The reason it had been chosen by the program agency was that its active World Affairs Council felt it necessary to spread the word that the shameful days of segregation were long past, and that they were representatives of a progressive New South. Also, Little Rock was home to Heifer International, a charity that provided livestock to African villagers. What else did Arkansas have of interest to Africa? Rice. As the foremost rice producer in the U.S., much of Arkansas' economy wound up on African dinner tables. A meeting for the ambassadors was arranged with the Arkansas Rice Council.

One concern of many of the ambassadors was the type of rice they received through the USAID program. They complained that it was mostly whole grain rice which was twice as costly as the broken rice their people preferred because much of African cuisine depended on the absorption of sauce by the broken rice. It was also the case that the expensive whole grain rice meant that they received less because of its cost. The head of the rice council explained that the surplus broken rice was highly sought after by the American beer industry whose strong lobby pressured Congress not to allow broken rice to be included in our surplus food program. He suggested the ambassadors mount their own lobbying effort to reverse that ban. The visit to Heifer International afforded the ambassadors the opportunity to learn of the mechanisms to access the very generous programs offered by that organization.

Little Rock Arkansas was known throughout the world for the infamous attempt in 1957 by Arkansas's governor, Orval Faubus, to prevent school integration. We visited Little Rock's high school, known as one of the finest high school buildings in America when it was built, and the one to which Governor Faubus had sought to bar the admission of Black students. The ambassadors were introduced to the student body president who was African American. They learned that the school population was 50 percent Black. Our ambassadors were divided into small groups, each of which observed a class in session and left persuaded that there had been some very healthy social changes in at least one American Southern town.

Upon our return to the hotel, I found I had a message waiting. I was to call the Governor's office. When I did, I learned the Governor wished us to have a reception in honor of the African visitors. I was asked if we could come to the mansion that evening. When we showed up, we were greeted warmly by Bill and Hillary Clinton. Governor Clinton impressed his guests by speaking knowledgeably about their countries and our relationship to Africa. When I returned to the hotel, I called my wife and told her I thought I had just met a future President of the United States. When I shared that with the ambassadors, they agreed. It was the highlight of our program up to then. It would soon be rivaled by what lay in store for us in Alabama.

Pritchard Alabama is a small town under the jurisdiction of Mobile. It has a remarkably unique connection to Africa. In 1860 slavers raided villages in what was then Dahomey and now the Republic of Benin and brought its cargo of enslaved people to America despite the fact that the Congress had banned the slave trade in 1807. Unlike other groups of slaves, that ship carried a community of Africans who spoke the same language and shared the same culture. As the Civil War raged from 1861 to 1865, the Pritchard slaves were soon emancipated. After more than a century, the culture of Pritchard still retained vestiges of its ancestral African origins. The boat that carried the tragic human cargo was named Clotilda. Its story is chronicled by historian Hannah Durkin in his definitive book *The Survivors of the Clotilda: The Lost Stories of the Last Captives of the American Slave Trade.*

At the time of our visit, Pritchard's main attraction was a young mayor, John Smith. After an impressive college football career at the University of Wisconsin, John was drafted by a professional football team. A knee injury led him to abandon a sports career and decide to return home and enter politics. Surprisingly, he ran and won as mayor becoming the only African American Republican mayor in Alabama. During his distinguished tenure he also served as Vice President of the National Republican Mayors Association and President of the Alabama Conference of Black Mayors. As John sounded like a liberal Democrat in all aspects of his political pronouncements, I asked why he chose to run as a Republican. He replied that it was a strategic choice since Ronald Reagan was president and he believed he could prevail on the Republican administration to provide more support for his people as a member of that party. Among the things he aspired to win from Washington was the acceptance of Pritchard's Africatown as a Historic District by the Department of the Interior. Eventually, he succeeded in that quest.

Our visit to Pritchard was timed to coincide with its hosting of a conference of African American mayors of Alabama. Despite his Republican affiliation, John had brought four dozen of his counterparts together to discuss mutual problems. Our ambassadors were invited to attend the meetings as observers. That provided valuable insights into the working of local governments and the role of African American politicians in the deepest South. During the opening session of their consultations, they were interrupted. Two white gentlemen asked if they could address the African ambassadors as representatives of the governor of Alabama. They then announced to our stupefaction, that the once infamous Governor George Wallace wished to welcome the African diplomats to Alabama and confer on them honorary citizenship of his state.

After presenting impressive certificates of honorary citizenship, they left. It was explained to the Africans that our political system is sometimes characterized by an important dimension of pragmatism. It seems that the icon of racism, George Wallace, wanted it known to the citizens of Alabama and the entire United States, that he had changed his stripes and he would welcome the votes of all races.

Upon our return to Washington, we assessed that the three weeks were marked by numerous accomplishments. First and foremost, we forged friendships with some key diplomats. That was especially important since African heads of state had often named as ambassadors to the U.S. important political figures, who one day could possibly become foreign ministers or even heads of state themselves. Second, we had provided them with valuable insights on how American society and politics works with the expectation that their more professional understanding of our country would serve to improve relationships. Third, we had allowed them to witness a key dimension of the African diaspora that once took the brutal form of slavery, but as a result of the civil rights movement, had evolved to take on an impressive weight in the politics of our nation.

We were pleased to learn that our project had been considered highly successful by the leaders of our own Agency. But then its success also had a downside. When some months later we requested funding for a repeat, we were turned down. The rejection was based on the fact that our success had whetted the appetite of other regional offices who wanted to emulate our program. We argued that the project was uniquely suited to Africa. We lost the argument and the next up was Latin America and the Caribbean. When that office of USIA sent invitations to the ambassadors of that region, they got six acceptances, none of them for the participation of their chiefs of mission, but rather for second or third secretaries. As we predicted, Latin American high-level diplomats usually already had impressive knowledge of the U.S., some of whom had attended university in our country.

As a consequence of our contact with the very impressive mayor, John Smith, I recommended him for our speaker's program to Africa. The very next day it was turned down. We had no explanation. It was our judgment that the Republican political appointee who headed the speaker program, Ronald Trowbridge, assumed an African American mayor from Alabama recommended by the Office of African Affairs must have been a Democrat. In his eyes, that was enough to disqualify our request since it would not pass his political litmus test. I prepared for battle assuming it would be difficult to overcome his objections.

The next day's *Washington Post's* front page changed everything. On it was depicted President Ronald Reagan signing a Congressional Housing bill. Next to him stood our friend, Mayor John Smith of Pritchard. Clearly, the White House was somewhat limited in its effort to find a Republican African American politician from the South. That seemed to vindicate John's choice to run as a Republican. I sent a clipping of the picture to Mr. Trowbridge with a note asking if I should contact the White House staff to inform them that USIA had refused to send John to Africa to speak on American local government and politics. The decision was reversed, and John travelled to Africa on our behalf, not once, but several times. A major stop each time was Benin, the ancestral home of many Pritchard citizens. They and their Benin counterparts have visited each other a number of times since.

The Reagan administration's political appointees came to office convinced that the program offices for Africa funded by USIA possessed an African American or Democratic party-oriented bias that directed funding to liberal organizations. They sought to funnel that money instead to conservative think tanks that had little or no experience working in Africa. I fought to retain the services of the African American Institute, and Operations Crossroads Africa despite pressure to diminish or eliminate their roles. We did agree to a better-balanced program and we prevailed to continue funding of the two program agencies that had served our needs in Africa for several decades.

# XI. Four Years in Dakar, Senegal (1984-88)

Dakar, the former French colonial capital of West Africa, appealed to me for several reasons. First, it had been the most stable country in the region, not having suffered from military coups or civil wars. Then there was its reputation as a center of culture and education. It had produced notable writers including its first president, poet Leopold Sedar Senghor and noted musicians, and film makers. Yet another consideration was based on our having five young children. Dakar was known for having the mildest climate in West Africa and as one of West Africa's healthiest countries.

The officer I replaced in Dakar was said to be a tough act to follow. He too was an Africanist, one of the service's most senior and most sociable. He left behind a well-developed project for a new cultural center, a new building that would be completed several months after my arrival. That cultural center was located just off the town's central square in a three-story edifice that would feature a large library, a multipurpose room, several classrooms for our English teaching program, as well as ample office space. I would have a staff of two American officers, one trainee, an excellent Senegalese staff, and a regional administrative officer. Several days after our arrival in Dakar we were invited to a reception after work. As we drove along the Corniche, we encountered one of the most spectacular sunsets we had ever seen. It lasted an astonishing half hour, displaying pinks and reds and purples before the sun set beneath the ocean. Never again during the following four years were we treated to another like it.

The great gift of being with the American mission in Dakar at that time was the presence of an outstanding and inspirational ambassador, Charles Bray. Bray was highly intelligent, fluent in French and conveyed advice that served me for the rest of my career. His point of departure was that too often diplomats reacted to events in an ad hoc manner. His concept of diplomacy was that we needed to be guided by a strategy. He advocated the adoption of an intellectual framework that should condition our actions. For someone like me, in the field of public diplomacy, that meant that our speakers, our exchange of persons, our press operations, our representational activities including who we took to lunch or invited to dinner, all should be thematically linked to the extent possible to achieve well-defined goals. He called it "developing an idea strategy."

Ambassador Bray had been a habitual smoker. He tried everything he knew to stop, to no avail. He shared his problem one day in conversation with his Senegalese driver. The driver suggested a way to combat his addiction. He proposed they go on Saturday to a nearby village to meet with someone who might have a powerful cure. The next Saturday they arrived at the village and were guided into a thatched hut. Seated in a corner was a wizened old man. Bray introduced himself and explained his inability to dispense with the habit. The old man looked deeply into the Ambassador's eyes and simply uttered these words: "the next time you smoke a cigarette you will die!" Bray said he left in a daze from the power of the experience. He said he was not sure if the prediction would come true, but he had decided not to take a chance. He had not smoked in the year since that visit.

In preparation for my arrival in Dakar, I anticipated I might be heading for a problem. Ronald Reagan had decided that the United States would withdraw from UNESCO. The issue had to do with what the U.S. rightfully considered to be the administrative abuses of UNESCO Director General Amadou-Mahtar M'Bow, a senior Senegalese politician who advocated "a new world information order," among other things. That concept meant that governments should insist that the media follow government policies in opposition to the concept of freedom of the press. Senegalese concerns were fueled by the fact that many Senegalese nationals worked for UNESCO and Senegalese organizations were recipients of generous UNESCO grants.

In fact, just before my arrival in Senegal, a petition was published in the major Senegalese daily signed by all the professors in the university's philosophy department protesting our decision to withdraw from that U.N. body. Just a couple of weeks later I met with the Dean responsible for that department and asked about the petition. He told me not to worry about it. He informed me that the philosophy department's journal was subsidized by UNESCO. Then he added: 'but it's not very good and deserves to be shut down."

To organize anticipated responses regarding Senegalese concerns about our withdrawal, I decided to stop in Paris to be briefed by our departing UNESCO staff before arriving in Dakar. The briefing was most helpful. It stressed that we not say our leaving UNESCO was because of M'Bow, but rather that we had many administrative concerns about the organization's operations. My briefing was from our educational officer to UNESCO who was literally packing his possessions in preparation for his departure. I had expected him to support our continued membership in the organization. He surprised me by approving of the decision to leave, citing our many efforts to correct what we believed were blatant abuses by the Secretary General.

The Paris stop turned out to have been a good decision. Two days after my arrival in Dakar, I was called by the Senegalese national television service and asked if they could interview me. I agreed and the next day they sent a team to my office for the interview. Sure enough, UNESCO was their major concern, and I was able to use the guidance provided to me to deflect the charge that it was our animosity toward the Senegalese Director General that caused our departure. After that interview, the TV producer came up to me and said I had been untruthful about our reason for leaving the organization. He argued that our opposition to its Senegalese Director M'Bow was the main reason, and he believed we were right to oppose him. He said M'Bow was a terrible man. He added that he knew that having grown up in his household.

In addition to the UNESCO issue, I was faced with another serious problem. Before leaving Washington, our Africa office was contacted by our furious USIA director, Charles Wick. He asked our Africa Office boss who he should fire in Dakar. The reason he gave was Dakar's failure to program the Agency's interactive satellite program known as WorldNet on Senegalese television. The answer given by my boss was not to fire anyone since Bob LaGamma was headed to Dakar and would solve the problem. When I arrived, I immediately investigated. It seemed my press attaché had insisted that the Senegalese TV presenter should be a recent one of our grantees to the U.S. The Senegalese television director had baulked at being told who on his staff should play that role. I then issued my Mickey Mouse decree. I told my press attaché to advise the television director that I didn't care if he named Mickey Mouse to conduct the interview. It was, after all, his prerogative not ours to make that decision. The second problem was that the Senegalese staff was being asked to give up their lunch hour to run the program, something they flatly refused to do. I therefore offered to provide them with lunch before they conducted the program. It cost me less than $20 to do so. They were pleased and the second problem was solved. As a result, USIS Dakar conducted six WorldNet projects in the next few months, more than any other USIS African office.

Soon after our arrival in Dakar we were invited to attend the opening of the 1984 season of the Senegalese National Theater. We were told that while the performance we were to see might not be world class, the entry of the audience into the theater would be. And so, it was. The elegance of Senegalese women when attending a public event is simply second to none; stunning and stylish with their dazzling boubous, decorated with sparkling, flowing, flowery designs. Dressed in their finest, their arrival was timed so that they entered one by one to be adored by ordinary mortals in the audience.

The opening of the National Theater season each year was and continues to be the most elegant fashion show on the African continent.

Dakar was an exceptional place to live. Our house was across the street from the national museum, a block from the American Embassy, facing the National Assembly and a block from the Catholic cathedral. Each workday I could walk to work breathing in the street's breakfast cooking, the venders of fresh bread and the newsstands. Not far from us was the fish market on the beach where we would regularly buy buckets of fresh shrimp and delectable swordfish steaks, all caught by the Senegalese fishermen in their colorfully painted pirogues. Anita captured the scene in this poem that won the prize conferred by the Jesuit magazine *America* as its best poem of the year:

**Morning Drive Along the Corniche, Dakar, Senegal**

The naked fou, serpentine hair matted
with mud, strides serenely in morning traffic;
a horse-drawn-cart with bushels of fish falters,
falls, spreading sea-life on sandy roads;
traffic slows—crisp French baguettes with
little children cross the road trailed
by ambling goats; a blind beggar raps
on windshields, one hand grips his young
guides head, the light turns red; corner
lepers lurch forward—one noseless, the other
with ski mask covering what is not there—
nquir yallah they cry moving to each car

until the light turns green, along the roadside.
peanut oil in cauldrons boils sweet, fresh dough—
street breakfast wrapped in oil soaked brown paper
for a penny; khaki-clad children eating butter-
drenched bread, shuffle in plastic flip-flops
to dark crowded school rooms; now past the stone
carvers' heads of fantasy, we turn off the corniche
seeing for the last time painted pirogues perilous
upon the wave, riding blue-green sea-serpents
to catch the great fish at the edge of the world.

The ocean currents that bring swordfish, marlin, and other great fish near land pass close to the Dakar coast, making it one of the premier sport fishing places in the world. When our good friend Charles Gusewelle came to visit he explored the commercial options for attempting to snare the sea beasts. He found the Dakar based French fishing boats extremely expensive. But studying a map, he found a Senegalese fishing village even closer to the currents. Together we explored the prospects of renting a wooden pirogue and found it could be done rather cheaply. He did so several times and each trip resulted in the catch of large swordfish. He gave them to the villagers and I asked that on the next trip he catch one for us. The very next day he came home with an eighty-pound swordfish which we cleaned and cut up, then stored in our freezer, giving us splendid meals for the next six weeks. I decided to try my own luck and together with my son Adrian we rented one of the pirogues. We motored ten minutes on a smooth Atlantic Ocean and were told by the boatman that we had arrived at the place where we could cast out poles. Twenty minutes later, Adrian's pole experienced a powerful tug. I helped him reel in what turned out to be a swordfish. We battled to bring it in when it dove under the pirogue and snapped the line. We lost it but had the experience of a lifetime, recalling Hemingway's *Old Man and the Sea*.

When our USIS office in Mauritania closed, it offered to transfer a vehicle to us. I had always wanted to visit that office on the Sahara, so accompanied by my wife Anita, a driver and two of my children, we headed north to spend an evening in Nouakchott. While there was a decent road through the Senegalese town of St. Louis, our problem developed when we missed the ferry that would take us across the Senegal River. After several hours it returned and we resumed our journey in the late afternoon. That was unfortunate since once on the Mauritanian side, we experienced the Sahara Desert. Anyone who has travelled on a road across the desert would know that winds blowing sometimes covers the road with sand, confusing the driver and causing him to veer into the desert.

After several such mishaps, we found our way to our destination just as night fell. Ironically, that evening we experienced one of the few rain showers of the year. Nouakchott is one of the least imposing capital cities in the world. A news story appeared in the *Paris Tribune* about the fate of an American naval ship's captain who made the mistake of navigating by sight to Nouakchott's port. The poor guy expected to see the city's skyline which does not exist. Instead, his ship landed on a sand bank and he lost his rank as captain.

Back in Dakar, our sparkling new cultural center was operational. Shortly after, we learned that Secretary of State Shultz was scheduled to visit Africa and Senegal was his first stop. I asked Ambassador

Lannon Walker who had replaced Bray, to request that the Secretary inaugurate the new American Cultural Center. When our idea was included in the Embassy's proposed schedule, the State Department quickly and I thought snootily, responded: "what is the precedent for the Secretary to inaugurate a cultural center?" I was frankly dumbfounded and began to prepare a long, acerbic argument about the importance of culture in Senegal to justify his involvement. Then I realized I had a better response, one that was short and sweet. To be precise, I walked over to the British Council's cultural center and copied the bronze inscription at its entrance. It read: "On this site, on the 13th of July of 1970 was inaugurated the British Council by her Majesty Queen Elizabeth II." We sent that as our reply and the Secretary's schedule was duly modified to include the American Cultural Center.

**Secretary of State George Schultz at Goree Island House of Slaves Museum**

In preparation for that visit, I arranged for the master kora player from Senegal's National Theater to perform as our guests arrived in the new library. He came armed with his splendid traditional stringed instrument and was garbed in colorful traditional robes. Then the Secretary's advance team drove up and the security officer ordered me to remove that gentleman. I ushered him into my office until the team left, then returned him to the library's entrance. Shortly after, the motorcade with Secretary Schultz arrived and encountered our musician. He had improvised a song in Wolof that repeatedly included the Secretary's name and Schultz, a man with a sense of humor, loved it, spending ten minutes listening before attending the main event and addressing the one hundred assembled dignitaries.

In his address to the assembled Senegalese elite, including the Minister of Culture, the Rector of the University and representatives of the media, Secretary Schultz precisely hit the right note. Understanding Senegal's pride in its cultural and intellectual traditions and gesturing to the library books that surrounded him, he spoke of the power of ideas to transform the world. Furthermore, he called the cultural center a meeting ground for the brightest and most creative Senegalese and Americans to enrich their mutual creativity. It was an absolutely ideal and helpful launching of our new center.

Shortly after, USIA Washington offered us the visit of a leading American sculptor, Richard Hunt. Hunt provided an array of small but exceptional works for exhibition. He was most amiable and interested in the local art scene. On our way to the gallery, we drove past some stone sculptures offered for sale along the corniche. Hunt asked that we stop and he exited the car to converse with the young men who had produced the work. He also invited them to attend the opening of his show and they later did so. We were disappointed that the exhibition gallery failed to provide the promised assistance to set up Hunt's work. Instead, I and my staff had to spend hours late into the night to do so. Helping in that job was our newly arrived junior officer, Michael Pelletier.

As we left at midnight, I told Michael that ordinarily we would not expect him to work such long hours. His response was, "oh no, this was my dream when I entered the Foreign Service." That statement matched my own concept of our USIS work, my own dream. Forever after, I tended to judge the young officers under my supervision by the standard that the Foreign Service is a dream profession. Michael went on to serve as DCM in India and ultimately as Ambassador to Madagascar.

During the visit of Secretary Shultz, Ambassador Lannon Walker decided to seek support from him on an exciting and ambitious project. We had learned that the owner of a lovely house on Goree Island, the heir to the Gilby Gin fortune, wished to sell his house. Since the island had been a slavery entrepot, we developed an idea to use the house as a research center to explore the diaspora and focus on the evolving progress of African Americans. I explored the idea with John Hope Franklin of the Smithsonian Institution, and he agreed in principal that the Smithsonian could provide an exhibition for the new center. Ambassador Walker arranged for Secretary Schultz to join us for a picnic in the garden of the house and to explore his thoughts about our idea. His reaction was very supportive to the tune of his writing a ten-thousand-dollar check to launch our fundraising effort.

Further fundraising was put in the hands of a former ambassador working with the State Department. Alas, Walker and I went on to new assignments and our project to acquire the house never came to fruition. It was a bitter disappointment. That disappointment was somewhat mitigated when I learned that with the help of our Fulbright professor, David Robinson, an initiative to create an American research center in Dakar was kept alive. In 1992 the West African Research Center (WARC) was created in Dakar to facilitate the work of scholars, as well as fostering student study abroad. That Center has continued to function for the past three decades. While we failed to secure funding for the house, the essential idea came to fruition thanks to the hard work of American Africanists.

A highlight of my career involving cultural activities was the scheduling of the New Orleans Dejan Marching Brass Band for a

**Jazz train comes to Senegal**

week in Senegal. This had special resonance since the city St. Louis, once the capital of French West Africa during colonial times, was settled by the French at the same time as our New Orleans. Further, like New Orleans, it was known for its jazz festivals. Its houses resembled the architecture of New Orleans with their vibrant pastel colors and wrought iron balconies. Because of its cultural and historical parallels, we decided to make it the major stop on the band's itinerary in Senegal.

Ambassador Walker gave me a splendid idea on how to traverse the one hundred eleven miles from Dakar to St. Louis. We had learned that the government of Senegal was making a major effort to improve and promote its railroads and their usage. We decided to suggest they lend us a train for the voyage as a way of helping generate interest in the railroad. They agreed and thus began the saga of what we called "the Jazz Train." I asked the head of the railroad company to add a flat car to the back of the train and we devised a plan to have it stop at major towns along the way. At those stops, the musicians would exit their compartment and move on to the flat car where they would perform a tune or two before continuing their voyage.

I also arranged for national television to send a crew to travel with us to produce an hour and a half special on the Jazz Train featuring our concerts in St. Louis. But arriving in that town, we were apprised of a problem. Our band was to march through town the next afternoon at precisely the time that a major soccer match would be televised. The question was: would anyone attend our concert? To better publicize our event, I rented a donkey cart, a unique St. Louis public conveyance, placed one of our trumpet players in it, and traveled through the town while he played the "When the Saints Come Marching In." When the next afternoon rolled around, we attracted six local people for the beginning of the march but as it continued the numbers swelled to the hundreds and when we arrived in the center of the town, thousands marched with us, despite the televised soccer match.

When we arrived back in the capital, Dakar, we prepared for the next day's marching concert. Once again, we encountered a problem. A police strike threatened violence and the government imposed a curfew which banned large gatherings. We had planned a ferry ride to Goree Island, the departure point for slaves sent to America, and a march with our African American band to the infamous House of Slaves Museum. I knew the cultural advisor to the President and called him to make the case for our peaceful, musical march. He agreed to share my concern with President Diouf and within an hour, the curfew was lifted for our march. Accordingly, the band boarded the ferry and gave an abbreviated concert for those leaving and those waiting to board. Once arrived at Goree, they repeated their playing for those coming on and off the boat. From there they marched through the town, accompanied by hundreds of delighted people. The finale was a concert held for a standing room audience only at the National Theater, but without the marching.

While Anita and I had travelled widely in Senegal, we decided to have our children join us during their boarding school vacation for a treat. Driving North past St. Louis and close to the border of Mauritania and the Sahara, we encountered the wetlands that constitute Djoudj National Bird Sanctuary. Djoudj consists of a lake, some ponds, and streams, all fed by the Senegal River, where millions of winged creatures refreshed themselves after their flight from Europe and across the Sahara. Nowhere had we ever encountered such a concentration of birds. Everywhere we turned, riding the water on a pirogue, we encountered white pelicans, great egrets, radiant pink flamingos, purple herons, and massive numbers of nesting cormorants. We explored this ecological wonderland by boat and later sadly learned that dams and the incursion of sea water would endanger the sanctuary, at risk according to UNESCO.

Once back in Dakar, we learned a lesson that cultural perceptions can often be at dramatic variance. When an American who had frequently served as an interpreter-escort passed through Dakar on his way home, he dropped by my office. He informed me that he had once served as an escort-interpreter for a Senegalese professor when he was in the U.S. for a one-month visit on a USIA grant. That professor subsequently become a leading government member of the cabinet as Senegalese Minister of Education. It seemed that the professor and the escort had developed a friendship during that tour and he very much wanted to visit him while he was in Dakar.

I called the Minister, Iba der Thiam, who said he would be delighted to meet with his old friend. I was present when they met and fondly reminisced about their travels. Later when I spoke to the American, he told me a story about the trip. After three weeks they arrived in New Orleans. The American had friends there with whom he wished to have lunch. He asked the professor if he would excuse him for a few hours. Since they were in a hotel in the center of historic New Orleans, he suggested that the professor might wander around the town and have lunch on his own.

When the American came back three hours later, he found the professor still in his room where he had remained since they parted. He asked why he hadn't gone out. The Senegalese said he had heard there were homosexuals in New Orleans. His escort then asked him what harm he would have been exposed to. The professor said, "they could rape me." The American then told me that they had travelled together for a month across the United States and then he added, "I am gay." The American told me that the issue had never come up until that moment in New Orleans and the professor had been oblivious to his interpreter-escort's being gay.

Common in friendly ports of costal Africa were visits of the ships of the U.S. Sixth Fleet. Dakar regularly hosted those visits which consisted of calls on senior military officials. To take the edge off purely military-to-military activities the visits regularly included the very excellent navy band flown in from Naples. During my time in Dakar, we had the opportunity to arrange a concert for them at the National Theater that was standing room only and wildly successful. The ship's captain also co-hosted a reception with the Ambassador which featured delicacies from the ship's larder.

We accepted another notable musical group offered by USIA, the Howard University's Jazz Band. The Band consisted of both faculty and senior students and was one of the best college bands in our country. We arranged their concert at the National Theatre which drew a full house and was a great success. Before they left, I asked one of our Senegalese employees who was well connected to the Senegalese musical scene if he could arrange for several Senegalese musicians to hold a jam session with the Americans at the Cultural

Center. We met the Senegalese group and were surprised to learn they had just returned from a European tour. Both the Howard professors and students were stunned to see the instruments their Senegalese counterparts had brought with them. They were far superior to those that the Howard musicians could afford. Their exceptional playing was also world class and the encounter was a lesson to us that we Americans had no monopoly on jazz.

After my initial few months under Ambassador Bray, my concluding three years in Dakar were spent with another remarkable but very different ambassador, Lannon Walker. Lannon was a ten-idea-a-day man. Most of them were good. But he was also quite demanding and difficult for his staff to keep up with. He was fluent in French, and studied the local language, Wolof, important assets for Senegal. Mrs. Walker was French and a talented artist. While the Walkers were at home in francophone Africa, the Ambassador was not at all prepared to play second fiddle to his French counterpart who tended to be domineering given France's role as former colonial power and its substantial aid program.

France's dominant role in Senegal did not prevent Walker from posing a challenge. A French monopoly produced wheat and controlled the production of flour. That flour in turn was sold to Senegalese bakeries to produce baguettes that were sold on street corners throughout Senegalese cities. Knowing that the United States produced a surplus of wheat, Walker found that we could provide U.S. produced wheat flour as part of our aid to Senegal, saving that country a tidy sum, as wheat had replaced the traditional millet and sorghum as the grain of choice for most Senegalese. Accordingly, an offer was made to substitute American for French flour. Before the deal could be consummated a rumor circulated like wildfire. It was that baguettes could not possibly be made with American wheat.

To counter that disinformation Walker arranged for several sacks of American wheat flour to be airmailed to our embassy. Upon arrival it had been prearranged for the Ambassador's car to convey the flour to a nearby bakery. That bakery would use it to make baguettes early in the morning. They would then be driven with a note, attached by red ribbon to Senegal's President and all its cabinet Ministers. The note signed by the Ambassador simply read "this baguette was made with American wheat flour," And it was delicious! Our wheat served the Senegalese people for precisely one year. The French response to President Diouf was that if he allowed it to happen again, France would have to reduce its aid to Senegal. That ended our brief ascendency in the Senegalese grain market. The U.S. had lost its ability to provide surplus wheat to Senegal, but it had also showed that France would not stand to be outmaneuvered when it came to its role in a francophone African country where it could wield its influence through raw economic blackmail. In subsequent years French dominance over its former colonies came to be questioned and in several cases has been replaced by other countries, including China.

An incident involving a reception held on the roof of our cultural center provided the occasion for mirth. Prior to the arrival of our guests and as we prepared the buffet table, I noticed one of our staff placing food in a paper bag. I took him aside and asked what he was doing. He responded that following receptions we usually let him take leftovers home, but he thought it best to take the leftovers before the guests came since there might not be any later. I found his response so novel that I said, "OKAY" and allowed him to keep the food.

Senegalese artists in various disciplines had a well-earned reputation in Europe. I identified a leading contemporary painter, Mamadou Fall Dabo, who lived not far from our home and called on him. When I asked if I could see some of his latest paintings, he responded that they had just been hung up at the gallery for the annual national art show. That show had been delayed and later cancelled because of a police strike that affected all gatherings. He said if I wanted to see the paintings, he knew the janitor who would admit us into the gallery. He did and I was struck by two large and remarkable works by him, one that I especially admired of farmers planting crops. It was six feet long and was dazzling in its explosive green and red colors. I asked if he could sell it to me after the show was over. He responded that we could take it now and he would measure the space and replace it with a new one. I bought it and it's hung in our living room ever since.

Agriculture was critical to the well-being of the Senegalese people. An editorial in the country's leading newspaper quoted a senior government official as saying the soil, especially in the Dakar region, was poor and unsuited for growing crops of any kind. An enterprising journalist contradicted that statement when he investigated the area around the site of a new soccer stadium being built by the Chinese. It was the Chinese practice in Africa that they sometimes built sports facilities, and to do so brought their own labor force and all the necessary material needed for the construction. Since the

Dakar construction site was substantial, they had planted crops sufficient to feed their workers. Those crops had thrived, according to the Chinese embassy, on precisely the land the government declared was unfit for agriculture.

Concerning the agriculture in our own backyard, although our family enjoyed eating pesto pasta, fresh basil was not easily available to us. I therefore ordered basil seeds from the American seed company, Burpee. Our gardener cleared a patch of lawn and together we planted one hundred seeds. The basil plants grew and grew and grew until they reached seven feet tall with leaves as wide as my hands. We had enough for many pesto meals as did our colleagues and Senegalese friends.

Prior to my arrival in Dakar my predecessor held what he called a colloquium on American Studies at the University. I thought that an excellent initiative and decided to build on it. We would continue to sponsor similar *colloques* each year. For the first year I put together a committee of Senegalese scholars joined by our Fulbright professor, Roger Shattuck, a renowned professor at the University of Virginia. I decided that each colloque would have a theme. I also ordered hundreds of copies of books on American literature in translation from our Paris Books in French program for distribution to those attending the two-day conference. Roger Shattuck delivered a brilliant lecture after reading over 20 Senegalese novels, comparing them to American Puritan literature. While the first year's program focused on literature, other themes in future years included American elections, the role of religion (and the separation of church and state), and American pluralism. The well-attended colloquia served to provide key academics, both students and professors, with fundamentally important knowledge on some essential elements of American society and politics.

Working with the press in Senegal was one of our key responsibilities. Press freedom was observed in Senegal more than in most other African countries although radio, television and the major newspaper were all government owned. Nevertheless, editors of independent papers and even that of the government were allowed to criticize the government on a variety of issues. When President Mobutu visited Senegal, a harsh editorial in the major daily, *le Soleil*, critical of his repressive rule, provoked his complaint to President Diouf. The Senegalese President called an aide to bring in a file. He showed the file to the Congolese President. It contained many news stories and editorials from the Senegalese press lambasting Diouf as severely as the offending editorial hit on Mobutu.

An example of how Senegalese journalists valued their role vis-à-vis their government concerned a problem confronted by a young television newsman. He recounted how a shipment of UNICEF vaccines destined for Senegalese children, had arrived at the Dakar port. He learned it had been held up by the head of customs who was demanding a bribe to release it. Rather than confronting the corrupt official who was likely powerful, he devised a plan. He called the customs office and excitedly told them he had been informed of the arrival of the vaccines and would be coming to the port with his team to cover that important news story. He then assembled his crew and went to the port with a TV camera that had no film. When he arrived, a ceremony was organized to celebrate the arrival of the vaccines which had been cleared by customs.

While the major Senegalese newspaper was government owned, the country also boasted several privately owned papers. On one occasion a young journalist called on me to discuss the launching of a monthly news magazine called *SUD* (or south) that was intended for all of francophone Africa. He produced the initial copy and asked my opinion of it. I said I would read it that evening and meet with him the next day. I read the journal and told him that in my opinion it was highly intellectual and would find a limited readership. I asked him for additional copies to send to my USIS counterparts in other French speaking countries to gauge their opinion. A month later the results were in, and the verdict was like mine. The editor thanked me and said he would consider changes that would give the publication wider readership. Then he asked if it would be possible for us to provide funding for the magazine.

I told him that although it would be inappropriate for the U.S. government to fund a Senegalese publication, I would be pleased to ask the regional Ford Foundation representative, based in Dakar, if he might help. Specifically, I suggested he might seek support in the form of the relatively new desktop publishing technology. Ford did provide that help and the publication came out monthly for several issues before becoming a weekly. Within a year's time SUD became a Senegalese daily and sometime later became the leading daily newspaper in the country, a remarkable feat for an independent newspaper. The paper also developed the county's first private television station.

Given Senegal's reputation for independent journalism, UNESCO decided Dakar would be an excellent site for its creation of a new Pan African News Agency (PANA). This gave us a headache since its first director was a Marxist official from Congo Brazzaville, which at that time had close relations to the Soviet Union. That director found Soviet disinformation acceptable to disseminate throughout Africa. One instance was particularly galling. PANA carried an article, originally produced by the Soviet Union, then carried by a Zambian newspaper, that claimed the U.S. had deliberately spread AIDS to Africa. I called on the PANA director and asked if he had checked the story with any American official. He clearly had not. Then I proposed he carry our rebuttal and denunciation of this clearly Soviet produced falsehood. He said he would not.

At that I got up to walk away and said, "then I would be forced to take action." Before I reached the door, he called out to me to ask what action I planned to take. I said I would send the article to all American Embassies in Africa and report on our conversation and ask them to contact their host governments to protest PANA's refusal to follow ethical journalistic processes. The director then changed his mind and agreed to carry our rebuttal of the false charges in the Zambian article. Nevertheless, I did alert all my USIS counterparts to PANA's mendacity and suggested they follow its news coverage for other instances of it. The penetration of much of the African media by the Soviets was widespread and often involved payments to receptive journalists. Dealing with it was a regular function of USIS officers throughout the continent.

As Dakar is the closest city on continental Africa to the United States, it had served as an important part of the strategic supply chain to U.S. troops during World War II for the North Africa and Southern European campaigns. For that reason, U.S. military engineers were sent to Dakar to modernize its airport and lengthen its runways. It was therefore no surprise that forty years later, NASA sought Senegalese permission to use Dakar's airport as an emergency landing site in case engine failure led the Space Shuttle to abort. To prepare for that unlikely contingency, NASA sent an emergency team to Dakar prior to each Shuttle take-off.

Ambassador Walker regarded this as a potential nightmare since such a landing could be tragic. He anticipated that should such an event happen the world's press would descend on us within twenty-four hours. To consider the consequences, he asked NASA to include a high-level public affairs official in its next emergency team's visit. NASA responded that for budgetary and other reasons that would not be possible but offered to cover the costs of an embassy official to travel to the Kennedy Space Center. The ambassador named me for that job since I was, among other things, his press officer. As the next blastoff was soon, I prepared to travel to Florida where I arranged to meet with our newly named information officer Dudley Sims, who was preparing to leave his home in Florida for Dakar.

Once at the Kennedy Space Center, I was thoroughly briefed on Space Shuttle matters, provided with contact information by its public affairs staff and prepared for a worst-case scenario that we would jointly execute. While working with the NASA staff, I ran into a former colleague, Mal McConnell. He had been in my foreign service entry class and then after two overseas tours, resigned to write several novels. He was there, he told me, to write a feature story for the *Reader's Digest* on the Shuttle program which he said was beginning to be regarded as what he called "a bus ride," something that had become completely safe and uneventful. That widely accepted judgment had been reached just shortly before the

1986 Challenger disaster. The tragedy, although it did not involve an emergency landing, illustrated that Ambassador Walker's thinking about the unthinkable had been merited and justified our Kennedy Space Center trip.

One evening, as was our habit in Dakar, Anita and I took our after-dinner walk. It was dusk at which time flights of yellow warblers which nested in the city trees flew out for their evening feast of insects. Only an occasional car rushed its occupant to the start of an evening's relaxation. A few scattered pedestrians sauntered homeward among a flock of women in flowing boubous, flowered fantasies gliding like ornate bushes in bloom. A peddler lady rose to load her wares of unsold mangoes and peanuts, adjourning until tomorrow. Night guards were beginning to assume their stations at the gate of each house. Senegalese students of English at the nearby British Institute walked briskly home, some in designer jeans with tie-dye shirts.

As we reached the road paralleling the ocean, four young men accosted us. One of them approached and reached for Anita's necklace. It all happened so fast that my reflex was a fist to his chin as Anita called out for the police. For some reason, all four raced away. We returned to our house where I took my car to a nearby police station. I told them what had happened. They said they had no vehicle, but they knew the cave from which the thieves most likely came. They offered to go with us if they could come in our car. We drove to the site of the attempted robbery and in the direction they had run. The two policemen exited the car near the caves and as they descended, we saw young men emerge and flee into the town.

In my anger, I stepped on the gas and drove with the police in the direction the men had run. Suddenly, I saw an undulation on the street in front and hit the brakes just in time to avoid scores of men bent over at evening prayer. Having narrowly averted disaster, I vowed never again to lose my temper. The thieves were never caught but the next evening. I carried a baseball bat on our evening walk. A night guard that we passed joked by asking me, "monsieur, are you going to engage in sports?"

A 1984 country team meeting presented us with a dark omen. Our regional medical officer, commenting on the advance of AIDS, predicted that all of us, in the next year, would know someone who had died of that disease. Unfortunately, that prediction came true. In light of Dakar's important Institut Pasteur research center for tropical disease, America's Dr. Fauci visited Dakar to consult with French and Senegalese experts. The spread of AIDS across the African continent was to be devastating. We later learned that Zambian President Kaunda's son who had been one of Anita's students was one of the victims. Leaders of some African countries felt helpless in the face of AIDS. Some, including South Africa's Mbeki, rejected Western medicine in favor of useless traditional remedies with tragic results.

Perhaps the single greatest humanitarian contribution the United States has made over the years to an otherwise neglected African continent was the initiative of President George W. Bush. In 2003, President Bush launched the President's Emergency Plan for AIDS Relief. The program is estimated to have saved twenty-five million lives. It affected the peoples of Botswana, Ivory Coast, Ethiopia, Kenya, Mozambique, Namibia, Nigeria, Rwanda, South Africa,

Tanzania, Uganda, and Zambia. The powerful campaign was comparable to the U.S. supported initiative several decades earlier designed to eliminate smallpox and measles which also saved millions of African lives.

President Leopold Sedar Senghor, before he was President of Senegal from 1960 to 1980 had been a Minister in the French government. He was the founder of the doctrine of Negritude and arguably Africa's most notable poet. The fact that Senghor was Catholic in a Muslim country is a testament to his political adroitness. As the father of Senegal's independence, Senghor peacefully retired after twenty years as head of state, unlike most of his West African counterparts, many of whom were overthrown by their militaries. Senghor retired to France where he took on a role with the Academie Francaise, joining with French "immortals" to work on the French Dictionary.

While he was still in Dakar, I decided that I would try to meet this remarkable African leader and put in a request to his staff. The immediate response was an invitation to join him for tea. That initial meeting was one of the most impressive encounters of my life. I called on Senghor at his home along the Dakar corniche. He spoke to me of his profound regard for America, and his conviction that it would lead the world in establishing racial equality once we overcame some hurdles. Despite being a man in his late seventies, the former president's intelligence and charisma shone. The Senegalese people much loved Senghor. I told him how much I admired the role he had played in influencing and inspiring the diaspora, an important contribution to American culture and a bridge between Africa and the U.S.

On one occasion I was especially pleased with a visit from another remarkable Senegalese, Ousmane Sembene, the famed author and filmmaker. Sembene, who at times was a communist and anti-American, came to our office to ask a favor. He together with his colleague, Thierno Faty Sow, were planning a feature film to document an infamous massacre that occurred in Dakar in 1944. Senegalese troops who had been imprisoned by the Germans during World War II had returned home. It seemed that French soldiers who had endured the same fate had received back pay from their government. The film would chronicle how the Senegalese soldiers housed at Camp Thiaroye demanded an improvement of their living conditions and an equal amount of back pay. Late in the evening French tanks approached the camp and the Senegalese were gunned down mercilessly. The story is a devastating indictment of French colonialism, one that was sure to affect Senegalese attitudes toward France once the film was produced.

Sembene called on me to ask for a sample of American military uniforms and equipment from the period of the 1940s when American soldiers were in Senegal during the war, to expand Dakar's airport and harbor to facilitate the provision of supplies to the North African and European war zones. Those soldiers were present during the time of the massacre. The filmmaker also asked if we could provide several extras from the Embassy staff to play the role of the American soldiers. I contacted our desk officer in Washington who found he could get the requested uniforms and materials from a store in northern Virginia that specialized in historic military garb. Also, I was able to recruit some of the Embassy's Marine guards from our security staff to play the roles of the American soldiers in the film. Sembene's film the *Camp de Thiaroye* went on to win the 1988 Grand Jury prize at the Venice International Film Festival. Predictably, it was also banned in France for a decade and censored in Senegal.

Senegal had a reputation for stability and democracy. That reputation was tarnished by its elections often involving almost twenty contending political parties, most of which consisted of a few dozen friends and family members of the less successful candidates. Managed by the government, President Abdoulaye Diouf, who inherited his job from Senghor, had received a suspiciously high ninety percent of the vote in previous elections. Before the 1988 elections, our ambassador Walker called on him. He told the President that as he was popular and likely to win 60-70 percent of the vote, why not conduct an honest election eschewing the clearly rigged overwhelming election victories of the past? In response Diouf informed our ambassador that although he was confident that he would win with a lower percentage of the vote, but many of his National Assembly deputies would lose their seats since they were on the same ticket, and his political party could not tolerate that. In a 2024 startling upset defying the trend of military coups among Senegal's neighboring countries, a young reform party upended an establishment candidate for president after the sitting President Macky Sall tried and failed to indefinitely postpone the election.

Upon arrival in Dakar, I learned that I had inherited an English Teaching program that had some problems. Upon assessment I found it to be poorly run by a contractor. Until then, any earnings from directly run USIS English teaching had to be turned over to the Treasury. But a new policy allowed profits to be used by our office to fund cultural projects. I therefore requested that an Agency English teaching specialist help us set up a revised and expanded program to accomplish two things. First, to professionalize our program, and second to revise it to be more entrepreneurial so we could earn a profit that would be plowed back into our cultural and exchange programs. Within two years we had met both objectives, earning, $60,000 annually that we invested in cultural projects including travel for international visitors, U.S. support of the annual colloquium on American Studies, and an array of other activities.

Senegal was a congenial and infinitely interesting African country. When I learned that an old friend, a syndicated columnist with the Kansas City Star, Charles Gusewelle, was in Paris for a year writing his column from there, I thought he might serve as a lecturer for Senegalese audiences. At that time, he was publishing his thrice weekly columns under the title *A Paris Notebook.* I concluded that the idea for such a book might be appropriate for Senegal and invited him to spend a summer with us. He quickly accepted the notion and was granted permission by his editor to spend a summer in Dakar writing his thrice weekly syndicated column from there. So, Charles came to Dakar to write about daily life in Senegal as seen by an American correspondent.

Selected columns were later published as *A Dakar Notebook* and quickly became a best seller among a discerning audience of Peace Corps Volunteers. He wrote about sports fishing along one of the world's richest game fishing currents, he interviewed the night guard Mousa at our home about his military adventures in the French army in Algeria and Vietnam, and told dozens of other tales that illuminated life in a West African county. If the task of a diplomat overseas is to enhance mutual understanding, making Gusewelle's visit possible certainly accomplished that.

Gusewelle also accompanied me on a journey of mercy. Our embassy Consul called me one evening asking for help. She was involved in a crisis involving an American lady who was in conflict with her hotel. Apparently, she believed she was being overcharged and refused to pay her bill and had to catch an evening flight to New York. To our astonishment she turned out to be the once-famed singer, Nina Simone. Charles agreed to accompany me to the hotel. What we met with there was a woman crying and swearing and in a state of total confusion. We suspected she had taken drugs. We calmed her down, took care of her problem with the hotel and offered to drive her to the airport to catch her flight back to the States. On the way Nina told us many stories of her life. One especially concerned her. She told of traveling by air with her prized dog and arriving at her destination to find the dog dead. Charles who loved dogs empathized with her and told her about the death of his own dog.

Nina told us about her marriage to a Liberian cabinet minister and the wild parties they had on the beach before he was executed by a revolutionary government. She complained that she could not board the plane unless she was assured that Washington Mayor, Marion Barry, would send a car for her when she reached her destination. That sounded farfetched to us but I called the Consul and asked that they pass that message to Barry with her arrival time. A half hour later, the Consul called back to say, "yes indeed," Mayor Barry would have his car meet her. It became clear to us that Nina Simone had worked closely with Mayor Barry during the civil rights movement. We later learned with pleasure that Nina, upon her return, resumed her career at a high level.

One of our new junior officers was an attractive young woman who soon after arriving in Dakar managed to participate in a high-level Senegalese social swirl. Two months later while on vacation in Florence, I was called by our ambassador. He asked what I knew about the marriage of our officer to the brother of Senegalese President Diouf. I expressed astonishment. When I returned, I discussed the matter with Ambassador Walker. We agreed that given security concerns, an American officer could not serve in the country where her spouse was connected to a high-level government official. In light of that, the Ambassador sought to arrange a position for our officer in Washington. A special effort was made to find jobs for both the officer and her spouse in Washington. Since the job offered to our officer was a domestic and not foreign service position, she refused to accept the arrangement. Her husband called on me to indicate that maybe their marriage had been hasty and they would have to ponder their options. Some months later we learned of their divorce.

Toward the end of our time in Dakar a police strike paralyzed the capital. A large body of police assembled at the lower end of the central town square. Opposing military units, blocking their passage to the Presidential Palace stood at the opposite end of the square, some based immediately in front of our office. I noticed my driver speaking to one of the sergeants. When I learned that the sergeant was his brother, I asked him to find out what orders had been given to the military. He returned and told me they were ordered to shoot to kill if the police advanced further toward the Presidential Palace.

Fortunately, the conflagration was averted when the police dispersed and no life was lost in the standoff.

Professor Cheikh Anta Diop was an eminent African historian for which Senegal's major university was named. He was known for his controversial writing on the influence of ancient Egypt on West African civilization. Soon after my arrival, I arranged to have lunch with him and discovered he had never been to the United States. Knowing that he was greatly admired by American Africanist scholars, I asked if he would like to visit his U.S. counterparts if I could provide a grant. He responded that he would very much like to do so. I quickly got to work contacting some of the leading academics at African Studies programs at UCLA, Boston University, Northwestern, and the University of Florida whom I knew well. Their response was uniformly positive with UCLA prepared to host a special event to honor him.

I organized an international visitor's grant and gave detailed instructions to a program agency. The day after the renowned professor was to fly to New York to begin his discovery of America I saw our cultural attaché who had been slated to leave on the same flight. "What happened," I asked? She informed me that their flight had been canceled after takeoff when the plane had mechanical problems and had to return to Dakar. I then met with a colleague of Professor Diop who told me that Diop considered the failure of the flight to be an omen that he should not go to the U.S. and so all our work had to be undone and Diop never got to visit America.

Senegal has been aptly described by scholar Roger Shattuck in two words: "Liberty and Elegance." It lives up to its reputation as an intellectual and center of culture par excellence despite the country's high level of poverty. It is also a major center of the African diaspora. Finally, it has been a crossroads of Africa and France and many members of its elite regard Paris as a second home. For all these reasons it was a superb place to spend four years. But it is a country of few resources, with an economy that made it literally "a peanut republic" and unless its prospective oil revenues are successfully tapped and not subjected to massive corruption, it will remain poor. It therefore has been forced to depend on its wits. Represented by its educated and influential citizens who often occupy positions in international organizations, they harvest support, especially foreign assistance, directed to Senegal.

# XII. Nigeria (1988-91)

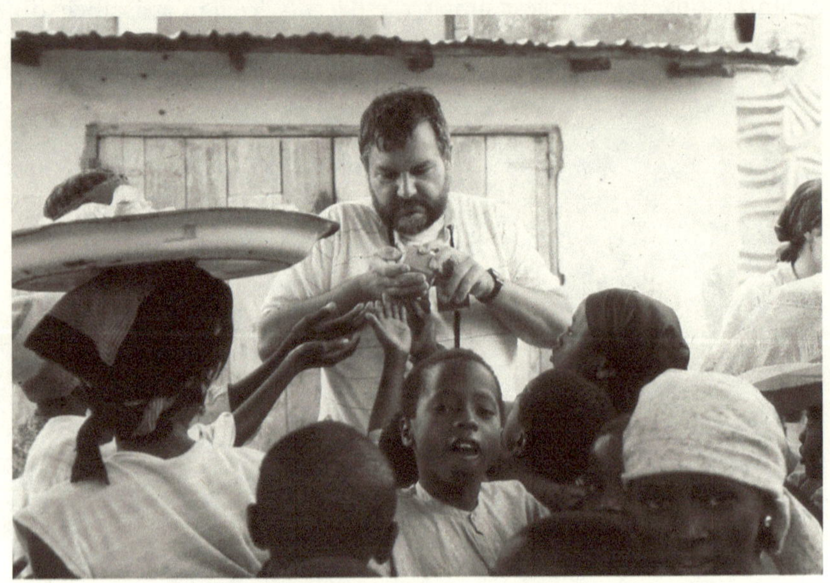

The author with Nigerian children

After the pleasures of life and work in Senegal, Nigeria was a sharp contrast. While Dakar was in some ways the Paris of Africa, Lagos was more like the tropical New York of Africa. That is the New York of the 19th century. While with its open sewers it was in no sense a beautiful city, it was the center of finance and of the media and while we were there, until the capital was shifted to Abuja, the center of government. Nigeria possessed a dynamic society with Africa's largest population and enormous diversity. It is a country of world class intellectual talent and cultural and artistic creativity. A lingering tragedy was the residue of Africa's most devastating civil war over the attempt of the East, which called itself Biafra, to secede from 1967-70 at the cost of an estimated two million lives. Despite the fact that Nigeria is made up of dozens of ethnicities, three of the largest groups, the Hausa-Fulani, Yoruba, and Ibo dominated their respective regions. Overall, though, the predominantly Islamic North dominated by the military, mainly exercised control of government. The civil war led to the consolidation of a political system and a military dominated by the Hausa-Fulani Islamic ethnic group.

In preparation for running a large USIS post with a dozen American officers, two branch posts and fifty Nigerian employees, I sought advice from my good friend Stanley Zuckerman. Stan had run several complex USIS operations. I asked him what I should know about managing such an extensive operation. His advice, which I sought to adopt, was that I had risen to a position where I presumably knew more than my subordinates about their jobs. It was his experience that many senior officers felt they knew better than their less experienced staffers and tried to massively intervene in the quotidian detail of all or many staff members. He urged me not to attempt to micromanage but rather provide guidance to allow my staff members to do their jobs without interference even if I might think I could do those jobs better. He reminded me that a good organization was the sum of its parts not one dominated by a single, know-it-all superior. What I most needed to do, he argued, was to get the best out of each staff member.

Our home in Lagos on Victoria Island was a spacious house with enough room for our family of seven. It was in a good neighborhood and near the American International School. Its front lawn had some citronella plants that kept away mosquitoes. I told the children that the plants repelled both bugs and tigers. However, while the house was adequate, it was in no sense safe. Each house in the area had guards assigned to it day and night. The area was known for armed robbery. Break-ins were so frequent that the military government decreed that armed robbery would be punished by death. While at first this sounded like a deterrent, it was pointed out to us it was instead an incentive for the thieves to murder all potential witnesses.

The second floor of the American diplomatic residences was protected by what was known as a "rape gate," a gate situated at the top of the stairs leading to the bedrooms intended to protect families at night which we assiduously kept locked. We were provided with a radio with which to call the marine guards at the embassy in the event of a break-in. But the marines were not authorized to intervene directly. They would be required to drive to the nearest police station and bring the Nigerian police to the place of the suspected break-in. But the Nigerian police lacked a sterling reputation. A Lagos newspaper report told of the capture of some robbers. When asked where they obtained their automatic weapons, they confessed they had rented them for the evening from the police.

The harshness of the Nigerian military government might best be illustrated by its decision to evict 300,000 inhabitants of

Maroko, a suburb of Lagos not far from our residence. It is captured in Anita's poem:

**Bulldozing roof Maroko: Lagos Nigeria, 1992**

*Today the military governor ordered the evacuation within 48 hours of theinhabitants of Maroko who have unlawfully occupied land on the eastern part of Victoria Island for the past 25 years.*

*The Daily Concord, Nigeria*

Beneath a pink and purple Lagosian sky
a silent army passed us by.
rotting wood and mattresses,
sheets of zinc and sacks of clothes
balanced neatly on each man's head.
Three hundred thousand
Looking neither left nor right,
not at the bulldozed site,
at books of prayer and Sunday hats,
at splintered frames in broken homes
of bamboo poles and rusted zinc.
Maroko of open sewers, each breeze
a threat to well-kept lawns, where
visions dance of marble halls to rise
on swamplands drained then made pure.

Several weeks after landing in Lagos our car arrived. A few days later a senior Nigerian employee came to my office to advise me that my staff wished to wash my car. I told him it was reasonably clean, but thanks anyhow. He said I didn't understand and told me the washing of the car was a Yoruba traditional ceremony for when one's car first arrived to protect its owner from harm. While I wasn't sure how this related to me, I thought it best to take Nigerian traditions seriously and accept their offer. We went downstairs where my entire staff was assembled and a ceremony commenced that involved some incantations in Yoruba and the pouring of some palm wine on my Volvo.

I was later to learn that the major cause of death for young men in Nigeria was road accidents. So serious was the problem that President Babangida called upon Nobel Prize laureate Wole Soyinka to serve as Road Safety Commissioner. Soyinka took his role seriously and worked with an American playwright to organize short dramas to be performed in marketplaces to educate the public on safe driving. One of those plays, *Babatunde You Are Very Great*, was a hilarious satire featuring a scofflaw driver who systematically violates all major rules of the road, with disastrous consequences. Despite the dangers, I drove on Nigerian highways for three years with no accidents, perhaps thanks to seeing the play combined with having my car washed.

We arrived in Nigeria on the eve of the Seoul Olympics. Olympic fever was in the air. Nigerians were led to believe that since their country was "the Giant of Africa," its athletes would surely bring home the gold, and lots of it. The impact on our operation was felt when two Nigerians we were sending to the U.S. on International Visitors professional visits turned up at our office to inform us their direct flight to New York on Nigerian Airways had been cancelled. They were told the problem was mechanical. The next day they were turned away again. We later learned that the flight scheduled for New York was instead commandeered to transport the Nigerian Olympic team to Seoul. We also learned that officials on that flight greatly outnumbered athletes in the Nigerian delegation.

The next day's news informed us that the flight had to land in the Middle East for refueling and when it landed, the Arab airport officials refused to accept their credit card knowing the reputation of Nigerians for fraud. They were told to wait several hours in the heat of the Gulf for the opening of the banks later that morning so they could get the cash needed to pay for fuel. Once they did so they were further delayed again by the failure to have filed flight plans.

Once in Seoul, the Nigerian officials in the delegation were bedazzled by the affordable electronics available that could only be purchased in Lagos for a king's ransom. As a result, several athletes missed their events when their coaches failed to take them to their venues. At the conclusion of the Seoul games the Nigerian medal count was zero. For the return to Lagos, the Nigerian officials had to hire a second aircraft to carry their purchases. Upon landing in Lagos, their plane was met by a host of media reporters.

As he left the plane the head of the delegation, the Sports Minister, in an interview was asked why Nigerians failed to win gold, silver or bronze, and instead came home with a load of electronics. The Minster responded by answering, "what Nigerian who had the opportunity to acquire gifts for family and friends would fail to do so?"

Prior to my arrival in Nigeria, the USIS Lagos office had developed a relationship with award winning documentary film maker Carroll Parrett Blue, who with support from Public Television and the Smithsonian Institution had embarked on a project that would result in a remarkable documentary film, an account of contemporary Nigerian art. We were asked to identify the artists who should be portrayed in the film and to help with some of the logistics. The result was an outstanding documentary, *Kindred Spirits*, that featured ten creative artists working in Nigeria who spoke of their work.

The film inspired a visit from a curator of the Harlem Studio Museum, Grace Stanislaus, who we assisted in contacting several of the artists featured in the film. Those artists were then invited to show their work in New York. That in turn led to two of them, sculptor El Anatsui, and print maker Bruce Onoabrakpeya, to be the first African artists to be invited to show their work at the Venice Biennale. Upon their return both thanked us, saying that we had been responsible for their selection for both the New York and Venice exhibitions. We took immense pride in having helped to elevate contemporary African artists, facilitating a take-off in their exposure to audiences in the U.S. and Europe.

Nigeria's historic kingdoms had produced arguably the greatest quality and variety of traditional art. Archeologists contend that not all of it has yet surfaced and that a great deal of the country's art treasure is yet to be discovered. My poet-wife Anita pondered the recovery of ancient Ife art in these words:

**Excavations: Ile-Ife, Nigeria 1953**

Earth reveals the fragile forms of deities
Disturbed, once released by potter's hands
Now fired clay is gently cleansed—the eyes,
The ears—from clotted mold of centuries.
Ploughman, paused to see the prize of unseasonable
harvest. Unchronicled, like sacred yam this find
will now survive, legend lived stored in marbled halls,
silent hollowed groves—spirits the hidden trove.
What Praxiteles shaped this ancient Yoruba head,
formed the mouth discretely closed,
the eyes that see what no man knows—
a Lazarus compelled to plead his cause.

In Ile-Ife, where man began, the Yoruba hold,
we shift the soil, upturn the earth.
Glad tidings made public the ploughman will say;
don't you know, can't you see we are all fired clay?

A weekend family excursion took us to the town of Osogbo. It was a place known as a center of Yoruba traditional religion which had inspired dynamic artistic creativity. Wandering through the town, we came upon the home of a well-known artist, Twins Seven Seven who kindly invited us in. He showed us his latest work, treated our children to soft drinks, and served Anita and me some palm wine. Twins had started out as a singer and dancer, then took up painting and sculpture after having been led to that professional direction by the German author and scholar Ulli Beier. Twins name was based on his having been the only surviving child of the seven twins to which his mother gave birth. His highly imaginative work drew upon traditional Yoruba religious beliefs and symbols. Combined with his personal qualities Twins was a charismatic creative force.

While in Osogbo we later encountered another exceptional Yoruba artist that we came to regard as a good friend. Nike Davies-Okundaye had been the wife of Twins Seven Seven. She created a magical world of brilliantly designed cloth. She designed her canvases with batik, the Yoruba indigo tradition of adire, and later embroidery. As did Twins Seven Seven, Nike drew her design themes from traditional Yoruba mythology. In the years after our meeting, she founded several schools for women to build on her legacy.

A major issue that affected U.S.-Nigerian relations was the fact that Africa's most populous nation was a military dictatorship during our time there. That meant human rights, freedom of speech, and other constitutional rights had been voided by military decrees. This was illustrated to me when I called on the President of the Nigerian Supreme Court. I asked him to tell me precisely what constitution guided the Court's decisions under the then military government. He said that was an excellent question and asked me to wait while he sought to provide the document for me. Five minutes later he returned with a tattered copy of Nigeria's former civilian constitution modified by dozens of amendments. That text had military decrees pasted over the parts that had been changed. He then told me that this was the only authoritative, working copy of what was Nigeria's ad hoc constitution, and that Nigerian citizens had no access to it.

Another problem we confronted, one that had dominated my predecessor's time in Lagos, was the issue of Soviet disinformation. The Soviets were regularly finding ways to sully the reputation of the United States through stories they planted in the African press. As Nigeria had more newspapers than any other country on the continent, the pickings were easy. One day as I poured through the sixteen Lagos dailies on my desk, I came across an egregious example of Soviet mischief in a most unexpected newspaper.

The paper was the *Champion*, owned by an Ibo billionaire. The front-page article, citing unnamed sources, alleged that the American government had developed the AIDS virus in a military laboratory aimed at infecting Africans. Since I had met the paper's owner several times and found him friendly, I called to lodge a protest and inform him that the story was fraudulent and produced by Moscow to harm us in Africa. He asked that I meet with him at his residence the next morning. When I arrived, I was surprised to see that the newspaper's editor and the two reporters who had written the story were present. Chief Emmanuel Iwuanyanwu, our host, introduced his newsmen. He asked that I explain the problem.

When I concluded he made a statement. He said this to his staff, "I love America. I go there frequently; my son studies there. I own a house in America. I don't own this newspaper to attack my friends." Then he told his paper's editor and reporters that if ever they were to write a controversial story about the U.S., they should check with Mr. LaGamma first before it was published. The paper printed a retraction and we never again had problems with it. I should have known that the result would be favorable since the owner was Ibo and a common expression about America among the Ibo was that America was known as "God's own country."

While we had continued problems with Soviet disinformation and the Nigerian media community had severe limitations imposed by the military government, the Nigerian press was the most highly developed in Africa. Arriving at the office each morning I found my desk covered with a pile of those newspapers. They reflected the social and political complexity of the country and the ambitions of wealthy Nigerian owners who sought to exert influence on whatever their military censors allowed.

On one occasion, I called on Doyin Abiola the editor-in-chief of the Lagos daily, *The Concord*. She was the dynamic wife of the paper's owner, Yoruba chief Moshood Abiola, a powerful businessman and politician who aspired to be his country's president. In fact, Chief Abiola appeared to win the 1993 election for president after which Nigerian General Sani Abacha seized power and Abiola was arrested and later died in 1998 after he was mistreated during imprisonment. While I was in Doyin's office two young reporters entered to ask for her urgent attention. I excused myself. When they left, I returned and she commented: "these young chaps don't realize we are working under a military regime." Clearly, she was concerned that what was published could result in the shutdown of her newspaper as was the case for others. *The Concord* itself was later banned and Abiola's other wife, pro-democracy activist, Kudirat, was assassinated allegedly at the order of Nigeria's head of state, Abacha.

It was the curious case that when a Nigerian newspaper was banned its editor's simply renamed the paper so it could be published under a new name. A particularly good friend had been editor of the two most important Nigerian newspapers, *The Times*, and *The Guardian*. After attempting to test the limits of censorship he resigned from *The Times*, applied for a visa to the United States and got a position as a professor of journalism in America. This was not only a commentary on the problems of practicing journalism in Nigeria. It also demonstrated that Nigeria had many world class journalists and other professionals who could take their talents to America, Britain, or other countries when they were fed up with corruption or the limitations imposed by their government on their ability to function professionally. For that reason, the U.S. and the U.K. benefit significantly from the Nigerian brain drain.

One egregious Nigerian problem was airport management. I personally experienced the difficulties when my family members and professional visitors arrived from the U.S. and departed from Lagos and when many other American visitors had the onerous experience of dealing with airport officialdom. One day brought a ray of hope for mitigating the problem. I met the congenial deputy director of the airport who helped diplomats with the problem of getting through security, customs, and immigration. His Ibo first name was Godknows and he had earned a Master's degree from the University of North Dakota in airport management some years earlier. He seemed a perfect candidate for a grant to update his professional experience, and I suggested a possible grant so he could consult with staff at several major U.S. airports. Godknows jumped at the chance and said that he could arrange to fly to New York on Nigerian Airways at no cost. I proposed the grant and it was arranged. When he returned he was ecstatic and full of ideas for improving Lagos airport management. A week later we learned he had been transferred to the Jos airport up north and all hope of navigating the Lagos airport was lost.

A telling anecdote exemplifies some of the chronic challenges Nigerians confront in their daily life. A fine journalist with the Lagos daily *The Vanguard* wrote about a friend who wished to start a Lagos business. He sought to replicate an American idea and launch a neighborhood sports bar. Knowing of the many problems that faced businesses, he carefully planned to avoid the potential pitfalls common to Nigeria. He knew water supplies were unpredictable so he had a well dug. He knew electricity was erratic so he purchased a generator. He understood he had to safeguard his bar against robbery, so he built a high wall topped with barbed wire and hired guards. It all went well until several days after his opening when he ran out of fuel for his generator and could find none. Despite being a major world oil producer gasoline was periodically unavailable. That was because Nigeria's oil refineries were frequently shut down, as was the case in this instance, and so were the businesses that depended on them. After that, the bar's owner seriously considered abandoning his business. That conundrum is reminiscent of Ben Franklin's "for want of a nail, the battle was lost."

The policy of the United States toward Nigeria was to bolster conditions that would support the building of democratic institutions. In other words, we sought to help what President Babangida himself had declared was his policy--a return to democratic civilian rule. Nigerian military rulers had reason to leave power since the threat of remaining in office incentivized other ambitious military officers to seize power. Such coups had several precedents. While that was the stated objective of the Babangida regime, a decision to hold free elections had been systematically postponed. We came to call it Nigeria's "permanent transition."

Accordingly, I sought to find the means of showing U.S. support for institutional change and to work with civil society to stimulate action. The problem for USIS was one of lack of resources. Following the money for things needed in Africa most often led to one agency, USAID. However, as one of the world's leading oil producers, Nigeria lacked an economic assistance program. USAID Washington did have a regional program office to support democracy in Africa but Lagos had no local USAID office and therefore no one to administer such a program. With the help of Ambassador Walker, I began exploring ways in which my USIS office could be granted USAID funding to advance democracy in Nigeria.

To do so I would have to develop a strategic plan. Such a plan would have to simplify what was usually a complex bureaucratic process and be relatively easy to administer. The proposal I concocted involved linkages between U.S. and Nigerian institutions. An example was to link the U.S. League of Women's Voters to the Nigerian National Women's Movement. Its objective would be to engage more Nigerian women in the country's political process, something they had been working towards with limited success. I reasoned that women in Nigeria had not been tainted by massive corruption and could therefore become agents of change toward clean government.

Other linkages would involve the transition toward drafting a new Constitution, ways to develop a more effective form of federalism, an electoral partnership to improve national elections, a linkage between the American Bar Association and its Nigerian counterpart, a partnership between the Washington-based Center for Foreign Journalists and the Nigerian Press Association, and several other linkages involving academic institutions. Our primary objective was to energize civil society in its effort to prepare Nigeria for and promote democratic civilian rule.

Our proposal was approved by Washington, together with a budget of three million dollars. Once the funding was approved, we quickly arranged the marriages of institutions over three years to cover travel, conferences, research, and other relevant activities that would stimulate the dialogue on the return to democracy and help bolster the institutions necessary for that transition. We encountered no Nigerian government opposition and the partnerships worked well. While the transformation was continually postponed by the various military regimes until elections were held eight years later, we believe we had made a modest, but significant contribution to the ultimate transition. I was to observe those elections following my Foreign Service retirement on behalf of the Carter Center.

One of the highlights of my career overseas was to welcome the all-time great jazz artist, Dizzy Gillespie to Nigeria. USIA's Arts America program offered him to African posts, and I insisted he spend at least a week with us. He came as part of a quartet that included brilliant saxophonist, James Moody and two skilled young musicians at bass and drums. Meeting him at Lagos airport was an honor. But it was slightly complicated by airport bureaucracy which insisted on knowing how much cash Dizzy was bringing into the country. Dizzy began to show them his massive wad of cash and credit cards but I told him, "No, no, no." I informed the officials that Mr. Gillespie was a world-famous musician who is bringing the gift of music to the people of Nigeria. That, along with our American Embassy credentials solved the problem. From the start it was clear to us that Dizzy was a friendly, humble, decent person, a great storyteller, and one seeking to connect with his African roots.

Our first concert in Lagos was timed to allow Dizzy to be the featured performer in Nigeria's annual jazz festival at the Nigerian National Theater. The concert was brilliant and much appreciated by the audience. Following it, the success was muddied backstage by an insulting remark made to the quartet's young drummer by an American staff member who had drunk one beer too many. Dizzy was rightfully angered and threatened to cancel the program. I intervened to apologize. Following the incident, I asked the offending official to leave and told Dizzy that I would gladly travel with the quartet in his place during his tour of Nigeria.

It should be noted that a tour like the one we had planned for Nigeria had to take account of poor roads, uncertain local support, electric power failures and a host of other potential problems, and that Gillespie while seemingly healthy was in his seventies. The next stop for Dizzy was a Yoruba town a half hour's drive from Lagos where our staff arranged for him to be honored. We entered the town to the thundering, rhythmic sounds of the famed Yoruba "talking drums." Our Cultural Affairs Officer, Nick Robertson had arranged for Dizzy to be granted an honorary Yoruba chieftainship and be proclaimed the "Baasheere of Iperu" which means "Chief of Entertainers." While he was a man who had many honors bestowed on him during his career, Dizzy announced that this one was the very greatest as he thought of it as coming from the land of his ancestors.

Our next destination, the eastern city of Port Harcourt would have been a difficult road trip for any man of his age. For that reason, I had arranged for us to fly there on a Mobil Oil aircraft. I was seated in front of Dizzy when halfway through the flight I felt his hand grip my shoulder and heard him shout, "oh my god Bob." I turned thinking he was experiencing a health crisis only to learn he had left his wallet containing several thousand dollars and lots of credit cards on the airport counter. I then went to the cockpit to ask the pilot to radio Lagos to ask the Mobil people at the airport to find and secure the wallet. Soon after, we learned they had done so. Dizzy responded, "I knew they would find it." I, on the other hand, considered it the miracle of Lagos. I was pleasantly surprised to hear the pilot ask

Dizzy Gillespie with Oba of Benin

if he should return to get it. Several hours later it was back in Dizzy's hands completely intact.

Following a cancellation due to a power failure, Dizzy had a successful Port Harcourt concert. Then it was on to Benin City, a town famous for a once powerful empire and one of Africa's greatest centers of traditional art. The day before our concert we took Dizzy to peruse the local art market where he came upon a few bronze bells that he thought he might use in future concerts. Our concert in Benin was scheduled at the University. The usual unanticipated logistical problems caused us to delay the start of the concert. When the quartet was set to begin the performance, the student audience was restless and unruly because of the delay. This caused Dizzy to wait for the students to calm down. When he resumed playing and there was an even louder audience buzz, he halted and left the stage with the other musicians. He then came out again to lecture the audience on its rudeness, noting he had been told that this was a great university in one of Africa's greatest cultural centers. A roar of disapproval left us wondering if it would not be best to start the engines of our cars to avoid what we anticipated might be a riot. We held our collective breath. Instead, the students quieted down and obeyed Dizzy's call for them to listen attentively to the concert. It all ended well with rousing applause and a student delegation coming backstage to make their profound apologies on behalf of the audience to Dizzy. It was an amazing turnaround arranged by an inspired master musician.

The outstanding visit of Dizzy Gillespie to Nigeria closed a profound cultural circle. The diaspora had produced jazz born from African roots and one of its leading practitioners had returned the favor to Africa by presenting that music performed by one of its great American exponents and artists.

Shortly after my arrival in Lagos a question presented itself. As was the tradition of USIS cultural centers, especially in Africa, we would mark Black History Month. We had several months to prepare. The issue before us was how could we best celebrate it? I had met a young African American resident in Nigeria, Chuck Mike, who had a strong background in theatrical productions and directed a Nigerian drama company. I discussed with him the prospect of his producing several plays by African American authors to be held at our cultural center. He enthusiastically agreed to round up the actors and select and direct the plays. The plays he selected were by August Wilson. As Chuck had a close relationship with Nobel Prize winning author Wole Soyinka, I thought nothing could better promote the plays than an introductory lecture by Soyinka and asked Chuck if he could arrange it. He did so.

Soyinka's extraordinary presentation took the form of a powerful defense of freedom of expression. It took place in the aftermath of the fatwa issued by the Iranian Ayatollah against Salman Rushdie for his publication of *The Satanic Verses*. In his lecture, Soyinka made a dramatic comparison. He recalled being in New York at a time that an African American playwright, Amari Baraka, was accused of anti-Semitism. He then asked his Nigerian audience: "what would we Africans think if the state of Israel had pronounced a death sentence on the African American Baraka for what he wrote?" His comparison was not lost on the audience. This powerful, and I thought newsworthy concept was apparently lost on the *New York Times* correspondent who attended the lecture and who failed to report anything on what this Nobel Prize winning author had to say in defense of Rushdie.

While Soyinka has been the first Black African to win the Nobel Prize for literature, his writing is somewhat complex and sophisticated. When he won the Nobel Prize, the *Paris Herald Tribune* interviewed some Nigerians. One was asked what she thought was his most important work. She responded, *Things Fall Apart*, which had actually been written by Achebe. In fact, many Nigerians tended to identify with the more accessible writings of Chinua Achebe.

When traveling in Eastern Nigeria, I was pleased to be present at Achebe's sixtieth birthday celebration attended by several hundred elite Nigerians. In the midst of the celebration there was some turmoil. Wole Soyinka had delivered a birthday present. It was a white goat. The Ibo celebrants were stunned and did not know how to react. The gift of a white goat symbolized good luck to Soyinka's Yoruba ethnic group. Ironically, a white goat was considered bad luck to Achebe's Ibo group.

A few weeks later Achebe called on me to ask a favor. He was in Lagos only briefly before returning to his home in Eastern Nigeria. But he had been invited to the United States for a teaching engagement and needed a quick turnaround for a visa. I told him it would be no problem for me to arrange to renew his visa. He left and the next thing I heard was he had been the victim of a car crash on the road back to Lagos. The accident had left him paralyzed, but despite his grave injury, he later made it to the U.S. where he had a long fifteen-year career at Bard College and later at Brown University. In his time in the U.S., he published a volume of poetry, a couple of novels, a book of essays and a superb critique summing up the problems of his home country, *The Trouble with Nigeria*.

While many African authors in the 1960's, 70's, and 80's depended heavily on publishing in Europe and readership in Europe and North America, Nigeria had a large enough literate population for its authors to depend on sales and even publication in its own country. This was especially true among the Eastern Ibos and the Western Yoruba. Most prominent was the Onitsha market literature, most often written for popular and semi-literate audiences. Some more sophisticated popular writers included my good friend Cyprian Ekwensi who like his fellow Ibo, Achebe, was from the East. Ekwensi was the most prolific of Nigerian authors. He was responsible for hundreds of popular short stories and more than twenty novels. His 1961 novel *Jagua Nana* was serialized by Nigerian television and became the most viewed television program of its time. At a dinner with him and two of his daughters, we discussed some of his work and the young women were harshly critical of his famous *Jagua Nana* character, a prostitute with a heart of gold.

Another prominent Nigerian writer who wrote for readers of his own country was Ken Saro-Wiwa, whose reputation also extended to Europe and America. Ken's arrest and execution resulted in Nigeria being internationally condemned. Ken had been sentenced to death for his role as leader of his ethnic group as it attempted to protect its interests in the eastern oil region. His highly successful novel *Sozaboy: A Novel in Rotten English* was a widely popular book, the subject of which was the Nigerian Civil War.

As one of the world's largest petroleum producers, Nigeria depended heavily on its oil revenue. It did so in a way tomaximize production regardless of its environmental or social impacts. Petroleum exploitation in the area of the Ogoni people of eastern Nigeria severely damaged the environment, having a devastating impact on agriculture and fishing and affecting the health of the region's population. Royal Dutch Shell Oil went all out to produce without regard for that devastation. Furthermore, the company failed to provide jobs for the poor population affected by the oil production, relying instead on better educated Nigerians from outside the area. The Ogoni people sought reform or compensation from the company and the Nigerian government. The highly regarded Ken Saro-Wiwa became the articulate spokesman for his Ogoni people as founder of the Movement for the Survival of the Ogoni people. I met with Ken shortly after he had taken on the cause. He explained his people's plight and presented me with a not-yet made public, newly drafted, "Ogoni Declaration of Rights." The Declaration sought redress of the grievances.

The well-developed plea fell on deaf ears. It was considered subversive by the military regime which sent military units to the region to prevent sabotage of its oil installations. I presented Ken's Declaration to our Ambassador with the request that we attempt to persuade the government to pay attention to the legitimate demands of the Ogoni people. He thought it would be difficult as the company involved, Royal Dutch Shell, was not American but British and Dutch, and had a track record of ruthless disregard for social or environmental impacts of their operations. He sought the help of his British counterpart who said he could not provide any assistance. Regardless of international opinion, Nigeria's military government refused to accept the legitimacy of the peaceful protest.

Several years later when several Ogoni chiefs who supported the government were killed, the Nigerian military government blamed Ken and his closest supporters, condemned them to death, and despite appeals from world leaders including the Pope, the U.S., and Europeans, executed them. Ken Saro-Wiwa's final recorded words were "Lord take my soul, but the struggle continues." It was a dramatic example of the ruthlessness of dictatorship and the desirability of democratic processes, especially the rule of law. True to Ken's prediction the struggle indeed continued and has only increased in violence since then.

When Nigeria first struck it rich on oil, its leaders were able to satisfy the demands of its young people for university education abroad by investing in a generous scholarship program for them in the United States and elsewhere. A government established Nigerian University Commission in Washington arranged to place students and recruit American faculty to teach in Nigerian Universities. Many students were enrolled in some of the best American colleges. The University of Wisconsin with its outstanding African Studies Program had its fair share of them.

Crawford Young, a political scientist and one of America's leading Africanists, was a seminal figure in mentoring Nigerian PhD candidates at the University of Wisconsin, many of whom later became faculty members at Nigerian universities. With that in mind and having spent a year in Dakar with Crawford as a Fulbright professor, I invited him to lecture in Nigeria. In addition to Lagos, we travelled widely to the North and to Ibadan, where aside from the success of his lectures, he was warmly welcomed by numerous former students who had risen to senior academic positions after having been mentored by him.

Throughout my career I strove to involve American Africanist scholars to deepen my knowledge and that of my Embassy colleagues in the complexity of the African societies in which we lived. In the words of another American scholar: "scholarship gives intellectual context to policy." As I had often found, American academic specialists were valuable resources and strong allies in our efforts to work with Embassy officials. I recall one instance in Nigeria when I invited an historian, David Robinson, to lunch with our Political Officer. The three of us began to discuss the role of Islam in Nigeria and Senegal. Robinson had written the definitive books on the Senegalese Muslim brotherhoods and their origins in Nigeria. Our Political Officer, John Campbell, who later become Ambassador to Nigeria, had a comprehensive knowledge of the key contemporary role of Nigeria's Muslim brotherhoods. Robinson's deep knowledge of the historical background combined with Campbell's detailed contemporary understanding of the brotherhoods, proved complementary to the enrichment of both professionals to their mutual advantage.

I had business in the Eastern city of Port Harcourt. In planning the trip, I learned of the presence of an American graduate student doing research on masking traditions in the area who happened to be a colleague of my daughter who was also working on her doctorate at Columbia University. Since she was located on the way to our destination, I set off to visit her with my wife and five children. We had made a reservation at a hotel called Dimdu's Cottage that had been recommended. When we arrived in the village it seemed there was no record of our reservation, but the manager said nonetheless they would accommodate us. He showed us to a large room next to a well-attended bar. The room had a bathroom, but the manager explained that it also served patrons of the bar in the evening. He expressed the hope that we wouldn't mind if they passed through our bedroom at night. We passed on his kind invitation, and we continued on our way to Port Harcourt.

One of our trips to eastern Nigeria resulted in serendipitously stumbling upon one of Africa's outstanding weaving traditions. The spectacular Akwete tradition derives from the village of the same name. Upon entering the village, we noted virtually all of the houses had verandas. On closer inspection, we heard the clicking of weaving heddles everywhere and saw weaving looms on most of those verandas. We subsequently learned that Akwete weaving is done not in strips that are sewn together as in almost all African traditions, but rather in a single wide width. That width depends on the span of the female weaver's arms. The stunning colors and designs reflect Ibo traditions. When asked where they get their compositions, one woman responded that they appear to the weavers in their dreams. We purchased a number of the Akwete cloths which we later donated to New York's Metropolitan Museum of Art. Another contribution to that museum was made by us in Abidjan in the name of our son Adrian, who was born there. It was a powerful Baule Goli helmet mask that we acquired from a ragged trader who appeared one night at our house.

One day, out of the blue, a call came for me from Chicago. It was the mother of the graduate student from Columbia University who had been stricken with a serious illness while in Eastern Nigeria.

I contacted our American embassy doctor and he flew with me to Port Harcourt where we rented a car and were at the hospital later in the day. The diagnosis was that her immune system was compromised. As the Nigerian hospital seemed unable to do much for her, the Embassy doctor and I decided to abduct her from the hospital and fly her back to Lagos to a private, well-regarded clinic. Soon thereafter she made a recovery, significant enough to enable her to return to the U.S.

That very afternoon, it had been arranged that the U.S. and Soviet embassies, in the new spirit of Glasnost, would engage in "friendship games" consisting of volleyball and tennis tournaments at the U.S. embassy's recreation center. Because of my trip to the East, I arrived late in the afternoon towards the end of the competition. While the Soviets dominated the volleyball competition, I arrived when the tennis tournament was tied, and one Soviet had not yet played. I was asked if I would play against him to break the tie and I agreed. Unfortunately, I had had a couple of beers and when the ball came at me, I saw three of them and lost the first set. I then ran into the shower room to sober up and came out refreshed. I dominated the next two sets, giving us a victory in the tennis tournament. Curiously, during those concluding sets, I noticed that whenever I won a point, I was cheered by the Russians. I asked our intelligence officer why the Russians had supported me. He informed me I had just beaten the KGB chief whom they all despised.

Suddenly a new chapter in the history of the world had begun. The Cold War was over. Decades of ferocious Soviet American Cold War competition in Africa, as elsewhere, was ending. To celebrate the anniversary of the October Revolution, the Soviets invited our embassy staff to a reception. We attended gladly. Midway through the evening the Soviet Ambassador and other senior staff disappeared. We later learned of the attempted coup that resulted in Yeltsin defiantly standing on a tank and ending the Russian military's effort to overthrow his government. It seemed that the Soviet Embassy staff had no idea what the outcome would be. Friendly relations were restored for the moment. I was told by the *Izvestia* correspondent that most of the Soviet diplomats had voted for Yeltsin in the recent election.

A trip I took to Kano shook me to the core. Northern Nigerian Islam had become decidedly anti-Western and anti-American. Up until then I had lived in the South among the dominant Yoruba, some half of which were Muslim, and mostly openly friendly and pro-Western. The Ibos in the east were fervently pro-American. But divisions in Nigeria were regional, ethnic, and religious. It was often said that fifty percent of Nigerians subscribed to Christianity, fifty percent to Islam and one hundred percent to indigenous or animist religions, reflecting the fact that almost all Nigerians retained aspects of their traditional beliefs.

Upon the completion of the building of a church by our friends, the American Jesuits in Lagos, they were enthusiastic when early on it was filled at every mass. They later learned that shortly after their mass many of the attendees went from their Catholic church to the nearby Protestant church for its service. For many Nigerians even in the South, the Christian/ Muslim rivalry did not prevent the occasional marriage of those of the opposing faiths. Attending two church services of different Christian faiths on Sunday simply meant that Lagosians were going to church for both social and religious purposes; a good thing to do on Sunday morning.

While we were there, the American Jesuits also launched Loyola College a secondary school with high admission standards for bright Nigerian students near the new capital, Abuja. During its first years a number of its students applied to Ivy League schools in the U.S. and were admitted. Then one year tragedy struck. On their way home to Eastern Nigeria during the Christmas break, their plane crashed killing some 59 of their students.

My trip to the major northern Nigerian city Kano exposed me to a hostility I had never before experienced in all my time in Africa. I met with several elite young journalists who advocated that Nigeria become an Islamic state. They were militantly anti-Western and anti-American. Until this visit, educated Africans I had known were primarily concerned about the governance of their own country. To the extent they cared about foreign affairs, their main issue was apartheid South Africa. However, the northern Nigerians I met were focused on the international Islamic movement and the Israeli-Palestine problem. This was also evident in the editorial policy of the hostile and often anti-American Kaduna based national newspaper, the *New Nigerian.* Radical elements of this political Islamic persuasion were to grow in strength and began large-scale kidnapping and religious violence, that even the Nigerian military was at a loss to control. That radical brand of Islam was to subsequently spread across Sahelian West Africa to Niger, Mali, Togo, the Central African Republic, and other countries, causing turbulence and instability over a wide area that France, the U.S. and even Russia were called upon to combat.

That mindset was manifested earlier during the first Gulf War. Siding with Iraq, an enraged Islamist mob in Kaduna attacked our Consulate in that northern city. While they were attempting to breach the walls, Ambassador Walker urgently called on the government to provide security forces to protect our diplomats. When they failed to act to prevent the violence, our ambassador had the State Department issue a travel advisory warning American citizens against travel to Nigeria. Nigerian President Babangida was furious, but he did reluctantly send security units to protect the Consulate and luckily none of our people were harmed.

In a rather bizarre media development, *The New York Times* West African correspondent inaccurately reported that the demonstration against our Kaduna Consulate was peaceful and that our Embassy had overreacted which was manifestly false. As that journalist hadn't contacted us to check on the story, I sent an angry letter to the editor of *Times* pointing out that the lives of American diplomats had been threatened in an attack that could have been deadly. The next time I met the reporter he apologized and asked me not to write to his boss again. I said I would not if he practiced ethical reporting.

Corruption was deeply imbedded in the fabric of Nigeria's government. One day I learned that Nigeria's Vice President, Admiral, Augustus Aikhomu, was to hold a press conference on the economy. It was during the first Gulf War when oil prices were at a peak. One of the reporters, a British correspondent, raised the issue to the Vice President of Nigeria having earned several billion dollars more than anticipated due to the windfall oil profits resulting from the war. The reporter noted that the government's budget report showed that more than a billion dollars had not been accounted for and he asked the Vice President to explain the disparity. Admiral Aikhomu hemmed and hawed and changed the subject. That journalist had a military escort to the airport the next morning when he was expelled from Nigeria and put on the first plane to London.

The issue of corruption that was widespread in Africa affects our foreign aid considerations giving most African governments a devastating reputation. While government corruption certainly exists in every region of the world it is especially egregious for most African countries. During the visit of an American academic, Victor Levine, I learned of the book he had published, *Political Corruption: The Case of Ghana*, that casts light on the nature of corruption in Africa. His book deals with corruption of government ministers in Ghana after the fall of the Nkrumah regime. The military, which had seized power, arrested a number of those ministers, and imprisoned them for having embezzled governmental funding.

After their release, Professor Levine contacted them. He pledged he would not reveal their identity under the pain of having them collect a substantial sum of money which was held in escrow. With that assurance, they all spoke candidly. The former ministers all admitted they illegally took government money. When asked if they would do so again, they all answered, "yes." The thrust of their testimony was that their position gave them control of substantial resources.

They responded that their actions were not motivated primarily by the quest for personal enrichment, but their traditional morality committed them to provide for their extended family, their hometown or village, their ethnic group, and their region. Not to have done so would have been considered a betrayal of traditional obligations, especially given the poverty of the people, constituents who had legitimate expectations of their help. It should be noted that corruption of the sort experienced in Ghana in the 1960's was of the order of ten percent. That was the amount of funding that might have been taken from a foreign contractor that was granted a contract by the minister. Levine noted that these loyalties held also for Nigeria and more broadly for most of Africa. Gradually over time, that early corruption has been overtaken by a massive diversion of government funding to high level officials, that has created billionaires who own villas in Europe, and high-end apartments in New York, especially in countries with valuable natural resources.

This has been the case especially in Nigeria with its vast petroleum resources and other mineral rich countries such as the Republic of the Congo and Angola. Some of that has been mitigated by the conditionality imposed by donor countries as part of their aid programs. Still, most African countries are rated low by Transparency International with Nigeria rated at 150 out of 180 countries in their 2020-2022 evaluation.

While the repatriation of African art, especially the art of Nigeria, has become a major issue in recent years, how to recover it and care for it is extremely complex. This was driven home to me when I received a call one evening from an American professor of African art history at Amherst College. Professor John Pemberton informed me that a stolen Nigerian Benin bronze head of great value was to be auctioned in Zurich the following month. The work was listed on the Art Loss Register for stolen art. He informed me that it could be recovered only if Nigeria claimed it before the auction. Once the auction took place, Swiss law could no longer enforce Nigeria's claim. He asked that I inform the proper authorities to enable them to claim the work and to do so quickly. The next day I contacted the Nigerian Ministry of Culture urging that they provide the Zurich auction house with the information needed to make their claim. Two weeks later came a second call from Amherst. Nothing had been done. Could I prompt Nigeria to act, he asked?

I recalled that the wife of Nigerian Vice President Aikhomu was from Benin City and owned a Lagos art gallery. I told my staff to contact her and stress the urgency for action. That did it. The Nigerian Cultural Attaché from London was tasked to travel to Zurich to make the claim. He did so with two days to spare before the auction. The work was recovered and returned to the National Museum. The museum director kindly invited me to the celebratory welcome home ceremony for the precious bronze head.

The ceremony was attended by the media and numerous officials. I was seated next to the Minister of Culture, Major General Y.Y. Kure representing the military government. Toward the end of the ceremony when I was warmly thanked by the museum director, along with Professor Pemberton, the Minister turned to me and asked: "Mr. LaGamma, how much do you think this sculpture is worth?" I shrugged and told him it was one of a kind, priceless, but if it had been sold at auction it likely would have fetched more than a million dollars. He responded with disdain: "I wouldn't give one naira for it." Then I realized that Nigeria's Minister of Culture, was Muslim. As such, he held the religious belief that rejected as blasphemous any depiction of a human image. I was stunned that we had worked so hard to recover this priceless work for all Nigerians and that the man responsible for the country's culture rejected it as worthless. I was left to wonder:

–how could a country demand restitution of its art when its key officials have contempt for art that depicts human images?
–how could countries demand the return of works of art when the security to protect them from theft was lacking?
–how could countries who give so few resources to museums and culture in general be expected to provide proper facilities, security and attract significant audiences for the art?

It seemed to me that these questions should be part of the equation when evaluating the issue of the repatriation of African art. As an alternative to repatriation, African countries should develop partnerships with Western counterpart institutions to provide training, arrange exchanges, and actively support their museums in order to protect their holdings and arrange for their citizens to understand and appreciate their heritage.

Towards the end of General Babangida's presidency, he decided he would like to pay a visit to the United States. The State Department considered it of value because of Nigeria's overall importance especially since it had become an important source of petroleum for us, but also to encourage the Nigerian President to act on his commitment to a democratic transition and end of military rule. President Clinton agreed, and a State Visit was scheduled for February 17th. I decided it would enhance the visit if I could travel to Washington and work with the Voice of America and USIA's press operation to assure appropriate press coverage. I arrived in Washington several days prior to the scheduled visit, only to learn that the visit had been cancelled.

As cancelling a State Visit is virtually unheard of, I sought an explanation. I got one at the State Department. The informed speculation was that apparently, the Nigerian ambassador to Washington had urged that the visit be cancelled. His tour as ambassador was nearing an end and he thought if the visit could be postponed, he might stay at his post another year. Accordingly, he advised President Babangida that mid-winter was a bad time for a visit given the cold weather which would preclude an impressive ceremony on the White House lawn. I was still in Washington on February 17th when contrary to all expectations, it was seventy-two degrees and sunny. On that perfect day I enjoyed lunch on a bench at the National Mall.

It was in the last months of our time in Lagos when we were hit by the most nightmarish crisis of our time overseas. My wife Anita was suffering from abdominal pains. We consulted the embassy doctor. He sent us to a Nigerian clinic that he said had just obtained some up-to-date American equipment. She underwent the X-rays and awaited the results. We returned home and the next day, to our dismay, we learned the clinic had determined that Anita had a massive tumor that was most likely cancerous. We were called by the doctor and told that his diagnosis was that she likely had no more than four months to live. That diagnosis led to the embassy arranging for her medical evacuation to the U.S. When our Jesuit missionary friends learned of this, they offered to give Anita last rites which we accepted and remarkably left her in a state of tranquility. I could not imagine anyone braver than her under the circumstances. I was not authorized to travel with her and had to pay my own way to accompany her home to New York. Meanwhile, her family in New

York had arranged an emergency appointment for her at Columbia Presbyterian Hospital.

The day after we arrived in New York, we met with the doctor who had her take a CAT scan. The results were known the next day. We were jubilant. There was no trace of a tumor. Looking at the Lagos X-ray our doctor speculated that someone's elbow had intervened and was interpreted as a tumor. His diagnosis was diverticulitis, an annoying but treatable medical condition. Reflecting on the Nigerian process that predicted a death sentence, I concluded our incompetent embassy doctor had placed his faith on newly acquired machinery and had ignored the well-known problems of the Nigerian medical system. While we had gone through hell and back, Anita had displayed remarkable courage throughout, emerging from the crisis grateful for whatever life was left to us.

# XIII. Washington 1991-95

I returned from Nigeria to assume the role of Deputy Director of USIA's Office of African Affairs for a year before spending the final two and a half Washington years as Director of that office. That role was the fulfillment of a career-long aspiration. It allowed me to witness and participate at a policy level in the major issues of U.S.-Africa relations, at least from the perspective of public diplomacy.

During that period four issues emerged of the greatest significance to the United States in our relations to Africa. They were the crisis of Somalia, the Rwanda genocide, the ending of apartheid in South Africa and the wave of democratization that swept the continent.

The Somali crisis is a difficult one to unravel. In the 1960's a leading authority on the horn of Africa, Professor William Zartman, a frequent consultant to the Department of State, wrote of his assessment of the fragility of African states. He wrote that given that most African countries had no sense of national unity based on complex ethnic, linguistic, cultural, and religious differences, fragmentation and conflict was inevitable for most of Africa. He went on to note that there was one country that lacked those divisions. He cited the example of Somalia as perhaps the prime case of a country that was united ethnically, linguistically, culturally, and religiously. When I next crossed paths with Professor Zartman, a scholar whom I respected, I reminded him of what he had written and asked why he had come to that conclusion given Somalia's complete lapse into an anarchic failed state. He seemed embarrassed by my recollection of what should have been a long-forgotten mistake in judgment that should not be held against him. In fact, the existence of rival Somali clans headed by warlords appeared to be the answer to the country's collapse, combined by the emergence of militant Islam.

In any event, the early 1990s saw drought causing Somalia to experience mass famine with warlord political power dependent on their control of food supplies. To feed the Somali people, both Presidents Clinton and Bush had decided to have U.S. military aircraft deliver humanitarian supplies to areas not controlled by warlords.

Nevertheless, international efforts led by the United States to feed starving Somalis were frequently stymied. That led President Bush on December 4th, 1992, in the last months of his presidency, to send in the Marines, the first ever dispatch of American ground troops to sub-Saharan Africa. I had represented USIA in several meetings of the Deputies Committee at the National Security Council. The main concern of that committee, led by the Department of Defense, had been how to overcome barriers to safely deliver food supplies to the starving Somali population.

At the time of our intervention, I had been making my quarterly visit to our African posts and was at lunch at the residence of our Ambassador to Ghana when he pulled me aside. He asked what I knew about our sending troops to Somalia. I responded that it was news to me despite having attended many high-level meetings on the crisis, and I told him military intervention was never suggested as a policy option. When I returned to Washington, I called on USIA's Director Joe Duffey. I asked him what had changed so profoundly that led to sending marines. He answered that President George Herbet Walker Bush made his historic decision because he could no longer tolerate the suffering of starving Somali children that he was witnessing each day on CNN. That historic decision, one that would not ultimately turn out well, must serve as a prime example of compassion in an American president.

A year later, during the presidency of Bill Clinton, we witnessed a dwindling support for the U.S. military presence in Somalia. At that time, our new ambassador to Somalia was my USIA good friend and former colleague, Robert Gosende. The ambush and murder of Turkish U.N. peacekeepers by Somali warlord Mohamad Farah Aidid triggered the effort of the American military to capture Aidid. Despite Bob's most energetic efforts to solve the problem, Washington failed to provide the support that was requested. Gosende had sent an urgent message indicating that tanks were required to deal with Aidid. The failure to heed his request resulted in the great tragedy known as "Black Hawk Down," a clash that resulted in the death of eighteen Americans. That failure was to later reverberate, preventing President Clinton from intervening to prevent the Rwanda genocide. Outrageously, and rather cynically, Robert Gosende was made a scapegoat for the tragedy and our subsequent withdrawal. That left Somalia abandoned to the warlords and pirates at the expense of its long-suffering people who were left mired in anarchy.

A surprising call to our front office conveyed a request from Supreme Court Justice Sandra Day O'Conner. She expressed a wish to visit Rwanda to see its famous gorillas. I was asked to call on her at her office at the Court. It was a pleasant conversation in which I explained to Justice O'Conner that we could not justify her travel without a professional dimension to it. Accordingly, I suggested that on the way to Rwanda she should consider a stop in Nairobi where we could arrange for her to interact with Kenyan jurists and lecture on the role of our Supreme Court and rule of law in the United States. Further, before her visit to the gorillas, we would benefit from arranging a luncheon in Kigali for legal officials, possibly offered by the ambassador. If that was agreeable, I would seek to arrange such a program, after which she could spend a weekend with the great apes. She readily agreed. I scheduled the proposed events and her program was highly effective in advancing our ideas about the importance of the concept of rule of law in our country. Not long after her trip, came the genocide in Rwanda. I happened to run into the Justice at Dulles Airport several months later. I reminded her of her trip and she immediately told me how terrible it was to think of some of the jurists she had met in Rwanda who had been victims of the horrific genocide.

If there is something worse than anarchy, it's genocide. Hatred borne of the colonial heritage that installed the Tutsi ethnic group as superior to the Hutus who comprised 85 percent of the population, had festered in the decades since Rwanda's independence. In 1994, the shooting down of an aircraft that carried the prime ministers of both Rwanda and Burundi who were returning home after a peace conference, triggered the massacre of 500,000 to a million Rwandan Tutsis.

When the magnitude of the slaughter was made clear, I assumed that President Clinton, like President Bush before him had done in the case of Somalia, would be moved to intervene militarily to save thousands of lives. Such an intervention was called for because the U.S. was the only country with troops available and aircraft to fly them to Rwanda. While ideally the U.N. should have had a mandate to act, it would have taken an estimated six months for the international body to assemble an intervention force without our involvement. But to President Clinton's everlasting disgrace, he declined to act fearing a repeat of Somalia's Black Hawk Down incident. That decision severely damaged America's reputation in Africa and around the world as we watched with horror the massive killings in Rwanda.

While the tragedies of Somalia and Rwanda were failures of American policy and Africa's reputation in the world, the peaceful transition of South Africa from apartheid to majority rule inspired the belief that humanity had the capacity to overcome its worst qualities. Further, the election of Nelson Mandela as President of South Africa was inspirational to all who believe in democracy. The attainment of majority rule in that country had long been my dream, but the tenacity of the white racist regime led me to believe it seemed unlikely that apartheid would be upended in my lifetime. That seemed especially the case once the apartheid regime acquired nuclear weapons, with the help of Israel, to defend itself against its external enemies.

The transformation was even more miraculous as it was achieved without great violence. And so, while I considered myself to be an Africanist, I had never sought assignment to Pretoria until the miracle of the 1994 election. Once that happened, in my capacity as

USIA Director for Africa, I worked hard in making it a priority of the U.S. government that majority rule in South Africa succeed. During a visit to South Africa, prior to my assignment there, I was briefed by our embassy political officer. I wanted to know how hard U.S. sanctions had hit the South African government, especially since South Africa was not a producer of petroleum. He informed me that while the South African government had evaded sanctions, it had cost dearly. He estimated they had to spend an additional five billion dollars a year to overcome U.S. sanctions.

The South African transition together with the U.S. encouragement of democracy and human rights, became the twin themes of my time as USIA Director for African Affairs. Once the historic moment of Mandela's 1994 election came, I decided I wanted nothing more than to be assigned to South Africa as Public Affairs Officer once the position was available. I did apply and was assigned to go there in the summer of 1995.

One example of my involvement while still in Washington, was my experience with a USIS/Pretoria grant that brought four senior officers of the reformed South African military to the United States to make professional contacts. Two were Afrikaner from the former apartheid regime, while the others had been officers in the ANC military wing. When they arrived in Washington, we helped to shape their visit which focused on civilian control of the military and how racial integration of our military had been implemented and functioned.

In welcoming the officers, I told them I would appreciate the opportunity to debrief them when they returned to Washington upon completion of their travels, and to hear the most important things they had learned. Three weeks later, we held that meeting. In answer to my question, the senior Afrikaans officer responded: "the most important thing we learned was from our African colleagues. We had thought we had been highly successful in protecting our civilian population." They informed us that the ANC was under orders not to attack civilian targets. That order clearly reflected Mandela's desire to avoid bitterness with white South Africans once, as he was sure it would, majority rule was attained.

On October 4th, 1994, Nelson Mandela began his State visit to the United States. I was among the hundreds that attended that joyous White House event hosted by President Bill Clinton. While the American president fittingly expressed his enthusiasm for the great transformation represented by the legendary Mandela, there was a lingering frustration hovering over the gathering. Clearly those of us who were familiar with complex transitions understood South Africa would require support and Mandela expected significant help from the United States. But precisely at this historic turning point, the fulfillment of the hopes and dreams of the once subjugated African population of South Africa and of the worldwide anti-apartheid movement, failed to be met.

Clinton was stymied by a Congress unwilling to respond generously to the need. The American assistance package that was thrown together was assembled from cuts to various other budgets and was unworthy of the great moment before us. In fact, during Mandela's visit, he wore a symbol of his disappointment, a lapel pin in the form of a peanut. It signified that he considered the American aid offered to be massively short of expectations. I was among those who believed the new South Africa deserved an American Marshall Plan.

Shortly after the April 27th, 1994, the first majority rule election brought Nelson Mandela to power, in the absence a large foreign assistance program from the United States, we sought to find ways to meet at least some of South African needs. Accordingly, USIA Director, Joseph Duffey, decided to hold a gathering he called "Investing in People: US-South African Conference on Democracy and Economic Development," to which we would invite potential investors in South Africa. It was initially decided to hold the meeting in Chicago. I felt the ideal place for such an event would be Atlanta. I made the case that Atlanta was a bastion of the civil rights movement, the long-time base of Dr. King, Andy Young, and Congressman John Lewis, and the center of a strong Black business community, as well as the Carter Center. Duffey agreed and we began planning to hold the gathering in Atlanta in June of 1994. While President Mandela. who had just come to office would not be available, he agreed to send Vice President Thabo Mbeki.

On the opening day I was asked to meet Vice President Mbeki at the airport. I was surprised to find that he would arrive by commercial air. I contacted the airline and asked that he be allowed to exit the aircraft first. I was even more surprised to find that he exited the plane alone, with no staff and no security. Having often experienced the visits of U.S. high level officials, I was expecting Mbeki to be surrounded by a large entourage. We drove to the conference hall while I briefed him on what to expect and shared an amiable conversation. The conference was attended by 800 people including Vice President Al Gore, CEOs of major corporations, and a host of civil society and civil rights leaders including: Georgia's Governor, Jesse Jackson, Andrew Young and John Lewis. It was also graced by the inimitable Archbishop Desmond Tutu with whom I had the great privilege of shepherding to and from the conference and enjoying his lively sense of humor. In his book *Partner to History: the U.S. Role in South Africa's Transition to Democracy*, U.S. Ambassador to South Africa, Princeton Lyman, writes that the conference: "...was a huge public relations success and brought people together to discuss all aspects of the new South Africa." One of the results was to generate an enormous amount of media coverage both in the U.S. and South Africa. We sought above all to greatly generate American trade and investment in South Africa,

While we departed the Atlanta Conference with a sense of its success, it was difficult to assess in the long run how effectively it inspired U.S. investment in South Africa. Clearly though with the end of apartheid American companies flowed into South Africa in great numbers. One clear result of the Atlanta Conference was that it served as the cradle of a Clinton concept. That concept was a governmental agreement entered into by the U.S. and South Africa, discussed in detail by Vice Presidents Mbeki and Gore, to form what was called a Binational Commission. A similar commission had been established by President Clinton with Russia at the end of the Cold War. The South African Commission would take on a similar format. It would be headed by Vice President Gore and Mbeki and include relevant Cabinet members from both countries. Their agenda would be the search for solutions to South African problems such as housing, education, the environment, energy, and an array of economic and political issues.

Shortly after the Atlanta Conference on South Africa, I received a call from Don Steinberg, the Africa Director of the National

Security Council. He spelled out the idea for a two-day White House Conference on Africa, the first ever to be held by an American president. He asked if my office could organize it. I said an enthusiastic "yes," honored to be tasked with such a responsibility. And with a mere ten days' notice I set out to collaborate with a team consisting of three exceptional members of my staff to work with the NSC and the State Department.

The conference had twin goals. It would focus the attention of President Clinton and other senior U.S. government officials on Africa and would enlist the many U.S. groups interested in the continent in a concerted effort to provide targeted assistance and stimulate trade and investment in Africa. According to many participants, it was successful in achieving those goals. In the judgment of the Council on Strategic International Studies:

> "Never before had so many senior officials from so many different departments of government gathered to discuss policy toward Africa. It is doubtful that there has been any prior occasion when the President, Vice President, Secretary of State and National Security Adviser gave public speeches on the same issue at the same event."

President Clinton addressed the 160 participants who attended including: Andrew Young, David Dinkins, Jesse Jackson, Maxine Walters, the NAACP's Benjamin Chavis, Senator Carol Mosley-Braun, leaders of private development organizations, as well as education, human rights and relief organizations involved in Africa. Twenty important business leaders also attended. In addition to senior U.S. officials and selected African ambassadors, USIA arranged to bring several outstanding members of African civil society to the conference.

Two inconsequential incidents proved to be irritants in the organization of the conference. Since it would open on a Monday, I arranged with my staff to take care of the last-minute preparation of background documents on the preceding Saturday. It was a blazing hot end of June day and after the first two hours, we began to sweat. I called the building's custodial staff to ask if there was a problem with the air conditioning. I was informed that unless ordered otherwise the building was not to be air-conditioned on weekends. I asked if I could order it to be switched on and was told only the Director of USIA could do so. I then sought to contact Dr. Duffey, but he was travelling and could not be reached. Since no windows could be opened, I asked our staff to work faster before we sweltered or ran out of air.

The second irritant involved preparations for the reception we were offering at the NSC at the end of the conference. We believed that a social event would properly conclude our two days and serve to convey to the African ambassadors present the seriousness of the Clinton administration's commitment to assist Africa. But here we were in the annex to the White House, arguably the most powerful real estate in the world, and on the morning of the last day's event, there was no supporting staff to help with food and drink, nor we learned, was there a budget to acquire refreshments. So, the NSC Director for Africa and several others of us took out our wallets and identified a staff member to go out and acquire something minimally suitable. Both incidents served to remind us of a couple of inadequacies that plague our government in the conduct of foreign affairs: the lack of funding for what we call representational activities (i.e. food and drink) and support staff.

With the ascent of South Africa to majority rule, a wave of democratic developments swept across the African continent and opportunities abounded for further developments. Toward the conclusion of the Bush Administration, Assistant Secretary of State for African Affairs, Herman Cohen, decided to produce an updated Africa policy for the new President Clinton before Cohen's retirement. He convened the entire community of officials who dealt with Africa throughout the U.S. government to draft the proposed policy document. I represented USIA during that process. At our concluding session, a near final draft document was circulated.

I read through the document quickly during a break in discussions and noted a striking omission. When we reconvened, I asked Secretary Cohen, "where's democracy?" It seemed that considering that most of our U.S. diplomats in Africa were confronting an increasing movement for free elections, transparent government, a free press and a concern for human rights and the rule of law, our policy should reflect the fact that we supported democratization in Africa. Cohn responded: "okay, Bob, give us language for the draft." I did and was delighted that for the first time ever a democracy policy recommendation for Africa figured as priority number one in the document that went to the White House and was formally adopted as our policy toward the continent.

Herman Cohen, in my estimation, was an exceptional Assistant Secretary for African Affairs who had a vast comprehension of African politics and exercised a superlative influence on our relations with many countries. When he was nearing the end of his mandate, I was invited to attend a farewell gathering for him. I asked where it was to be held. I was told the plan was to hold it in a small conference room. I reacted strongly, asking the caller if this was to be a farewell for Hank Cohen. He asked why I raised that question. I said that Hank was greatly respected and would doubtless have much to say that many throughout the State Department could learn from. I suggested it be held in the Dean Acheson auditorium which seats several hundred. The venue was changed, and the Acheson auditorium was filled.

Cohen's reflections were wise and far ranging. What I recall most vividly was the surprise he expressed upon taking office. He found that very often his Country Directors, desk officers and others in the Africa Bureau would in effect, question what that bozo in country X had just said or done. His reaction was to inform those who offered such critiques that we had carefully selected those ambassadors and other senior career officials for our embassies in Africa. He argued that those officers had detailed knowledge of the contemporary situation they lived and worked in 24/7. He said he had learned that the second guessing that went on within the State bureaucracy was rarely correct and that we should trust the officers we placed in the field unless there was clearly a reason not to. Cohen also reflected his view to the assembled officers that democracy promotion was an important dimension of our recently developed foreign policy for Africa.

There were those who questioned why we at USIA and State put such a heavy emphasis on supporting democracy in Africa. I came to diplomacy at the time of the Kennedy administration amidst the birth of so many African states freed of colonialism. At that time, it was hoped that African countries might choose the path of democratic governance. It was also the peak of the Cold War when the question of potential Soviet domination or significant influence was of major concern to U.S. policy makers. African leaders had many options to choose from both regarding foreign policy orientation and much more importantly, internal government structure. Given those factors democracy promotion was hardly a major policy concern. At that time *realpolitik* was the order of the day. But the Cold War was over, and African publics were clamoring for governments that would be responsive to their needs.

Colonialism had drawn arbitrary borders between countries, borders that were to be often contested. It had distorted, destroyed, and manipulated critical ethnic differences, so important to the loyalty of virtually all Africans. Some colonial regimes favored and empowered ethnic groups that could no longer remain in power once colonialism ended. In Togo, for instance, the Germans and later the French, had favored the coastal Ewe/Mina group and drew upon them as administrators of their other colonies including Southwest Africa (later Namibia), Tanganyika (later Tanzania), Cameroon, and Rwanda and Burundi.

In Togo, a military coup later reversed an elected government after independence. It was led by Eyadema of the northern Kabiye ethnicity, a group that had been favored by the Germans and French for their supposed warrior orientation. Similarly, the British in Nigeria chose to align with the educated southern Yoruba and eastern Ibo ethnicities for their qualifications as officials. After independence, however, the northern Hausa-Fulani dominated the military and hence the government. This pattern recurred elsewhere on the continent creating tensions and sometimes internal tragic strife.

Africanist Crawford Young, in his excellent book *The Post Colonial State in Africa* best describes what came to be known as "The Third Wave of Democratization in Africa." He notes:

> When the urban street erupted in Algeria in October 1988, shattering the seeming revolutionary elan of a once invincible regime, few realized that this was the opening scene of a momentous transformation of the African political landscape. But a short two years later the surge of democratization appeared irresistible, and it spread across the continent.

Churchill's oft quoted maxim that "democracy is the worst form of government except for all the others" should be tested against the post-independence experiences of African countries. In the case of Africa "all the others" include military rule, one party states, and various kinds of dictatorships or one-man rule. In recent decades those "others" are synonymous with misrule, massive corruption, and the dominance of one group at the expense of others. How else could it be explained that when the rulers of Benin were offered to be provided with significant bribes, they accepted European nuclear waste and dumped it in an area inhabited by a rival ethnic group.

The early 1990's was a time, with the fall of the Berlin wall, in which the Eastern European states were able to liberate themselves from the Soviet orbit and to seek to join a democratic Western Europe and even NATO. That historic process was strongly encouraged and supported by the United States. Parallel to that, an ascension by civil society in many African countries, caused a realization that citizen participation in government was the path to the solution of many problems. There was a "let's try democracy" mood that spread across the continent.

When at a conference of our public affairs officers in Africa, USIA's Director Joseph Duffey asked me what our highest priority for Africa was, I responded that in this context of historic worldwide transformation, I had successfully urged the State Department to prioritize democracy promotion as our main mission. Duffey, apparently not understanding the groundswell of support for democracy by a broad spectrum of educated Africans, responded "missions are for missionaries." I was dismayed that a liberal Democrat could be so dismissive. And this at a time when our government was creating the National Endowment for Democracy, the International Republican Institute, and the National Democratic Institute. Also in the planning state was Madeline Albright's Community of Democracies, a coming together of Foreign Ministers from the world's democratic countries which had as its goal support for democratic movements around the globe.

To influence Dr. Duffey's understanding of the surge of democracy around the world and our role in supporting it, I thought we might invite political guru David Gergen to our senior staff meeting. Knowing Gergen's support for democracy promotion, I looked forward to his advocacy for that policy. I was stunned when Duffey again argued against U.S. active promotion of that policy.

Then one day I received a call from the Voice of America. I was informed that newly elected President Ousmane of Niger was in town for an official visit. Ousmane wanted to call on us to thank the USIA Director as well as the Hausa service of the Voice of America for their help in explaining pluralism and democracy at the time of Niger's latest election campaign. He expressed his appreciation, saying "your coverage helped the people tremendously to understand their basic rights and the tenants of democracy, and thus despite severe economic problems it is now well established in Niger." The President explained that it had been impossible to have what he stood for reflected in his country's media since it had been completely controlled by the ruling party. He had high praise for the VOA's Hausa service which he said helped voters to understand their rights and the tenants of democracy. I sought to arrange for a meeting of the Niger President with Director Duffey, but his office said he was too busy. I had to argue hard to get Deputy Director Penn Kemble to take the time to join me to receive Niger's President.

The visit was confirmation that our role in supporting democratic processes had accomplished an important goal of what we called public diplomacy. This was happening at a time in which publics, meaning the views of civil society in Africa, had begun to weigh heavily on decision-making at the highest level. I sought to convey the importance of the move to democratization in Africa to our Deputy Director Kemble. When I learned that my friend, Professor Richard Joseph, at that time director of the African Governance Program at the Carter Center, was in town. I arranged for him to meet Kemble. Joseph was a leading expert on the African democracy transition. He briefed Kemble on that transition. Regretfully, I later learned that briefing made little impression given his lack of interest in what I considered to be an historic development that deserved U.S. support.

I wanted the concept of African democratization to be loudly echoed in the halls of the Department of State. The Department had initiated an Open Forum that seemed to be an excellent venue in which to spread that message. To build support for the concept of democracy promotion, especially in Africa, I proposed that Stanford's Larry Diamond serve as its first annual speaker. Larry was a professor of politics at Stanford and a pre-eminent authority on democratization, especially in Africa. Both the Forum and Larry accepted, and he superbly articulated how American diplomacy could promote democracy at the close of the 20th century. I firmly believe his argument found some favor among those hardnosed State officers whose careers were built on the concept of realpolitik.

With that to work with, I decided we at USIA had a free hand to coordinate our efforts with our wealthy cousins at USAID on democracy enhancement projects. One of my favorites was democracy education which I considered to be a necessary underpinning for African citizens to successfully build democratic institutions. Support for freedom of information and a robust civil society was another way we could support democratic development. A free press was a theme we were especially qualified to pursue since our public affairs officers all had primary responsibility for handling the press at our embassies.

Our office had a good deal of experience with organizing journalism seminars as we often involved senior U.S. journalists in them. I encouraged our posts to stress lectures on press freedom and organize workshops for journalists. We were able to fund a good many of them to help prepare African journalists to convert from working in government-controlled media to an environment that enabled greater press freedom. This was especially the case as we were witnessing a proliferation of private community radio stations in many African countries.

On one of my trips, I visited Mali which had recently seen the creation of sixteen Bamako community radio stations. At one of them the director was proud to show me a table he had acquired as a gift from a local restaurant owner. It seemed the restaurant's ads, broadcast on that station, had yielded many new customers. Now, based on the restaurant's gift, he told me, he could move the station's transmitter off the floor and place it onto the table. At a second radio station I noted its windows were broken. I asked what had happened. I was told that a new show had solicited calls from listeners. One issue on which many listeners voiced their opinions was the subject of a strike of truck drivers. A market woman had called in to say the truckers were a dirty bunch and she would never allow her daughter to marry one. As the truck drivers headquarters was nearby, when they heard that broadcast, they marched on the station to smash its windows. Not the ideal means of free expression, but at least the incident proved the station had listeners and influence, even though such an issue would never have been broadcast on government radio.

Yet another element that deserved strengthening was the role of women in the political process. We believed that if women participated more actively in voting, running for office, and in the political process in general it could help diminish corruption. And we thought it could also lead to the promotion of democracy by eventually doubling political participation.

Our speaker program, International Visitor Program, and even some of our scholarship programs, began to focus more heavily on issues of human rights, rule of law, local government, and the role of political parties. The latter issue was one we could work on with the newly established National Democratic Institute and the International Republican Institute, both of which had the development of democratic political parties as part of their mandate. While we knew that many of our African posts were involved with civil society, we encouraged them to expand those efforts since we saw that as an element critical to democratic development.

I also worked with State and USAID to arrange for the transfer of five million dollars to fund linkage grants that would strengthen democratic institutions. My colleagues at USAID, knowing we were a comparatively low budget agency, often asked how we would manage such large sums. Having recently read that USAID had invested in office space costing five million dollars I would sarcastically answer: "I would simply replicate your model and spend it on renting a new building."

The way we organized the expenditure was to identify one U.S. institution to manage several hundred thousand dollars over several years to carry out a democracy related project developed in partnership with an African counterpart. One early example was a multi-country series of journalism seminars contracted with the Center for Foreign Journalists over several years. I did encounter some resistance from USIA's Bureau of Educational and Cultural Affairs. They properly noted that they had been tasked to administer the grants but had no funding for the additional staff costs needed for management. Their point was well taken. I went back to USAID to build in a modest percentage of each grant to be devoted to administrative costs so our Bureau could hire one or two staffers to manage the program. Often this role was filled by part-time Foreign Service retirees.

Violence in Liberia caused our Voice of America transmitter to be damaged and shut down. This severely limited VOA's ability to effectively reach much of its audience. Surprisingly, I received a call from Jan Hartman our PAO in Gabon. In addition to Gabon, she was also responsible for the island nation of Sao Tomé where she had developed close ties with that country's leadership. When she learned about the VOA crisis, she proposed she could persuade the friendly government of the island nation to host a transmitter. She was confident she could arrange to get permission. I contacted VOA and their study of the situation led them to believe that the island was an excellent alternative to Monrovia.

While the government of Sao Tomé acceded to the plan, its execution ran into some minor difficulties. For one thing, while the study for the VOA installation was in progress, our PAO had arranged for an environmental expert to visit the island. Since concrete was needed for the site of the transmitter, he asked where the sand would be acquired to make it. He was told it would come from Sao Tomé beaches. The environmentalist vetoed that idea as harmful to the island. Consequently, sand had to be imported from the U.S. The second issue was the existence of a rare animal on the site selected which the expert argued could be further endangered by the project. The site, therefore, was relocated to protect the creature. Within the year a contract was approved and the problem was solved to everyone's satisfaction.

Gabon was one of the posts that had not recently been visited by our office. I was able to include Libreville on my itinerary of visits which was especially gratifying since my daughter Alisa was spending a year in Gabon to carry out research for her doctoral degree in art history from Columbia University. Alisa had been born in the Congo and grew up during my assignments to Ivory Coast, Togo, Milan, and Florence, and visited us during our time in Senegal, Nigeria, and South Africa so she was well acquainted with life in Africa. I arranged to spend a couple of days with her in a rain forest village in the south of Gabon where she studied the art of the Punu ethnic group famed for their mask making tradition performed ceremonially by dancers on stilts. When she completed that research and earned her doctorate, she began her career as a curator of African art at the Metropolitan Museum of Art in New York City.

After the catastrophic events of Somalia and Rwanda, a series of highly positive developments provided opportunities for improved U.S. relations with the African continent. The miracle of South African transformation and the end of military rule in Nigeria coupled with a strong democracy movement elsewhere, however fragile, generated a rare Afro-optimism unmatched since the independence movement thirty-four years earlier.

South African apartheid had been the subject of outrage throughout the African continent. The fact that the South African government had developed nuclear weapons seemed to indicate it was ultimately prepared to unloose Armageddon if its privileged dominance by the white minority was challenged. The fact that Mandela early on decided to abandon those weapons was a symbol that a less dangerous, peaceful order was beginning to define a way forward. I was privileged to have played a major role in organizing the historic Atlanta Conference to welcome South Africa at the end of apartheid, the White House Conference on Africa, and the drafting of a new African policy paper for the White House that for the first time made democracy promotion a priority for the U.S. in Africa. These developments combined to demonstrate, at least for the time being, that when internal and external conditions are right African countries can overcome dictatorships and massive corruption.

Aside from dealing with the public affairs aspects of major African issues, my responsibilities included the overall management of our USIS posts across the continent. To do so effectively required arranging sub-regional conferences and visits to as many USIS offices as possible. In addition to briefing the PAOs on policy issues and hearing from them about their opportunities and difficulties, there were obligatory meetings with ambassadors, U.S. staff, and with foreign service nationals. These were usually enormously informative, energizing, and very often full of surprises. As Deputy Director for Africa, I was responsible for more than forty evaluations of our desk officers and public affairs officers each year, evaluations that were central to the career development of the officers in the field and those in Washington. Subsequently as Director for African Affairs, I had oversight of all of our African operations both in Washington and abroad.

One unusually interesting visit was my very first trip to Eritrea. It was not long after that country's war with Ethiopia in which the Eritreans acquitted themselves better than expected against their more populous neighbor, as shown by the many destroyed Soviet tanks abandoned by the Ethiopians. Our PAO in Asmara was an especially bright and energetic young man in one of our more difficult posts, given the recently concluded war, one of Africa's most costly in terms of loss of life. After a day at the office, the PAO asked if I would like to take a drive on Saturday down the escarpment upon which Asmara stands. It was a dramatic mountain-top drop down to the coast.

Part way down we ran into two boys waving at us. The PAO stopped the car, spoke briefly to them, then returned to the car carrying something. I asked what it was. He showed me a baby eagle that was being sold for food. He continued our drive and stopped after rounding a bend. He then exited the car and freed the young eagle, a noble act although not exactly in his job description. That earned him points in my estimation of his human value. To top off our decent, we stopped for lunch in a restaurant embedded in an escarpment cave that served the best pasta I had ever had in Africa, a vestige of the brief and ill- designed Italian occupation of the Horn of Africa.

Once I returned to Washington, I dealt with an incident that involved post- genocide Rwanda. It concerned our Nairobi information officer, someone who had been a European specialist, but had come to me for a PAO assignment in his efforts to seek promotion. Since he had had no previous African experience, I offered him the Nairobi assignment as press officer. He was present when a Congressional delegation stopped in Nairobi on the way to Rwanda as that devastated country sought to recover from the genocide. The officer offered his assistance to the delegation since he had a good grip on the French language. Based on his past record, I viewed this as an attempt to ingratiate himself with key Congressmen. I contacted his boss in Nairobi and noted he had not gotten the required permission to leave his post and travel to another country. When I spoke to him his explanation was that he was so moved by Rwandan suffering that he felt obliged to go there. I contacted our Africa personnel officer and noted that we had a vacancy for our PAO position in Rwanda and decided to assign him there. When he learned of the assignment he begged to be excused and allowed to remain in Nairobi.

# XIV. The New South Africa (1995-97)

Arriving in Nelson Mandela's New South Africa with the rank of Minister-Counselor and our embassy's Public Affairs Officer in the summer of 1995 was the fulfillment of a life-long dream. As Director of USIA's Office of African Affairs in my previous assignment, I found a good deal of my energies had been devoted to the architecture of our new relationship with what was arguably Africa's most important and most complex country. The transformation from minority to majority rule was at the heart of that complexity. So was the change from a society defined by violent adversarial relationships toward one aspiring to multiculturalism and racial harmony.

At the time of my arrival a new constitution was being promulgated, Bishop Tutu was conducting his Truth and Reconciliation Committee, and President Mandela and his partner in transition, F.W. De Klerk, were reassuring their respective communities that the new dispensation was working. A unifying cause for jubilation by all South Africans was their team's victory in the rugby World Cup.

The challenge of change confronting Mandela and the ruling ANC was massive, but there was also much jubilation captured so well by Hollywood in the film Invictus. That film highlighted the victory of host country, South Africa, in the Rugby World Championship. Mandela skillfully used sports, so important to South Africa, as a racially unifying force when he wore the shirt with the number of the Afrikaner team star. Of the three major sports in South Africa, soccer had been dominated by Black athletes, Cricket by those of British background, and Rugby by Afrikaners. When Mandela came out to cheer for the predominantly white Rugby team that the Black population had previously rooted against, it was a powerful symbol of national unity.

Many American companies returned to majority ruled South Africa. One example was captured in Anita's jovial poem:

**Vernissage: Opening of McDonald's in Pretoria**

VIP's gathered where the golden arches rose
glinting in sun, reflecting robot's evening light—
a beacon for all those marching toward Pretoria
caught in the new South Africa's euphoria.
A Big Mac in his mouth, the mayor struck a pose,
gold chains corseting his robust chest. Carter Drew
commended his Mac-gowned crew who'd given
their best, then the mayor expounded on how
the quarter pounder would make the economy
sounder: 'Let us raise a glass in praise of food

> that's fast, forget our past and in this place create
> a new domicile where men can reconcile." Corks
> popped, hips began to sway to the rock band beat
> beneath the Southern Cross by the Big Mac sign.

While freedom was exhilarating, expectations of the Black population were unrealistically high. Certain needs were fast-tracked. Priority was given to the provision of clean water and electric power in the townships and rural areas, as well as the beginning of integrated education. The end of apartheid meant a vast influx to urban areas, an influx of mainly unemployed families and individuals seeking work. Suddenly, the new majority rule government had to deal with massive housing, healthcare and education problems that were not solvable in the short run and which were at odds with the high expectations at the end of apartheid. Inevitably, the concentration of population in urban areas, especially in Johannesburg, Durban, Pretoria, and Cape Town, led to a spike in crime.

Our family, consisting of Anita, Florence, and I, moved into a lovely house in what was formerly an all-white neighborhood but had begun to change. It reminded me of my own move to Washington D.C. in 1962. It was a time of change from legal to de facto residential segregation with one dramatic difference. With the unprecedented number of newly independent African countries, came an influx of new embassies and their staffs. This also had occurred during the time of President Kennedy whose administration was alert to preventing the newly arrived African diplomats from being ghettoized. Accordingly, they were not prevented from integrating previously all-white neighborhoods. A parallel development resulted when

South Africa become a majority ruled country. Once South Africa abandoned apartheid, it had become a legitimate African country. When that happened diplomats from all over Africa flooded into the country's twin capitals, Pretoria and Cape Town, including the previously all-white suburb we lived in. Those Africans, together with the new senior South African Black government officials were no longer constrained by previous housing discrimination.

Majority rule came to South Africa the Mandela way, without great bloodletting. But that did not mean that the white minority conceded power without attempting to subvert the realization of full equality. We brought a lecturer with experience in economic transformation to discuss how the private sector could be adapted to the new political dispensation. James Dwinell shared his ideas on integrating Black South Africans into the private sector hierarchy. We had him speak to government officials and others who exerted economic influence. Then came an interesting call. I was contacted by a corporate representative who asked if James could speak to a Johannesburg gathering of the CEOs of major corporations. He accepted and after meeting with them, returned to brief me.

He told me that the corporate representatives explained what they considered their dilemma. They said they could not resist the political pressure to be more inclusive. They needed some Black faces in prominent corporate positions. They asked for Dwinell's advice on how they could create positions that would accommodate that need without yielding real decision-making power, which they wished would remain in the hands of the white executives. They said they were willing to create positions with high salaries and benefits but did not want to give up real authority. I was pleased to learn that when James heard that, his response was that he wouldn't be party to such a sham operation.

In the post-apartheid South Africa there continued to be a dynamic arts scene, but its nature had been transformed. Prior to the political transformation, a good deal of that dynamic related to opposition to apartheid. Further, the publicly funded cultural institutions tended to cater to the tastes of the white minority. With the change, a major issue was how best to manage the arts institutions when the majority population had distinctly different tastes in the arts. My colleague, Cultural Affairs Officer, Rosemary Crockett, arranged a brilliant program to address that issue. She invited one of America's outstanding arts administrators, Michael Kaiser, to come to South Africa.

Kaiser expressed interest in doing so, but he explained that he would only be able come for a number of short visits rather than for an extended period. To do so he persuaded South African Airways to provide him with close to free fare. USIS would then cover his per diem. Crockett arranged for the University of Witwatersrand to host a series of Kaiser's symposia on managing the arts for representatives of institutions throughout the country. She also had those sessions video recorded. The program was a huge success. I had copies made of the videos for distribution to USIS cultural centers throughout Africa, knowing that there was an appetite for Kaiser's ideas everywhere on the continent.

South Africa has produced two Nobel laureates in literature, notably Nadine Gordimer and J.M. Coetzee, but my own favorite South African writer has to be perhaps the greatest living South African playwright Athol Fugard. I had the good fortune to attend a performance of his magisterial *Master Harold and the Boys*. Towards the end of our time in Pretoria, we also experienced one of his autobiographical plays, the brilliant *Captain's Tiger, A Memoir for the Stage*. The play chronicles young Fugard's adventure as he travels the 4,000 miles from Cape Town to Cairo where he tries to fulfill his dream of seeing the world while serving as an assistant to the ship's captain in order to generate a literary career. We sat in the first row while Fugard himself served as narrator, and at one point the actor playing him reaches the conclusion that his attempts at writing were unworthy. He then tossed those writings into the ocean, which on that occasion happened to be in my lap. I felt like the recipient of fragments of the early writing of the great dramatist.

Before arriving in Pretoria, we had to solve an administrative problem. It involved the Dance Theater of Harlem's highly successful tour of South Africa. Our Cultural Affairs Officer strongly advocated for that tour but did not fully plan to cover all expenses. That left the dance company unable to cover the costs of shipping its costumes and equipment back to New York. I was able to prevail on the USIA Director to dip into his emergency fund to meet that need. Two years later when the Alvin Ailey company also toured South Africa, funding for it was completely covered by an American bank, unlike our ballet company that had to struggle to cover all its costs.

Personnel changes also followed the end of apartheid. When I learned that jazz trumpeter Hugh Masekela had been named director of Pretoria's National Theater, I contacted him to seek an appointment. Masekela's story is legendary. He is known as the father of South African jazz. As a boy growing up in a township, he saw the 1950 film *Young Man with a Horn* with Kirk Douglas who played a young man who aspired to play the trumpet. Masekela was inspired to take the same path. He conveyed that dream to the eminent Bishop Huddleston who managed to find a used trumpet for him. In his first years with the instrument, he was self-taught. He later studied at the Manhattan School of Music where he became a jazz virtuoso. With his increasing fame both abroad and in South Africa as a musician and composer, Masekela was also a voice of opposition to apartheid.

Early in my career in Washington I was briefly assigned to the USIA motion picture office. I had the good fortune to assist in the filming of a documentary on Masekela's career in the U.S. Our film crew covered his concerts in Los Angeles and visited him at his Malibu home. While Masekela remembered little of our encounter thirty years previously, he graciously invited my wife and I to dinner at the theater where we had the opportunity to discuss his new vision for what the National Theater was to become under his leadership. His objective was to satisfy the tastes of the majority Black population. He found it a difficult challenge since he lacked any of the administrative experience necessary to succeed in what he faced as an exceedingly difficult task.

South Africa was a treasure trove of ancient examples of the origins of human art. We got to know David Lewis Williams, the leading scholar of the rock painting form. An even earlier manifestation of this tradition was excavated east of Cape Town in a place known as Blombos Cave. Abstract engravings on ochre dated 73,000 years ago found there are thought to be the earliest instance of art produced by the modern human race. That discovery led to the establishment of a museum at Witwatersrand University in Johannesburg known as the Origins Center, which traces the development of art in southern Africa and focuses on the earliest populations to live and express themselves visually across the region.

One small effort we made to advise on how to deal with crime was bringing former New York City Police Commissioner Bill Bratton to South Africa. Bratton shared his experience on crime reduction, including his ideas on community policing and the "broken windows" theory about limiting petty crime which if uncurbed would lead to more serious infractions.

To give advice to solve the many problems that grew out of its apartheid past, we offered grants to newly named African officials to visit the United States for them to observe how we attempt to come to grips with problems of racism among other issues. We also arranged for USIA Washington to design professional programs to allow newly named, inexperienced Black South African government officials to observe how their U.S. counterparts dealt with similar problems. Most of those programs were designed to directly support the fields identified by the Vice President Gore/Vice President Mbeki's headed Binational Commission. Those fields included education, energy, health, housing, commerce, and the environment.

To acquire the resources necessary to fund a greatly expanded exchange program we persuaded our USAID colleagues to provide a significant addition to our budget. We also made a deal with various South African ministries to cover international travel costs of the officials they wished to send to the U.S., while we covered the in-country expenses once they arrived and arranged for their professional contacts.

The Binational Commission sought, through the collaboration of the Cabinet Ministries of both countries to work in priority fields of cooperation for the U.S. and South Africa that were designed to help with the transition. The idea was to designate heads of Cabinet departments that would integrate those subjects for cooperation into their agendas. Although USAID was also involved, the Clinton Administration had decided that unlike our relations with most African countries, traditional aid programs would not assume a major role in our relationship. This was in part because of the reluctance of a Republican controlled Congress to provide the magnitude of financial assistance many of us would have liked. While the Binational Commission appeared to be a bold, innovative way to forge a new relationship with South Africa, it was a new and unproven concept. An agreement to provide South Africa with Peace Corps volunteers was also part of our initiative to build a new relationship.

The American Embassy in Pretoria was spanking new when I arrived. It was a handsome structure but one lacking windows, designed to be a hyper-secure fifty-million-dollar fortress. While the offices were modern and comfortable the public access was difficult. Security even plagued embassy officers at the time. One told me he had to enter five combinations including one in the elevator before he could begin his workday. The high priority given to security in its construction derived from the fact that South Africa was considered at the time to have the potential for bloody racial violence before attaining majority rule. It was one of a series of new embassies built with security in mind in the age of terrorism. We occupied a brand new "Inman embassy" named after Admiral Bobby Ray Inman who chaired a committee that produced a study following the bombing of the U.S. Embassy in Beirut. That study defined ways in which our embassies could best be protected. It required a building with a significant set-back from the gate, one with few windows and having fortress-like walls. Access to it was limited to those who had well-defined business with us and they had to pass through metal detectors and leave phones and other devices at the entrance. The formidable building prevented access to the normal USIS foreign visitors who had traditionally come to our library or attended cultural events at our center.

The bombings of embassies in Kenya and Tanzania clearly made security a foremost consideration for our African facilities. South Africa's peaceful transition, had it been anticipated, might have obviated some of the heavier security measures so irksome to our South African public in the time of Mandela. Our previous embassy had been in a downtown office building, occupied also by the South African security service and said to be replete with listening devices planted by them. The new building had a grassy set-back with a lawn that was home to my favorite ha-de-da birds. The USIS library, once open to the public, was reduced to a research center.

One of our greatest and most pleasurable travel discoveries, one that we revisited frequently during our weekends, occurred while driving to Durban. We saw a sign for Royal Natal National Park in the Drakensburg Mountains. Established in 1879, the park was the second oldest national park in the world. We drove to it and after surveying its wonders determined we would have to stay in this majestic park. We learned that its Royal name was conferred as a result of having been the site for a stay by Princess Elizabeth and her sister before Elizabeth was crowned Queen.

Several weeks later we returned and stayed in the cabin occupied by the royals and hiked on the mountain trails among herds of baboons and expanses of tropical flowers. Unknown to us, and only discovered during our next visit, was a cluster of villas higher up in the mountain that could be rented, consisting of several bedrooms, a living room, a fully equipped kitchen, an outdoor fireplace, and a deck from which to look out at the mountain vistas. Our children especially came to love that place. Once when our daughter Alisa visited us on New Year's Eve, we shared an evening gazing at an unobstructed, wondrous view of all the thousands of stars visible in the southern hemisphere's sky. For us, Royal Natal was our favorite place to spend a long weekend in South Africa, even surpassing our appreciation for its outstanding game parks.

Our ambassador, when I arrived in South Africa was Princeton Lyman, one of our most seasoned and brilliant career ambassadors. I had the pleasure of serving with Princeton during his concluding year as ambassador to Nigeria. His reflections on how we attempted to help South Africa during its transition are a model of diplomacy. He detailed what I saw as his diplomatic prowess in his book *Partner to History: the U.S. Role in South Africa's Transition to Democracy.* I very much regretted his departure only a few months after my arrival in South Africa. He was replaced by James Joseph, an African American who had served as the President of the U.S. Council on Foundations. Joseph was an interesting choice as he had been an active member of the American anti-apartheid movement.

After several months as President Clinton's ambassador to South Africa, Joseph expressed his disappointment that his past efforts to end apartheid and support majority rule and his energetic enthusiasm to be helpful to the democratic transition seemed not to be fully appreciated by the senior ANC government officials with whom he interacted.

One day I attended lunch at his residence and was seated next to Vice President Mbeki's brother and senior advisor. I asked him why we Americans who sought to be accepted as friends and partners by key South Africans were often held at arm's length. I expected him to say that Chet Crocker's constructive engagement policy under President Reagan accounted for the perceived mistrust. While that might have shaped the lack of warmth in our relationship to some degree, his answer was something that should have been obvious to me.

He said many senior ANC officials had sought refuge not in the United States or Western Europe but in the Soviet Union and Eastern Europe where they were provided with educational and other opportunities. And although the U.S. anti-apartheid movement was appreciated, it was the Communist governments that provided unambiguous support to the ANC members who sought material support and refuge in their countries. The absence of all but a relatively small number of refugees from apartheid obtaining scholarships to the United States (as part of the SASP, or Southern African Student Program which included students from Mozambique, Angola, Namibia, and South Africa) was clearly short sighted on the part of American administrations. It should have been clear that one day apartheid would end. If we had the foresight to educate the new governing elite, relations between South Africa and the U.S. would have benefitted from our provision of educational opportunities.

Likely even more important to our relationship was the great disappointment President Mandela felt and expressed over the failure of the United States to provide more substantial assistance to South Africa in its time of greatest need, the complex transition that the country was undergoing. The unwillingness of Congress to provide funding despite President Clinton's appeals, prevented Mandela from acceding to as close a relationship as he would have wanted with the U.S., since he was under pressure from the radical wing of the ANC which expected more generous assistance from America.

That history explained the less than enthusiastic relationship of many key ruling party leaders toward the United States. South Africa, after all, had a small but influential Communist Party. But it happened that world communism was on the wane in the 1990's and with the end of the Soviet Union, many of the ties developed during the Cold War were cut. Nevertheless, the ANC had come to power with many of its key members in favor of state ownership of major corporations. During the transition, the U.S. sent several prestigious economists to consult with Mandela and his key advisors. They spelled out that seizure of major corporations by the state would yield revenue equivalent to several hundred dollars for every South African. But that benefit would be realized one time only. Subsequently, they predicted the inevitable collapse of the economy due to the absence of an entrepreneurial class. Following those consultations, the ANC announced that it would no longer support government confiscation of major corporations.

The euphoria of the years immediately after the end of apartheid depended on two things: the persona of the charismatic Mandela, and the ability of the new government to begin to seriously address the basic needs of the majority of South Africans. It was clear that enormous efforts had been required to bring the ANC to power, but also clear was that the hard part was yet to come for South Africa in order for it to become the success story that so many of us wished for and to realize the dreams of Mandela, Tutu, or the children of Soweto.

Our South African USIS operations, in addition to our main office/cultural center in Pretoria included important centers in Johannesburg, Soweto, Durban, and Cape Town, with Cape Town serving as the Parliamentary capital when the government shifted to the Cape with the opening of the parliament. It also included a USIS library in the township of Soweto, to serve the youth of that community. It was a place of great symbolic importance to the U.S. presence in South Africa. Given that significance, I developed an idea that would bring reading rooms to other townships. In consultation with the cutting-edge computer company Oracle, I proposed the acquisition of shipping containers that could be modified to serve as lending libraries and research centers. The containers would be air-conditioned and equipped with antennas that would connect to the Internet, a generator to provide power, and several computers. My plan was to connect those townships to the wider world and give young people an invaluable learning tool. Unfortunately, I could not follow-up as my tour had come to an end, and I had to return to Washington to conclude my career and ready myself for retirement.

While still in South Africa, my wife Anita came across a brief notice in the local newspaper. It announced that a poetry workshop would take place the following year in the southern South African town of Grahamstown (now known as Makhamda). Not knowing the geography, she asked if we could go. I looked it up on Google and learned it was about a twenty-hour drive. I then considered if we could work it into an overdue visit to Cape Town where I needed to make a periodic visit. Further research showed that the workshop was being given by Robert Berold, an anti-apartheid stalwart, one of South Africa's leading poets and editor of a cutting-edge poetry journal, *New Coin*. We decided to make the trip. We had flown to Grahamstown once before for its annual arts festival, the largest in Africa. It was also host to Rhodes University, one of South Africa's most important institutions of higher education.

Our long two-day drive taught us much about the incredible variety of the South African landscape. When it found us in Grahamstown, the hard part of the journey was yet to come. Our final destination was Berold's farm for which he had given us directions. After a few miles we came to railroad tracks and a junction with an unlikely dirt road. With no other choice, we took it and found ourselves combating huge potholes, the roughest surface my Volvo had ever encountered. After a quarter of an impossible mile, we reached the farm. There we were welcomed by farmer-poet Berold and ten young, aspiring Africans poets from neighboring Port Elisabeth that Berold would coach along with Anita for the next few days. As for me, I was assigned the task of gathering provisions for our meals in the town. The workshop was a success and we learned a great deal about both poetry and the South African imagination and the concerns and talents of ten exceptional young South Africans.

Among the throngs of celebrities who flocked to the newly born democratic South Africa was First Lady Hillary Clinton. In March 1997 she visited Johannesburg and Soweto and gave an address at the University of Cape Town. In that speech she told the students that they had the chance to forge the new South Africa and help shape the course of history. She reminded them that:

> The world is watching, and the democratic world stands with you. It has been given to you, as to few other people in history, the opportunity to hold in your hands your own futures and the futures and dreams of countless millions of others."

Mrs. Clinton's visit to Cape Town, Johannesburg and Pretoria was exceptionally well received and served to support our relationship with the new South Africa.

One final and disappointing episode put me in conflict with Ambassador Joseph. At a country team meeting I learned that the FBI, Treasury, and the Drug Enforcement Agency would be establishing offices in Pretoria. Those agencies together with others that dealt with such issues as counterfeiting, drug trafficking and international criminal activity, comprised a large presence of security related offices new to our South African diplomatic presence. I asked the Ambassador how the government of South Africa felt about the establishment of that new presence. He told me they welcomed it as an important dimension of our cooperation on security related issues. Since that was the case, I suggested that we hold a press conference with the support of our South African partners to explain our new cooperative relationship. The ambassador agreed. We proceeded to invite the press for a briefing devoted to the new developments. Soon after, the media began announcing the journalists who planned to attend.

Then came the problem. *The Mail and Guardian*, one of South Africa's most important newspapers, said they would send their new security correspondent, Stephen Laufer. I learned that Laufer had returned to South Africa after having worked as a local USIS press officer in Berlin for our embassy. He had done so for 13 years while at the same time working for the Soviet KGB. He had been convicted of espionage by West Germany in 1992 and given a suspended sentence for cooperating and providing information about the Russians for whom he had spied. I urged that we contact Laufer's newspaper and ask that they send someone else to the press conference. Joseph told me he would not risk our relationship with the newspaper. He declared the Cold War was over and we should not allow our relationship to be tainted by declaring that Laufer was unwelcome.

I argued that Laufer had betrayed his employers, USIS, the American Embassy in Berlin, and the U.S. government over the course of 13 years. Further, I had met Laufer when he disrupted a lecture by Secretary of State Warren Christopher a few weeks earlier by coming to it very late and making a big fuss at his entry. At that time his utterances made it clear he had an anti-American chip on his shoulder. My argument fell on deaf ears and the Ambassador overruled me. While I never considered myself a Cold Warrior, I did consider betrayal a cardinal sin and had I not been at the point of returning home, I would have used the dissent channel to oppose what I considered to be the bad judgment of Ambassador Joseph. I later learned that Laufer's period of espionage happened to have corresponded with Vladmir Putin's time with the KGB in East Germany.

After my failure to reverse the decision, I learned I was not alone in my position. The following week the station chief sent me a thank you note and an envelope containing CIA paraphernalia, including an Agency cap. It was small compensation but appreciated.

Among the highlights of my two years in South Africa was the CIVITAS conference I organized in Pretoria in 1997. The initiative came from USIA Washington, part of a project favored by our Deputy Director Penn Kemble and sponsored by the California based CIVITAS NGO. The 1990's democracy movements faced the problem that the broad spectrum of the population failed to understand their role in assuring that their democracy take root by continuing to support it. American revolutionary Thomas Paine and leaders of the French Revolution had as an article of faith, the belief that ordinary people should have a right to seek to influence decisions that affect their lives. Accordingly, civic education was necessary to enable the engagement of citizenry in the political process by voting in free elections, freely expressing their views, and involving themselves in the political process at local and national levels.

We organized the Pretoria conference first by holding a full day meeting to consult with six leading South African democracy organizations. I prepared and distributed an agenda for our discussions on how they might engage with democracy supporters from a dozen African countries. One of our partners in that meeting responded to my agenda by saying, "Bob, we won't need your agenda. We know how to organize such a conference." I was delighted to hear that, knowing it indicated they would relish taking the leading role in the two-day gathering.

As I expected, South Africa was the ideal host for such a conference as the Mandela government was vigorously attempting to educate and engage its people in the new democratic world after overcoming apartheid. To avoid a conference that was merely a talk-fest we especially engaged the help of the dynamic Paul Graham, president of the South African NGO, the Institute for Democracy in South Africa (IDASA) which had been a leader in the struggle against apartheid.

IDASA arranged to transport groups of participants to Soweto to meet with leaders to discuss how South Africans had organized to oppose the former racist government. David McQuaid-Mason, law professor at Durban University, who for many years worked on democracy education to organize opposition to apartheid, also organized meetings with major South African leaders of their country's democracy movement. Other innovations were that conference participants attend "street theater," performed in marketplaces and other public venues, designed to inform South Africans about their rights and met with the designers of the new South African constitution.

The conference served to illuminate the key role of democracy education in solidifying a newly established democracy. We had invited Nelson Mandela to address the conference, and while he had initially accepted, we had a last-minute call that having just returned from an international trip, he would be unable to attend. Instead, he sent a remarkable and highly articulate substitute, his wife, Graca Machel, who had experienced democratic transformation in Mozambique as the former first lady there before her late husband's death.

I learned from the passionate belief of the various African participants that to be a successful democracy, citizens of African countries needed to understand the new role of civil society in a post-authoritarian society, a role very different than their struggles to adopt democracy. While independence and majority rule, often obtained by struggle might be the end of one kind of oppression, to avoid another required hard work which was the responsibility of the citizenry. They stressed that the process was not over with freedom. Yet another national effort was required to secure that freedom. As I had previously suggested to Thabo Mbeki at our Atlanta conference, we had learned that once freedom was achieved, to preserve it, the hard part, was yet to come.

One last hurrah while we were in South Africa was our learning from a tourist agency about an affordable trip to Victoria Falls coupled with several days in Botswana's Chobe game park. The temptation was too great to resist. I had taken Anita to Victoria Falls almost forty years earlier and it had been the thrill of a lifetime. Our second visit was simply to revisit paradise. Victoria, the grandest of falls, twice as high as Niagara, and more than a mile wide, was given the Lozi name *Mosi-oa-Tunya*, "the Smoke that Thunders." We reveled in walking along the edge of the falls on a trail along a rain forest created by its perennial mists. We later rode a canoe along the mighty Zambezi River and were welcomed by its resident hippos and crocodiles.

Then it was on to the Botswana lodge that had been the site of Elizabeth Taylor's second honeymoon with Richard Burton. It was a thrill to be in the Okavango Delta. We were treated to boat rides on the Zambezi again accompanied by crocodiles and hippos, and a sky filled with exotic birds. While we saw an elephant or two, we were disappointed to learn that it was the time of year that the herds were at the point of leaving the area. Then dramatically, as our guide drove through a rain shower, he heard his radio crackle with news of a sighting of a large elephant herd. It was nearing the hour of darkness so our driver raced to where he was directed and there in the dusk were perhaps a hundred phantom pachyderms. It was a transcendent experience described in my wife Anita's poem:

**Along the Chobe River: Botswana**

We drive along the Chobe River
where fifty thousand elephants
drink and uproot the land. But too late.
The mopane and acacia woodlands
are already abandoned, ravaged. We move
through a trampled wood. The rains
have sent the last of the great pachyderms.
south to the Okavanga Delta.

We look for the lingering drifters. We scan
the bushveld, the Savannah, the forest
and see the sky tumbling as lilac-breasted
rollers fly upward, then dive gathering

speed with folded wings. Everywhere
they perch on dead branches and tree stumps.
Rain falls and we pull the tarp across
The top of our land rover. We race

with the rain along the sandy beach,
into the veldt and suddenly elephants
erupt before us—in the rain darkened day

matriarchs and calves and protective bulls.
Ten strides away, one hundred blackened
by mud lumber toward the river. Rain soaked.
we watch shadowed silhouettes dancing
in the dark and sense the bulk of our own bodies.

We just sat there contemplating what was before us, as our time together in Africa ended on the most majestic note imaginable.

# XV. Homecoming: Ending a Diplomatic Career and New Beginnings

I came home from South Africa reluctantly. I had come to love my work passionately and was considered USIA's senior African specialist. My career ended when the promotion panel recommended me for promotion, but it was decided by the Agency's leadership that no officers would be promoted from my grade as Minister Counselor. I was told this was a concession to the State Department at the time we were preparing for USIA's integration into the Department, since it was argued that we had a surfeit of officers at the higher grades.

The integration of USIA into the State Department led to widespread disappointment among many of our colleagues. One of them sought to define our relevance to the new dispensation by having tee shirts made defining our deeply held, if slightly exaggerated belief. They read "ALL DIPLOMACY IS PUBLIC DIPLOMACY," That slogan was meant to define an institutional culture that was quite different than that of the State Department's. The end of my Foreign

Service career, combined with the end of the agency I cared deeply about, left me and many of my friends deeply saddened.

The integration of USIA into the Department of State was in my opinion a great mistake, one that has cost our country significant influence in the world. It has greatly weakened U.S. efforts to support civil society at a time when it had the capacity to influence democratization in Africa. To cite one example, at the time of the design of the Millennium Challenge initiative a number of criteria were proposed for countries to be eligible for its rather significant assistance grants. A major criterion, appropriately, was the absence of massive corruption and the efficiency of government to deliver services to its population. When we were consulted on those criteria, I noted neither human rights, rule of law, nor democracy were among them. We argued for their inclusion. It was the USIA perspective that led to their adoption.

Having been Public Affairs Officer in Nigeria, our largest operation in Africa, I was aghast that after integration with the State Department all but a skeleton public affairs staff was retained both in Lagos and the new capital of Abuja. When at several times after my retirement I recommended that our embassies assist and make use of prominent American scholars who were planning visits to their countries, I learned that U.S. missions in Nigeria, Ethiopia, Senegal, and Cameroon, no longer had the inclination or resources to make use of those visitors. I learned that our new public diplomacy officers attached to embassies were often inexperienced administrative or consular officers. Furthermore, they were sidelined by having to depend on the embassy's motor pool rather than having vehicles assigned to them. What had been our regional offices were transferred to a State Department annex building and contrary to my advice, its responsibilities were not integrated into State's Africa Bureau. As such, more often than not, its role was simply advisory and not at all central to decision making.

Throughout my three and a half decades in the Foreign Service I drew inspiration from the beginnings of my career when Edward R. Murrow set the tone for our profession and met with us new officers to convey his vision of our role in the world. Known for his integrity as a journalist and USIA's director, he reportedly gave President Kennedy a word of advice. It was: "never do anything you don't want to see on the front page of the *New York Times*."

My disappointment with leaving the profession was tempered with a culminating honor at the end of my career. I was surprised and deeply honored when before leaving the Agency I was informed I would receive the annual Edward R. Murrow award for Excellence in Public Diplomacy, in my estimation, the highest award conferred by my Agency. It was therefore with great pride and humility that I accepted the award in Boston at a Tufts University ceremony in the presence of my family. I placed the award certificate on my study wall next to a photo of me shaking hands with Murrow at the onset of my career, 35 years earlier. I later learned that the award was advocated and promoted by a former colleague, someone I was proud to call a friend, Larry Schwartz.

My regret at ending my USIA career came at a time when Congressional pressure led by Senator Jesse Helms and his allies in the Senate forced President Clinton to choose between shutting down USAID or USIA. Without an effective challenge from the Democrats or from USIA Director Duffey, the decision had been made to integrate USIA into the State Department. The argument made by Senator Helms was that the Cold War was over, hence there was no longer the need for an American propaganda agency. Admittedly our Agency, out of necessity had its share of Cold Warriors, but neither I nor most of my colleagues were among them. We prided ourselves on our expertise in doing what we enjoyed most, interacting with the people of Africa, Asia, Latin America, and the Middle East on their own terms.

The decision to transfer USIA into State completely ignored the fact that with the end of the Cold War, USIA was optimally positioned for public diplomacy's maximum impact. That failure occurred at precisely the time when publics, the people, and the institutions of most countries were beginning to be highly influential. It ignored the fact that the State Department and its traditional diplomacy placed heavy emphasis on dealing with foreign leaders, and the immediate challenges confronting our nation. In contrast, what USIA did best was relate to civil society, the press, the academic community, and youth, notably those parts of societies that had longer-term consequences for our relationships. Our focus was on youth and change agents, those who would shape the future.

This was especially relevant at a time when the people of the Middle East had launched the Arab Spring. It was the time of the transformation of Eastern Europe and the end of Soviet imposed Communism at the Cold War's end. And it was the time of the challenge that confronted African countries attempting to grapple with widespread democratization. So, at the very moment when civil society and publics were exerting an influence rarely seen in modern history, our government in its wisdom, decided to abandon public diplomacy. We had developed a finely honed discipline to deal with such change in a manner favorable to how the United States wished the world shaped at a time when it could be most impactful. Lacking that perspective caused the United States to abandon a powerful diplomatic tool. While I had not favored our agency's heavy emphasis on countering Soviet disinformation during the Cold War, USIA would have been in an excellent position to respond effectively to Putin's effort to use disinformation to influence our elections, especially the election of Donald Trump.

Despite its promise at that optimal historic moment, public diplomacy was integrated into the State Department. However, the integration by its very nature significantly downgraded and subordinated what I most valued in USIA, its autonomy overseas. That autonomy allowed it to do those things that once integrated into the State Department, were relegated to a much lower priority. While realpolitik deals with elites, public diplomacy's longer-term impact was considerably diluted by the integration.

And so, it was that at the age of fifty-seven that I sought to be on to other things. What I had in mind was some continued involvement in Africa and in the promotion of democracy. In the short run I was interested in the relatively new National Endowment for Democracy based in Washington. My good friend and one of the foremost authorities on democracy promotion and Africa, Larry Diamond of Stanford University, recommended me to NED as a researcher, which provided me with an office and an environment replete with activities that allowed me to keep abreast of my interests in the year immediately following my retirement.

During that period, my good friend David Michael Wilson asked me to work with him on a study of the visa program that required foreign students, after graduation from American universities, to return to their home country for a period of time. We found that requirement, originally designed to avoid the brain drain depriving developing countries of needed talent after their study in the United States, was no longer desirable from the U.S. perspective. Canada, we found, had no such requirement and was recruiting students immediately after graduation to apply for Canadian jobs, especially in the Canadian equivalent of Silicon Valley.

While working on that project I recall reading what Bill Gates had to say when asked if he feared competition from Japan. He answered: "no, our Japanese are better than their Japanese." In our report we argued that the traditional reasons for sending foreign graduates back ignored two things. First, it would be in our national interest to keep some of those foreign graduates from U.S. universities who were highly sought after by U.S. tech companies. Secondly, the old rule sought to prevent a brain drain from countries who badly needed highly trained graduates. Those outdated rules ignored the development of modern communication which allows talented foreign researchers, and young corporate managers to connect on a daily basis with their home institutions to share the knowledge they acquire while working in the U.S. At this writing our recommendations to eliminate the return policy have not yet been adopted.

Another opportunity made available to me was the chance to serve on the interview panel for entrance to the Foreign Service for those who had passed the written examination. Our panel was to conduct interviews in Washington D.C., Denver, and San Francisco. I was curious to participate in the process that thirty-five years earlier had opened the door for me to enter the Foreign Service.

We found candidates that were qualified and were able to recommend them. However, I was surprised to find that what attracted candidates to foreign affairs during the Kennedy Presidency was fundamentally different from the motivation of the candidates in the year 2000. For one thing, the average age had risen. Some of those we interviewed were in search of a new profession. Others were retirees in their fifties. Another major change was the lack of sense of adventure among the candidates. I recalled going off to Africa with all the difficulties of communicating with friends and family back home. The coming of the internet allows daily interaction with home. I also thought of the lifeline that was the *International Herald Tribune* out of Paris that kept us informed about what was happening around the world. Other than that, there was a cultural vacuum about the wider world, especially the world we left behind back home.

In the past, when we returned home after several years, we felt the need to catch up on theater, films, the arts, and societal changes. While overseas, our boys had no opportunity to play baseball and our girls were similarly out of touch. Many of the things we lacked have now become available to those who live overseas due to technology. It seemed to me that the adventure associated with representing our country abroad has been greatly diminished. That sense of immersion in another culture and the sense of adventure associated with representing the United States abroad was something uniquely important in my own career.

In the attempt to define the ideal public affairs officer, I would stress he or she should be endowed with a genuine passion to understand and interact with those of another culture on behalf of our country. Murrow thought of it as the interaction between our representative and that of the other culture, the communication at the level "of the last three feet." It is that face-to-face communication that explains who we are and why it has relevance to others.

I found that during our interviews I tended to refer back to my experience in supervising new officers in Senegal. After an unusually heavy workload, soon after the arrival of a new officer in Dakar, I apologized to him, saying it would not always be so difficult. His response to me was that it was his dream. His passion for the work and intelligence made Michael Pelletier most suitable to become an ambassador. I truly sought to identify other candidates who fit that model and who shared that dream.

One example of a candidate we interviewed in Washington who did not fit into any past category, was a former mid-level diplomat from the Philippines. He had become an American citizen and therefore was eligible for our Foreign Service. He was able to respond skillfully to all our questions and simulations. He objectively earned high marks from us. When the interviews were over for the day, and we had recommended him for an appointment, he asked to speak to me. His question was: would a divorce disqualify him? I asked what he meant. He responded that his wife was a doctor and if he had to go abroad, she would divorce him. I answered that our responsibility was limited to his objective qualifications on the oral exam. What I left unsaid was that I felt I had contributed to the breakup of a family and that this was not the kind of issue we faced when I entered the Foreign Service.

Once concluded with the interview project, I sought and was granted a position on the State Department's Inspection Team for what was then our largest overseas post, Egypt. My contribution to our report was to inspect the USIS operation. I found most of our officers well prepared with excellent Arabic language skills. I was especially interested in determining how well the staff used the full range of Agency resources and their concern for promoting respect for human rights. I was pleased to give our USIS Cairo operation high marks for their effectiveness as our group did for the entire Embassy operation, especially as it was working under difficult circumstances including the threat of terrorism.

I was handicapped when early in the inspection, while taking a walk along the Nile with a colleague, I tripped on rocky ground and broke my elbow. When I was hospitalized the American embassy doctor made sure I got excellent treatment from a skilled Egyptian orthopedic surgeon who was summoned to Cairo from his vacation in Alexandria. That enabled me to resume work with the inspection two days later. When my wife Anita learned of my accident, she flew to Cairo to join me. Later, when we had a long weekend, we had the great good fortune to travel with the team to Upper Egypt to explore the incomparable Valley of the Kings. It was the unexpected thrill of a lifetime, matched only by one other unexpected treat.

The end of our time in Cairo coincided with the one hundredth anniversary of the first performance of Giuseppe Verdi's *Aida* which we learned had been first performed in Cairo. A commemorative

**Bob and Anita in Cairo**

performance was arranged for the evening of the anniversary to be held at the pyramids. Since Egypt had recently experienced acts of terrorism, we the members of the audience, were protected by Egyptian soldiers guarding the temporary theater with their automatic weapons. Anita was especially thrilled since her opera loving father had promised when she was a child that one day, he would take her to Egypt. Thus, two dreams, coming to Egypt, and witnessing *Aida* at the pyramids, had come true for her.

As I had never been in the Middle East, Cairo was an exceptional experience, especially since Egypt was clearly the keystone of the region, exerting great political and intellectual influence on its Arab neighbors. The experience led to my discovery of an Egyptian author I have come to consider one of the great writers of our time, Naguib Mahfouz.

When we returned from Egypt, I was ready to take on another task. It came in the form of a call from the National Democratic Institute (NDI), the Democratic Party's democracy promotion institute that is part of the umbrella organization, the National Endowment for Democracy. (NED). I had great respect for the work of that organization, especially its efforts to promote democracy on the African continent. But the project they proposed I lead was extremely challenging.

The National Democratic Institute (NDI) sought to encourage some measure of democratic change in the Republic of the Congo, a country that had not known democratic governance in its history and had been ruled by the corrupt authoritarian regime of Joseph Mobutu. But Africa was in the process of experiencing a wave of democratic change at the end of the 20th century. An opportunity for change also existed in light of the end of the long reign of the Mobutu regime in 1997, when Laurent Kabila took over as head of state. NDI thought to bring to the Congo the experience of another francophone country that had recently undergone democratic transition. It was determined that since Benin had such a transition in 1991, it could reasonably serve as a model for the Congo.

Since independence, and before becoming a democracy, Benin had been a one-party state and Marxist dictatorship, and had also known military rule. Accordingly, the NDI Kinshasa office identified ten non-governmental Congolese representing NGOs, opposition political parties, civil society, and journalism to travel to Cotonou where I would meet with them. My job was to arrange a series of briefings to introduce them to Benin's democratic constitution, its political parties, and its admirable free and fair electoral system. I would then lead them back to Kinshasa and work with the NDI representative to observe how their Benin experience related to their home institutions and how they might convey the Benin experience to the Congo.

Our first difficulty was to return with our grantees to the Congo. After our excellent briefings in Benin, our Air Afrique flight was to connect with a flight to Kinshasa in Douala, Cameroon. Our flight was delayed and the connection was missed. We were told that we were booked on a flight the next morning to Kinshasa. The problem then was accommodation. We had not budgeted for an overnight stay. We therefore expected that the airline responsible for our missing the connection would take responsibility for our hotel costs. The Air Afrique manager refused at first, until I called for a sit-in at his office. He then found it possible to reserve rooms at a local hotel. It was far from a five-star hotel, but it seemed adequate. That is until the evening when we discovered that a Cameroonian youth group had organized a roof top rock concert just above my room.

Since most of us had rooms on the top floor when we returned after dinner, we found the ceiling, walls, and floors shook from the rock music as if in an earthquake. My own closet door was unhinged by the vibrations and fell crashing beside me in my bed just missing my head.

Early the next morning, after a sleepless night, we found the hotel elevator jammed with departing revelers and musicians' instruments, so we risked having to wait and almost miss our flight. By luck the flight was delayed enough so we were on our way to Kinshasa. Shortly before boarding though one member of our group received a telephonic warning from Kinshasa. It said authorities might be waiting at the airport to arrest some of us. It was a sign that the Kinshasa government considered our project to be subversive to its governing system. We arrived to find that the rumor of arrest turned out to be unfounded.

The first part of the program took place as planned, and while it was clear that it generated press accounts on the virtues of the Benin democratic transition and a good deal of discussion within political circles, the dictatorship was too deeply engrained for our project to produce fundamental change, at least not in the short term.

I experienced an indication of the nature of the Congo government when I was invited to a lunch by our U.S. ambassador. I was seated next to the newly named governor of the nearby Bas-Congo region. He was excited and told me he had just been given his instructions by the President. I asked if he could tell me what those instructions were. He replied that he was instructed to exercise control of his territory. I asked him what that meant. I imagined that as governor he would say he was to maintain roads, provide education, and health care, possibly arrange for wells or electric power. His answer was that he was simply expected to collect taxes.

Our Congo project had proved imaginative and well organized but ran into an obdurate dictatorship opposed to any change that would challenge its legitimacy. I had last served in the Congo in 1965-67 and found the country had not fundamentally changed. It was the very definition of kleptocracy. Its government provided few if any services and still failed to exercise control over most of the interior of the country. Its vast resources were controlled by external forces who occupied parts of the interior and inflicted violence on the population. Anarchy was still the order of the day for the unfortunate Congolese people.

Soon after I returned home, I found another invitation awaiting me. The Carter Center was renowned for monitoring elections around the world. I was asked if I would manage their monitoring of the 1999-2000 Nigerian elections. Our monitoring would be a joint project with the National Democratic Institute (NDI). I considered the return to democratic civilian rule in Nigeria, the most populous country in Africa, coupled with the recent transition to democracy in South Africa, to mark the key advances in the democratization of the continent. Having served for three years in Nigeria during what we called President Babangida's "permanent transition" to civilian rule, I felt a strong commitment to observe these historic elections; the first to elect a new president, the second election to select members of a parliament.

The 1999-2000 elections followed a long period of military rule. Political change was made possible by the death of dictator Sani Abacha who was replaced General Abdulsalami Abubakar, a military

Jimmy Carter with General Obasanjo

leader who was genuinely committed to elections and the transition to civilian rule.

The first phase of our mission took place in Nigeria's vast former capital, Lagos. President Carter launched his presence in the process by asking that I arrange appointments for him with the presidential candidates. I set up meetings with all six candidates who had initially thrown their hats in the ring. President Carter wanted to hear about what each stood for, but he especially made a strong pitch that the elections be honestly conducted. Clearly two candidates stood out: former President General Olusegun Obasanjo and Chief Oluyemisi Falae, the Secretary of the government.

I vividly recall Obasanjo's presentation. He told Carter he was the only one who could serve as President. When asked why, he responded that "I am the only one who knows how to fear the military." I immediately understood what he meant. He alluded to the fact that if the winner of the election was not favored by the northern military officers, a newly elected civilian President would have to tread with extreme care, less they intervene to overthrow his government. Obasanjo, who had previously served as Vice President, had assumed the presidency in 1976 when President Murtala Muhammed was assassinated. The National Museum in Lagos displays Muhammed's bullet ridden Mercedes in which he had been killed. Obasanjo turned over power to a civilian government three years later, in part because he feared a coup if he remained in office.

Obasanjo's main opponent in 1999, Chief Falae, a former Finance Minister and chief Secretary of the government, had the reputation of being an astute technocrat who had been a stabilizing influence during the latest military regime. The elections were administered by the Independent National Electoral Commission (INEC) that was considered to be neutral. We consulted INEC frequently to check that the rules governing the election were adhered to. In addition to the Carter Center and the National Democratic Institute (NDI), the election was monitored by the U.S. International Republican Institute (IRI), both of which I collaborated with. Other monitoring groups represented the European Union, the Commonwealth (both the EU and Commonwealth had been instructed to endorse the results and restore normal relations with Nigeria), and the West African ECOWAS group which was not known for its high standards.

Over the course of the election campaign, those of us who served as monitors shifted operations from Lagos to the new capital, Abuja. Once there I hired a cab driver to allow me to cover the territory and employed a young Nigerian university graduate who was familiar with the area. The cab driver immediately proved his skill at dealing with our situation. Although Nigeria was a leading oil producer, it often faced shortages due to the frequent breakdown of its refineries. Such was the case during the election campaign. This resulted in long lines of cars awaiting supplies at gas stations, some of them manned by drivers who slept in them overnight. My driver knew a way around that. He learned that the entrance to the nearby military camp was occupied by the wives of officers who sold gas out of well-supplied jerry cans at a slightly padded price.

While in Abuja, I met several more times with President Carter who had taken a lively interest in the campaign. I arranged meetings for him with party leaders, the electoral commission, and other key observers. Most enjoyable were the amiable dinners I shared with him at the Sheraton Hotel. I reminded him of the time we first met when I was serving in Lagos in 1990. I observed that he seemed happier to be an ex-president than when he had been President of the United States. His response was that as President he had to do everything, while as ex-President he could pick and choose what he wanted to do.

A hint that not all was going well came with a knock at my hotel door one evening. It was a young lawyer I had worked with in Lagos. He had been chosen to run for the Nigerian Senate by his local party. However recently, he was outraged when some military vehicles had driven up to his party headquarters and a high-ranking officer had imposed a military man to replace him as the candidate. When he complained to the national party leadership, they said nothing could be done but they would find another suitable office for him. As compensation, he was later given a position as Minister in the new government. This incident demonstrated the power of the Nigerian military despite the return to civilian rule.

A highlight of the campaign was to have been a nationally televised debate between General Obasanjo and Chief Falae. I arranged to attend the debate, but when I got to the venue, I learned that Obasanjo had chosen not to attend. The speculation was that he had withdrawn, convinced that the debate format would greatly favor his opponent. After some scrambling the organizers decided to devote the time slot to questions for Falae only. He acquitted himself well, but the next day Obasanjo insisted he be granted an equivalent time slot on national T.V.

The General was granted the time. Rather than responding to questions about his presidential plans, he discussed his time as a prisoner of the military government. He told the audience that everyone knew how very fond he is of pounded yam, a stable of his Yoruba people. He recalled that the women who brought yams to his prison cell also laboriously pounded them for him. Then he said he had discovered that there was a Japanese produced electric yam pounder on the market. He exclaimed that Nigerians knew that the Japanese did not eat pounded yam and wondered why Nigerians hadn't themselves produced an electric yam pounder. He concluded with the promise that as President he would make sure that the things Nigerians needed would be produced in Nigeria and not imported. Obasanjo was clearly favored to win, in large part because he was better known. Nevertheless, his party was taking no chances and their dirty tricks were apparent.

President Carter returned to Abuja just before election day. He issued a call to both sides that the election be conducted honestly. When the day came, independent Nigerian and international observers went to selected polling places to monitor the voting. Each polling place was staffed by a representative of the Electoral Commission, one or more police officers, and a member of each political party. I drove to a site with my young Nigerian assistant. As we arrived at the school where voting was taking place, the young man directed my attention to a school room a hundred feet from the polling place. He had detected some suspicious activity involving a group of young Nigerians. We headed there and upon entering saw several young men jump out the back window and race across an adjacent meadow. On the floor of the room were hundreds of ballots that had been filled out with the name Obasanjo. I grabbed several handfuls as evidence, exited to report to the folks at the polling place, but assumed that they had been accomplices.

I then drove to the Electoral Commission office in the town a few miles away. When we arrived the officer in charge offered to drive back with us. Upon arrival he commanded that the polling place be closed. We left with the thought that this ballot stuffing must be going on elsewhere throughout the country, but at least this one place had been caught and sanctioned. Two hours later we were disabused of the idea that we had even accomplished that when we returned to the offending polling place and found it had been reopened and was still managed by the same corrupt officials.

We reported our experience as did other monitors who had observed violations. When the results were tabulated, Obasanjo was judged to have won with a substantial majority. But fraud was apparent when one Nigerian state reported that Obasanjo alone had recorded more votes than the total number of registered voters in that state, indicating that the vote count itself had been corrupted.

Based on other reports of this nature, President Carter, as did NDI and IRI, issued a statement that the declared election result was illegitimate, and that the election had not been "free and fair." Apparently though the result was good enough for the West African and Commonwealth groups which gave it a passing grade as did the European observers. The Carter standard was clearly too high a bar for Nigeria at this stage in its history. While I shared the conclusion that fraud was endemic everywhere in the country, in hindsight, I look back on the result of the election as allowing Nigeria to emerge from a tyrannical military regime. While Obasanjo himself was a former general, his two terms as president were to provide stability and moderation as he balanced civilian and military interests. His rule was at least an improvement over the military regime he replaced.

As I write this, the Nigerian election results for the 2023 elections are in. Election observers from the joint U.S. institutions, NDI and IRI (the democracy promotion organizations of the Democratic and Republican parties) have issued a report noting substantial irregularities that clearly favored the ruling party. An op-ed in the *New York Times* of March first by Nigerian author Chimamanda Ngozi Adichie notes that at the time of the election: "A majority of Nigerians are below the age of 35. They are a bright, innovative, and talented generation, a hungry generation, starved of good leadership, who do not merely sit back and complain but who act and want to forge their own futures." Adichie also observes that: "Africa is full of young nation-states, and democracy takes time to establish its roots and even when it does, the fragility always remains." I find that conclusion hard to accept. Nigeria by 2023 had already experienced more than six decades of independence and its population was relatively well educated and sophisticated. And yet, it seemed to have perfected two skills: dishonest elections and corrupt governance at unprecedented levels. It is no wonder that at the same time a recent poll revealed that half of all young Nigerian adults expressed the wish to emigrate.

# XVI. A Second Venture into Democracy Promotion

Born in the shadow of Yankee stadium, one of my heroes has always been the great Lou Gehrig. While I was never gifted enough to play ball for the Yankees, I always identified with Gehrig's farewell statement: "I consider myself the luckiest man on the face of the earth." My own luck enabled a boy from a Bronx tenement to play a modest role in American diplomacy at the time of Africa's independence as well as the struggle of peoples everywhere for a share in a democratic world order.

The convergence of the international democracy movement and foreign policy was a theme that ran through the second half of my Foreign Service career with USIA. I therefore welcomed the opportunity to focus intensely on that theme at the start of the new millennium. That opportunity presented itself when in 2001 I was contacted by my good friend David Michael Wilson. He told me of the creation of a new institution, a small democracy promotion NGO. Knowing of my professional interests, he asked if I would like to apply for the position of Executive Director. He explained that a new non-governmental organization, the Council for a Community of Democracies (CCD) was being launched. David had helped it move into an office three blocks from the White House and just around the corner from the original headquarters of the United States Information Agency where we had both begun our professional careers almost four decades earlier.

Its modest office was located in the historic building, the Dacor Bacon House, the headquarters of a foreign service retirees' organization. Dacor Bacon house had served as the residence of founding fathers including the first chief justice of the Supreme Court, John Marshall, and not incidentally, had been the house where I had arranged for the reception following the wedding of our daughter Therese.

It sounded like the perfect segue following my thirty-five years in USIA during which I had made democracy promotion a major concern. Later that week I met with the CCD President, Walt Raymond, a career foreign affairs and intelligence official who had worked with the Department of Defense, the CIA, and the National Security Council. A senior official of the NSC once noted that too frequently that Council focused only on the latest crisis while Raymond would regularly interject "but what about democracy?" Most recently he had served with USIA where he was Assistant Director responsible for U.S. policy to encourage and assist with the democratic transition of Eastern European nations who had abandoned Communism after the break-up of the Soviet Union. His work on promoting democracy in those countries was parallel to his work and that of other remarkably committed CCD board members who had participated in the very successful rebuilding and democratization of Germany and Japan after World War II as well as the creation of NATO.

A formative example of the experience of one of our Board members, Richard Rowson, who at the death of Walt Raymond, became President of CCD, is instructive. Richard had served in the army at the end of World War II. He was assigned to post-war Japan. One day his commanding officer asked to see him. He assigned Rowson to a large town in southern Japan. His instruction was to see if he could introduce some democratic ideas in the management of the town. With his revolver on his hip, he called on the town leader. Rowson asked how decisions were made in the administration of the area under the leader's jurisdiction. He replied that when an issue arose, he reflected on it and simply decided. Then Rowson asked if he ever thought of sounding out the views of the local people before making the decision. He said no, but if the American thought it a good idea he would try it in future. Sometime later Rowson was summoned to Tokyo. There a senior officer asked him for a briefing on how he had gotten the town to adopt democracy. Not much later, perhaps using some of Rowson's methods, the entire Japanese government adopted democratic institutions albeit while retaining a figurehead Emperor.

Other CCD Board members had been active in the Marshall Plan's reconstruction of a democratic postwar Europe and the policy that eventually led to a free Eastern Europe once the Berlin Wall came down. I learned that board members had come together to test just how far democracy could be strengthened in new democracies and could encourage the promotion of democratic institutions elsewhere in the world at a time when a surge in democratic transitions was at a high point. Our bipartisan board consisted of a number of distinguished, idealistic, former diplomats and other foreign affairs specialists whose careers all involved support of democracy. Our Chairman, Robert Hunter was President Clinton's U.S. Ambassador to NATO from 1993 to 1998 during which he was architect and negotiator of the post-Cold War "new NATO."

At the time of the establishment of the Community of Democracies (CD) our dynamic Vice Chair was Mark Palmer, former ambassador to Hungary, who in 2003 published his book: *Breaking the Real Axis of Evil.* His subtitle spoke precisely to the policies he advocated: *How to Oust the World's Last Dictators by 2025.* The book was a clarion call for the democracies of the world to work together to promote democratic change. Palmer urged the U.S. government to make that a major foreign policy objective. His book earned high praise from important statesmen and leaders including Nancy Pelosi, Senator John McCain, former CIA Director James Woolsey, philanthropist George Soros, Professor Francis Fukuyama, former U.S. Ambassador to the United Nations Bill Richardson, and Ambassador Max Kampelman among others.

That new priority given to international democracy promotion was an initiative fostered at high levels of the U.S. and other democracies. At the end of the Clinton administration, Secretary of State Madeleine Albright and Poland's Foreign Minister Geremek jointly sponsored a ministerial meeting of one hundred six countries on June 27, 2000, to discuss creating a collective effort to strengthen and advance democracy around the world. The meeting produced a document expressing the consensus of the group: "The Warsaw

Declaration: Toward a Community of Democracies." So, the question to be answered by those of us outside of government was how we could best assist and contribute to what the democratic governments themselves declared they sought to accomplish in building an increasingly democratic world order.

We decided that our role would be to encourage our own government to make democracy a foreign policy priority. We also took on the task of helping create an international non-governmental organization network of some twenty key individuals to enter into a dialogue and work with the governmental Community of Democracies and attend its annual Ministerial meetings. Our NGO group led by the Council for a Community of Democracies included our own Council and representatives of democracy organizations from Chile, South Africa, India, Mali, Taiwan, Mexico, Italy, Hungary, Poland, Lithuania, the Philippines, as well as individuals pursuing human rights and democracy goals in non-democratic Singapore, Iran, and Russia.

Following the Warsaw founding meeting, Ministerials were held every couple of years as follows: South Korea (2002), Chile (2005), Mali (2007), Portugal (2009), Lithuania (2011), Mongolia (2013), El Salvador (2015), and the United States (2017). While the Warsaw Ministerial attracted high level Foreign Ministry officials, with the passage of time, diplomatic representation tended to diminish, with the low point being the poorly organized 2017 Washington meeting. In time, we would seek to identify other useful functions we could perform that transcended more traditional activities in the area of democracy promotion and human rights.

The first decade of the Community of Democracies was highly productive in encouraging democratic governance worldwide. CCD launched effective gatherings of NGOs in Colombia where narco-trafficking had previously reigned. We held meetings in Chile with the strong support of local NGOs in a country that greatly valued its resumption of democratic governance and was prepared to share its values with other nations. We held an especially important meeting in Indonesia, the most democratic Islamic nation. At one point, Nobel Peace Prize winner Aun San Suu Kyi asked me, "what about Africa, will it develop?" I responded that it was difficult to generalize about the entire continent, but that some countries would, but many were constrained by corruption and poor governance. It was a great honor to meet Suu Kyi, but years later I was deeply disappointed to learn that she had taken a position in support of Myanmar's military to suppress her country' Islamic minority.

The New Delhi NGO meeting was exceptional for having been held in the world's largest democracy. Mongolia hosted us, pleased to reinforce its post-Soviet status. The Mongolian leadership was energetically happy to play a role that it hoped would influence its region. Our El Salvador NGO gathering was important for its emphasis on democracy education, in a country with hopes to escape from authoritarianism. Our Taiwan hosts clearly wanted to vaunt their democratic form of government in contrast to that of Communist China. Its very democracy was considered a matter of national security, fundamental to its independence. Interestingly, we visited Taiwan's National Museum. Its treasures had been removed from the mainland, possibly sparing them from China's Cultural Revolution.

Our meetings in Quatar and Jordan were especially significant since we were breaking new ground in the Arab world. Those deliberations there were organized by Radwan Masmoudi, the brilliant Tunisian who founded the Center for the Study of Islam and Democracy. Radwan's network of Arab democrats allowed us to explore the meaning of the Arab Spring and to find ways of supporting it.

We realized that it was imperative that we not reinvent the wheel. Other well-established organizations had been playing an important role in the field including Freedom House, Human Rights Watch, and the government funded National Endowment for Democracy, with its Democratic and Republican party affiliates and its Labor and Commerce Department branches. In addition, another Washington organization, IFES, the International Foundation for Electoral Systems, had a distinguished record of monitoring international elections together with the Carter Center. There were also a number of related organizations that we wished to work with from time to time. We understood that as newcomers we needed to carefully coordinate our work with those entities and not appear to compete with them. I also felt the need to more clearly define how we could make unique contributions to the field.

To determine a set of priorities in the first months of our existence, we established a representative committee of Board Members. We met with that committee to define an initial agenda. That meeting was highly productive. In it I proposed that we encourage the United Nations to establish a democracy fund that would support NGOs that sought to expand freedom in their countries. It was noted that historically the U.N. had felt obliged to ignore the "D word." Democracy had been controversial for a comprehensive international body, some of whose members were authoritarian and had in the past objected to activities that involved the U.N. in democratization. Notwithstanding that history, some of our board members felt that the world climate had changed sufficiently to expect the United Nations to assist countries to adopt democratic institutions. We concluded that it might be possible with the help of the State Department to induce the U.N. to consider our idea.

It did, and rather miraculously, within a year a U.N. Democracy Fund office had been created that funded some twenty projects annually in amounts up to more than one hundred fifty thousand dollars each. That fund would support several of our CCD projects over the next few years that allowed CCD to organize NGO conferences on democracy and to focus on democracy education. To manage the new U.N. fund, an office was expanded within the U.N. Secretariat. That office concerned itself with organizing competitions to award grants to NGOs around the world to promote democratic ideas and institutions. This first meeting got us off to a good start.

A second goal we adopted early on was to create a network of non-governmental organization members that would come together on a regular basis to identify policies that we could raise with governments to promote democracy. Those topics would then be conveyed to the Secretariat of the governmental CCD and placed on the agenda to be debated at future annual ministerial meetings of the Community of Democracies for possible action by governments. The idea was to engage democratic governments in the process of supporting countries who wished to improve their democratic institutions or to help aspiring democrats with transitions from authoritarian to democratic government.

The Clinton administration was coming to an end and the campaign that would elect President George W. Bush was in full course. I decided that jointly with the National Endowment for Democracy and Freedom House we would address an appeal to all the candidates for president of both political parties to seek a continuation of the U.S. commitment to the Community of Democracies. In fact, our letter spelled out a dozen steps to strategically enable the U.S. government to use its influence to promote democracy around the world.

In addition to sending the letter to candidate George W. Bush, we also sent copies of that letter to Bush's key advisor, Karl Rove, as well as his future Secretary of State Condoleezza Rice. One concrete proposal contained in the letter was a call for a doubling of the budget of the National Endowment for Democracy (NED). Several months later once Bush was elected, he addressed an anniversary ceremony of NED. On that occasion the newly elected President Bush announced his support for virtually all the suggestions contained in our letter including the U.S. commitment to the Community of Democracies and the doubling of the NED budget. That was enormously gratifying. It demonstrated what a small, newly established NGO could do to exert influence on political leadership at the highest level to implement ways to promote democracy. My own experience in government was that an idea advocating such initiatives would be slowed or completely blocked by our complex bureaucracy and take forever to arrive at a decision or be altered or rejected. I was amazed at the fact that a simple letter could elicit such a swift response about an issue so important and be adopted.

While we rarely struck gold as dramatically as this, we again launched an updated appeal during each subsequent presidential campaign with letters sent to all viable candidates of both political parties and their key aides. The letters would urge U.S. continued leadership in the CD as well as some concrete actions the U.S might take to promote democracy. It was intended to assure that all presidential candidates would consider democracy promotion as an integral part of their party's foreign policy platform in the context of the Community of Democracies.

In between meetings of the Community of Democracies Ministerials, CCD also participated in the National Endowment for Democracies conferences which brought together non-governmental democracy representatives from throughout the world. One particularly significant conference was held in Kiev, Ukraine, then an aspiring democracy. Significantly, the democracy conference was held in what formerly had been the Lenin Museum. The building had been converted into the home of the Museum of the Ukranian Genocide to commemorate the genocide committed by the Soviet Union to wipe out Ukrainian peasant farmers who resisted collectivization of their land. That museum addressed the killing of an estimated ten million Ukrainians by the Stalin regime. My college Russian history professor, Jesse Clarkson, once wrote that "Stalin was a genius because only a genius could create a famine in the Ukraine."

Early on we also agreed that promotion of democracy education was essential to the democratization process. It was clear to us that we should devote ourselves to proposing best practices for democracy education so that people everywhere might understand what it takes to create and sustain democratic institutions. We were aware that education for democracy was found wanting in our own country where our democratic institutions were taken for granted, a problem that became acutely apparent in later years with the election of Donald Trump.

Our Board, consisting of a number of retired, seasoned diplomats, noted that at no point in their professional training had they been exposed to ways of promoting democracy as an element in our foreign policy. CCD therefore worked to develop an outstanding tool to be used in the training of senior diplomats and newly named ambassadors which we called *A Diplomat's Handbook for Democracy Development Support*. The concept for the Handbook was conceived by Ambassador Mark Palmer. The project was headed by former Canadian Ambassador Jeremy Kinsman and the case studies were prepared by our Director of Research, Kurt Bassuener. Kinsman was a dynamic member of our Board. He had served as ambassador to Moscow, Italy, the European Union, and as High Commissioner in London.

The second edition of the book was funded by the Smith Richardson Foundation as well as the governments of Canada, Poland, Lithuania, and Italy. It was published by Princeton University. It opened with a preface by the renowned leader of Czechoslovakia's Velvet Revolution, President Vaclav Havel and had a Ministers' forward by the Foreign Ministers of Portugal, Lithuania, and Poland. We were extremely proud of the handbooks whose spirit is captured by Ambassador Kinsman who wrote that diplomacy had developed a new dimension: "There is in practice a right to be helped as well as a right to help. The role of outsiders is never primary, but their catalytic support can be pivotal."

*The Handbook* stressed the role of cooperation embodied in the Community of Democracies. It documented successful examples in international solidarity to promote democratic change, the role of governments and embassies to support civil society, support for free elections, and help in democratic transitions. *The Handbook* also offered what we called a diplomat's "toolbox," that reflected the resources available to diplomats from democratic governments to support democratic ideas and processes. At its conclusion, I thought to add a resource list with internet addresses of dozens of organizations that aid democratic movements and institutions, beginning with the United Nations Democracy Fund that CCD had been responsible for creating. Also, we added what we called an "Annex: International Human Rights Law," beginning with the *Universal Declaration of Human Rights.*

Our case studies set the stage by providing context for each country and suggesting how diplomats might behave to promote democratic ideas or support nascent democratic institutions. Our studies included chapters on Cuba, Egypt, South Africa, Ukraine, Chile, Belarus, Burma/Myanmar, Zimbabwe, Tanzania, Sierra Leone, and China. Each represented very different traditions of diverse societies, some very difficult contexts to advance democratic ideas, and some examples of political transitions needing assistance to consolidate their transformation.

*The Handbook* was highly praised by Community of Democracy governments including the United States which used the Handbook in its Foreign Service Institute training program. Also, a number of CD foreign ministries translated and reproduced it for distribution to their embassies.

The support of the Rockefeller Brothers Foundation was especially helpful in making available its exceeding lovely Pocantico Center and providing funding for two of our international conferences, allowing us to gather leaders of non-governmental democracy organizations from around the world to develop an action agenda to promote democracy.

A CCD priority was the promotion of democracy education. I was positioned to further that goal when I was nominated in 2004 to serve as a Commissioner on the United States Commission for the United Nations Educational, Scientific and Cultural Organization (UNESCO). The role of the Commission was to provide advice to the U.S. government on matters related to UNESCO. In that capacity I defined a U.S. policy for the Department of State that urged the world body to make the teaching about democracy a priority as a UNESCO international educational objective. We regarded this opportunity as an example of how UNESCO could reinvigorate and reform itself after years of U.S. absence from the organization due to many issues concerning its management and priorities. The resumption of U.S. representation in UNESCO was vigorously promoted by First Lady Laura Bush who held a White House reception that I attended for the commissioners. Its purpose was to stress her sense of the importance of our role in the body. Mrs. Bush was especially interested in UNESCO's role in fostering equitable educational opportunities for women throughout the world.

**White House visit in honor of Liberia's president**

After its tumultuous past, Liberia was finally stabilized, under the leadership of Elen Johnson Sirleaf who was awarded the Nobel Peace Prize. To reinforce the historic U.S. ties to a democratic Liberia President George W. Bush held a State visit for the Liberian President that Anita and I attended.

While we were keen to assist other countries to adopt or strengthen democratic institutions, we always kept in mind that our own country was imperfect. For many years, Freedom House has published an annual study called *Freedom in the World* which evaluates all the world's countries for their adherence to democratic values.

Early in the new millennium, they for the first time included the United States in that review and in the years since, our country's ratings have declined, especially during the Trump years. His presidency also failed to support the work of democracy development carried out over decades by American diplomats in Africa and elsewhere.

We thought it important to the promotion of democracy around the world to identify and reward examples of individual diplomats who by their actions and often sacrifices, worked to advance and solidify democratic institutions. To do so we looked to a member of our own Board of Directors, Deputy Director Mark Palmer, and his work as ambassador to Communist Hungary. Mark had throughout his diplomatic career championed democratic values. During the Cold War he had never relinquished hope that Eastern Europe would leave the Soviet orbit. He had worked in Hungary with leaders who opposed Communism and rejoiced when at last the Russian domination was at an end. It was our decision to honor Mark and inspire other diplomats by creating the "Mark Palmer Prize." Each year we sought nominations from our NGO network as well as the Community of Democracies governments. The prize was an honor conferred jointly by CCD and the Community of Democracies governments on one or more diplomats who had made significant contributions to democracy during the year. I arranged with my artist son-in-law, Ard Berge, to design and produce a lithographic award for presentation to each recipient.

Our first awards were extended in 2011 to seven diplomats. They included the Czech and American ambassadors to a highly authoritarian Zimbabwe, Dutch and Peruvian diplomats to Cuba, an Indian diplomat to the United Nations, and a posthumous award to a Polish diplomat. In 2013 a Palmer Prize was awarded to a Mongolian Ambassador-at- large for his services to the Community of Democracies, another to the Swedish Ambassador to Belarus, and a posthumous one to U.S. Ambassador Chris Stevens who had been killed in Libya. Three Palmer prizes were awarded in 2015 to U.S. and Swedish ambassadors to Syria and Jordan and a third to the Lithuanian Foreign Minister. 2016 prizes went to the Canadian Ambassador to Afghanistan and the Secretary General of the Organization of American States. In 2017 Sweden's Ambassador Maria Leissner won the Palmer Prize for her work as Secretary General of the Community of Democracies.

Later when CCD closed its doors for lack of funding, I turned the Palmer Prize over to Freedom House which was pleased to continue to award the prize based on contributions to democracy. Furthermore, as we suggested, the American Foreign Service Association (AFSA) also began awarding Palmer Prizes to American diplomats.

In the course of our work, we serendipitously learned that the London headquarters of the World Bar Association (WBA) had announced the site of its 2008 annual meeting. We were stunned to learn it would be held in Singapore. We frequently had issues with Singapore since one member of our network was an opposition leader there. We were acutely aware of Singapore's opposition to one of the pillars of democracy, rule of law. We wondered what the world's leading law organization was thinking by organizing its world conference in a place opposed to the very idea of rule of law. As one of our board members had a good contact in the American Bar Association, we called him and asked for an explanation. We sharply criticized the idea of holding the meeting in Singapore and suggested that this was totally inappropriate and that the WBA should change the venue.

Our American friend checked with the WBA headquarters in London. It appeared they were embarrassed. As they had already paid for the venue, they asked what could be done. I urged that they allow our CCD network member Chee Soon Juan to address the conference about his concerns on Singapore's policy. Chee, a vocal opponent of the regime and head of a Singapore opposition party had been systematically harassed and several times imprisoned for seeking to raise issues of free expression and rule of law. This occurred in the context of Singapore's dismal record on human rights including preventive detention, suspension of judicial processes, and restrictions of free expression and media. I added that the WBA should also issue a report on those policies. They did both. Their scathing one-hundred-page report on Singapore's legal system was released to the media.

Based on my experience in Africa, one issue we chose to emphasize was education for democracy. We found the Albert Shanker Institute of the American Federation of Teachers had made it a matter of importance when it conducted a study of "civics programs" in all fifty American states. That study produced shameful results. On a scale of "A" to "F," the study found the educational systems with respect to civics education of most American states tended toward a "D."

When I sought support from USAID's official responsible for supporting democracy programs, I found him skeptical about funding democracy education programs. He told me that as a student in Michigan his civics class was absurd. He said it consisted of memorizing the names of the state's counties. I expressed shock that the imagination of educators could be so limited since democracy education in America could have been illustrated with examples from the civil rights, women's rights, environmental, and anti-Vietnam movements among many others at national, and perhaps more importantly, local levels. In March 2023 a report on U.S. treatment of civic education was headlined "Civic Education is Having its Moment" after having dropped the ball for decades in teaching students about democracy, and that it was becoming clearer that it was essential to repairing what it called "a battered democracy."

In virtually every country, there are of course heroes in the cause of freedom, exemplars to be studied from Gandhi to Mandela to Martin Luther King Jr. that can serve to imbue students with democratic values. Building on what I learned at the 1997 Pretoria CIVITAS conference I sounded out members of our NGO network on their experiences with education for democracy. I was given an excellent example from a Korean colleague. In a Korean civics classroom, the teacher raised the issue of a local marshland in the school's community which was slated to be devoted to new housing, pending citizen approval. Students were asked to conduct a study of the project. They learned that the marsh was rich in wildlife that would be damaged. They also found that a variety of other environmental damage would be done if the project were to be implemented. The results of that study were presented to the local government. Based on the students' report, the government abandoned the housing project in that area. This example of democracy at the local level illustrated how citizens, even students, could make an impact on decisions affecting the quality of life in their communities.

Education for Democracy was therefore prioritized at several of our NGO gatherings. One was held in Kosovo, another in Bogota, Colombia, and the final one held in Lima, Peru. The Lima conference led us to hold a major international conference on the subject at the University of Virginia in Charlottesville, involving twenty-seven experts from around the world. That conference led us to begin the process of assembling CCD's *Best Practices Manual on Democracy Education*, which was widely distributed to Community of Democracies countries. The manual was organized, assembled, and edited by a genius in the field, South African professor, David McQuoid-Mason. Funded by the United Nations Democracy Fund, the Manual drew upon the experiences of eighteen countries including the United States. Other examples were drawn from Bosnia and Herzegovina, Burundi, Columbia, Greece, Ghana, Hungary, Kenya, Lebanon, Mongolia, Nepal, Philippines, Russia, Senegal, Slovenia, South Sudan, Thailand, and the United Kingdom. What we found was there is no shortage of good ideas on how to teach the rudiments of democracy nor how to adapt strategies to local and national situations.

Further, our advocacy of education for democracy led to our holding a session in New York attended by seventy U.N. delegates which was followed by a United Nations November 2012 resolution on the subject, and its adoption as a priority issue by the Community of Democracies at its Ulaanbaatar Ministerial in 2013. CCD was charged with the task of organizing a panel on the subject by the Mongolian government at the Ministerial.

Perhaps the most profound experience I had in my years with CCD was my visit to Vilnius, Lithuania. It was my first time in that city. When we arrived at the Lithuanian Foreign Ministry, I was astonished to learn that I was expected to address the Parliament to inform Lithuanian Parliamentarians of Community of Democracy developments, especially the importance of Lithuania's founding role in the organization and also the role of civil society in the democracy promoting organization. I was humbled and honored to have been seated next to Algirdas Brazauskas, the courageous Prime Minister of Lithuania at the end of the Cold War who managed Lithuania's break with the Soviet Union.

With the fall of the Berlin Wall on May 18th, 1989, Brazauskas, was the first Warsaw Pact leader to defect from the Soviet Union and end Communist rule at the time when it was not yet known whether the Russians would again send tanks to restore their dominance in Eastern Europe. Our visit, and it appeared my briefing, seemed to be well received by the leaders of a country relieved to be part of democratic Western Europe. I was in awe to have been in the presence of Brazauskas, a leader who had risked everything in the quest for a democratic Lithuania. And I realized how significant it was for those of us in democratic countries to support such heroic figures, lest they be crushed by authoritarians who would deny their assertion of independence and democratic rights. That reality was reinforced when walking from my hotel I discovered the building that once housed the Vilnius KGB headquarters. On its wall was a plaque inscribed with the names of Lithuanians who had been tortured in that very building and put to death by that insidious Soviet intelligence organization.

Poland, which together with the United States had played the founding role in the Community of Democracies has created an institution that reflects its post-Cold War animosity toward the Russians. That institution is the Warsaw Uprising Museum, opened in 2004 on the sixtieth anniversary of the Warsaw uprising. The heroic and tragic revolt of the Warsaw Ghetto Jews toward the end of the second World War is rightfully known throughout the world but the other simultaneous and parallel Polish uprising against the Nazi occupation is less known. In 1944 as the Red Army reached the border of German occupied Poland, Polish patriots were inspired to rise up against the occupiers hoping to combine their resistance against the Germans with that of the Soviets. Instead, once the uprising began, the Soviets decided to allow the Germans with their superior force to wipe out the Polish insurgents.

Because of Soviet influence over the course of four decades, Polish students were taught that the resistance had been led and dominated by fascist-oriented Poles and not the anti-Nazi nationalists. Poland's post World War II education system and its curriculum were shaped by the Communist Party as dictated by the Soviet Union. The Uprising Museum attempts to rectify that distortion of history. The Museum rewrites that history and the teaching of it by portraying those who led and fought in the uprising as heroic patriots to be honored by their countrymen.

I attended the National Endowment for Democracy conference held in Crackow with Anita. It once again demonstrated Poland's central role in the Community of Democracies. On our way back to Warsaw we felt compelled to stop at Auschwitz. While we had read much and seen films about the horrors committed there, the emotional impact of being where it actually happened was unbelievably staggering. I came away from that hellish place feeling that "never again" could only be avoided if we build much stronger institutions than we now have.

CCD held an NGO network conference in Kosovo which had known ethnic cleansing. At the time of our gathering Kosovo had not yet been widely recognized as an independent nation after separating from Serbia. A reminder was a statue of Bill Clinton in Pristina, the capital's central square, a tribute to the American President's decision to intervene to stop the tragic violence by Serbian forces. We structured our gathering there to emphasize democracy education a subject that civil society considered vital to the country's future.

My first visit to Budapest, Hungary, yet another founder of the Community of Democracies, was also revelatory. Driving into town I noticed the many buildings that were pockmarked. I was informed that they were bullet scars left over from more than two generations past when in 1956, Russian tanks invaded to put down Hungary's attempt to assert its freedom from the Soviets. It seemed that it was government policy not to repair the walls but to leave them as reminders of what the Russians had done to crush the rebellion.

A powerful CCD contribution to democracy promotion was a concept that had been rarely discussed, but we felt needed intense consideration. It was the role of the military of democratic countries to provide support for democratic development. In 2013 our Chairman, Robert Hunter, identified an ideal individual to address that dimension. That person was retired Admiral Dennis Blair. Admiral Blair, a four-star officer and Rhodes scholar, had commanded the U.S. Seventh Fleet in the Pacific. After retirement he was named by President Obama as Director of National Intelligence. Following a disagreement with the Obama administration Blair left government and was available for our project. He produced two volumes published by the Brookings Institution entitled *Military Engagement: Influencing Armed Forces to Support Democratic Transitions.*

In those studies, Blair presents sound advice to defense officials and military leaders of democratic governments on how they might interact with those in both autocratic regimes and those that have made their break with those regimes. Blair defines his advice as follows:

> The approach described here is not about regime change by military means. It is not about supporting armed freedom fighters against dictatorships nor about invading authoritarian countries to establish democracy by force of arms. As is explained...nonviolent democratic transformations in recent decades have proved far more durable than armed overthrow of dictatorships. Rather the objective of the recommendations in this handbook is to persuade the armed forces of authoritarian governments that they should not oppose, and should even favor, peaceful transitions to democratic governments in their own countries. They should do so both because it is best for their countries and in the self-interest of the armed forces in which they serve.

Blair tells a story that demonstrates his commitment to democratic ideas and how the U.S. military in its frequent contacts with high level military leaders around the world can make a difference. While commanding the Pacific fleet he made frequent calls on military counterparts in the Pacific region as U.S. regional commanders frequently do. He recalls an encounter in Manila with the Chief of Staff of the Filipino military. The general told Blair he was faced with a dilemma. His autocratic chief of state, President Marcos, was troubled by numerous demonstrations against his government. He ordered that in future, he expected the army to fire on the demonstrators.

As he was reluctant to comply, he asked Blair what he should do. Admiral Blair's advice was, "don't do it." The general responded, "but it's my job to obey the orders of my chief of state." Blair advised him to find a way not to. Ambassador Palmer has written that American military thinking was influential among Filipino officers. He has written: "Some officers in the military had long chafed under Marcos resenting the political commanders foisted upon them; diluting a proud professionalism many brought from training at West Point and other American staff schools."

The next time Blair visited Manila he asked how the general had avoided carrying out the massacre of his country's peaceful citizens. The General responded that he referred the issue of whether the President's order was legal to the Filipino Supreme Court knowing how long they would take to ponder the issue. Before they could decide, the Marcos regime had been ousted and the Philippines had undergone peaceful change. It both surprised and pleased the American admiral that he might have had an influence on the general's decision. It left him with the conviction that military officers from the United States and other democratic countries could influence military decisions in authoritarian and fragile democratic countries in ways that could promote democratic outcomes when crises threatened. Blair was convinced that since the reputation of the American military was so great around the world they could, if the situation was right, influence democratic change, especially if other tools of diplomacy as outlined in our *Diplomat's Handbook for Democracy Development* were deployed.

As African countries have experienced more than their share of military coups, it was especially significant that we examined Senegal in a case study. It was of great interest that Senegal was a country where the military had never intervened to overturn its civilian democratic regime. An exploration of Senegal's armed forces history began with founding President Senghor's strategy in shaping important roles for the military. He defined these roles as helping build the country's infrastructure, providing disaster relief, and participating in United Nations peacekeeping ventures, a source of great pride for Senegalese soldiers. The Senegalese election of 2024 that resulted in the election of reform candidates was a reaffirmation of the viability of what I consider to be West Africa's best example of democracy. There was no military intervention, as was the tradition in Senegal. In the face of the attempt by President Macky Sall to postpone an election, public protests led to the holding of that election and the victory of insurgent reformist Bassirou Diomaye Faye, Africa's youngest president.

In his discussion of the armed forces in democratic transitions Blair observed:

> The armed forces are one of the most powerful institutions in any country. They have weapons and disciplined personnel and are organized for acting. To an extent that is hard for military officers in mature democratic countries to understand.

> The military leaders of new countries and new governments believe they have both the right and the responsibility to play a decisive role in the political development of their countries. Often their independence wars elevated military leaders as did military coups, and few other established institutions have their power and influence within the country. They will often assume or be thrust into a decisive role in a political crisis, and large sectors of society will look to them for leadership and action.

In 2017 with our concluding military and democracy education projects, the Council for a Community of Democracies slowly, painfully ran out of funding. We were unable to replace our founding Senior Advisors, most of whom had passed away and who had provided substantial contributions in our first years of operation. While we were able to find resources for program activities, we were unable to cover the modest costs of staff and administrative overhead. In those final months our staff consisted only of myself and two talented young program officers. I had taken no salary during my final two years as President of CCD.

A major part of the problem was the diminished appeal of the Community of Democracies which we were founded to support. Fewer foreign ministers attended the Ministerial meetings and a number of non-democratic governments managed to be admitted to the organization. Realpolitik considerations on the part of governments increasingly took priority over those for the advancement of democracy. The founding United States and its Department of State which had been in the Community's leadership appeared to lose interest in the Community. Democracy itself by this time seemed to have lost the momentum it had enjoyed in the world when the organization was launched at the start of the millennium.

# XVII. The Accomplishments of CCD During its Fifteen Years of Existence

1. We can take great pride in persuading the United Nations to establish a democracy fund (UNDEF).
2. We published two volumes of A *Diplomat's Handbook for Democracy Development Support* that was widely circulated to all Community of Democracies countries for the use of diplomats everywhere.
3. We influenced the United Nations and UNESCO to recognize the importance of the idea of democracy.
4. We persuaded the Bush administration to fully support democracy promotion and double the budget of the National Endowment for Democracy.

5. We were responsible for spreading the gospel of democracy education through international conferences and the publication of a widely distributed best practices manual.
6. We established the annual Mark Palmer Prize that was awarded to diplomats who had promoted democracy. That prize was later continued to be offered by Freedom House.
7. We were responsible for Admiral Blair's remarkable two volume *Military Engagement: Influencing Armed Forces to Support Democratic Transitions.*
8. We organized an international non-governmental network of democracy advocates that regularly made recommendations to governments.
9. We convinced the World Bar Association to publish a critique of Singapore's legal system for its failure to adhere to rule of law.
10. Through international conferences and workshops and our Best *Practices Manual on Democracy Education*, we greatly advanced and influenced teaching about democracy around the world.
11. We established an important precedent by regularly involving NGOs in policy discussions with high-ranking government officials on advancing democracy.

It was devastating to have to close our CCD doors after those major accomplishments, when our work had just begun to make an impact, but the democracy climate had decisively changed with key Community of Democracies countries such as Hungary and Poland developing authoritarian governments, and when the Trump administration came to office all hope of continuing U.S. efforts to promote democracy either at home or abroad were effectively abandoned.

# XVIII. Some Concluding Thoughts

As I reflect upon the past six decades, I recall beginning with idealism at the time of Kennedy and Murrow and Dr. King and Nkrumah, Senghor and Nyerere. Over the decades my idealism has traversed many potholes.

Throughout my Foreign Service career and its post governmental sequel I had three major goals:

> First, I sought to help the U.S. to advance the realization of the political and economic dreams of African people.
>
> Second, I supported the growth and spread of international democracy.
>
> Third, I worked in support of the concept of public diplomacy that was the essence of my career in the United States Information Agency.

All three have faced numerous setbacks. Nevertheless, the balance sheet does contain some positive elements that may be instructive and survive in future to reverse the negative tide.

I am convinced that seeds have been planted among many democracy NGOs in the world and that they can make a difference, especially when supported by democratic governments. I am confident that those seeds, despite inevitable setbacks, will eventually grow in all world regions. My confidence springs from the belief that in the twenty-first century, masses of citizens will grow increasingly aware that their participation in shaping decisions that affect their lives must reside in democratic institutions. The Internet continues to be critical in making information available worldwide. It allows individuals everywhere the opportunity to understand that their aspirations for greater freedom exists elsewhere and should be known to those in authoritarian regimes. In the past this has led those aspiring freedom to immigrate. In the information age it increasingly leads them to improve their status at home. I am betting on other Arab Springs as well as African and Asian Springs.

Let me conclude with some reflections on each of my professional goals. First, there is Africa. While it is impossible to generalize about an entire continent of fifty-four nations, we can discern certain trends. The British and French, unable to maintain their imperial grip, granted independence to most of their African colonies by the 1960's but sought to maintain influence and privileged relationships with them. The Angolans, Mozambicans and the people of Guinea Bissau had to engage in a long violent struggle to gain independence from Portugal. South Africa and Rhodesia remained dominated by white majorities until Mandela and Mugabe were able to lead their countries to majority rule.

Fundamental to the problems confronting newly independent African states were the artificial boundaries inherited from the European colonialists. Further were the ethnic and religious divisions that have led to internal struggles in most African countries. Ethnic diversity continues to be a major impediment to national unity. Increasingly also are religious divisions especially with the rise of militant Islam in so many countries. Adding to those difficulties has been the absence of an educated population, a large middle class, as well as health care and basic infrastructure. Furthermore, democratic governance has proven difficult precisely given the weakness of the African state. When African states have lacked resources, governments have had difficulty exercising control of their territory and providing basic services to their populations. When they enjoy rich natural resources, corruption has most often prevented the exploitation of those resources from benefiting all but a handful of elites who have siphoned off that wealth for their own purposes. States are weak and vulnerable to coups, external exploitation, or Islamic radicalism.

Many of us regarded the decolonization of the 1960's which conferred freedom on so many African states as an historic turning point. We were euphoric. We hoped independence would lead to democratic governance of one form or another, and with the end of colonial exploitation, some measure of economic growth. We simply failed to comprehend the complexity, and challenges facing African leaders. Our hope and expectation was that the life of the average African would improve. Instead, for several decades what politically had characterized too many African states was military rule, one party states, dictatorships, and other forms of authoritarian government. On the economic front, colonial exploitation was replaced in many countries by neocolonialism combined with corruption at the highest levels especially with respect to those countries endowed with petroleum or other mineral resources. The failures and shortcomings of the initial decades of independence, when confronted with the end of the Soviet empire and the Arab Spring, led in the 1990's to a wave of democratization that swept across the continent with varied results.

Some forms of democracy including rule of law, freedom of expression and of the press, the existence of opposition parties, and a semblance of free elections characterized the political forms of governance in many African states. However, too often economic benefits failed to flow to the mass of citizens. Botswana and Mauritius have sustained their democratic forms of government since independence. Ghana, Senegal, and Benin have been models of imperfect democracies. Importantly, the African Union has adopted a policy of denying membership to countries that experience military coups. But the South Africa of Mandela has fallen on hard times, especially after the corrupt rule of former President Zuma. Nigeria, overcoming a tragic civil war, has abandoned military rule several times and held elections, however imperfect.

The tragedies of Somalia, Sudan, Ethiopia, and the Rwanda genocide, as well as the continued chaos of the Congo have dominated the headlines leading to pessimism about the ability of many African countries to achieve stable governments. Perhaps the ultimate exasperation and cynicism was expressed in the Congo some years ago when I heard one Congolese ask, "when is the independence going to be over?" I saw that remark not as the endorsement of colonial rule, but rather the reality that under colonialism most areas of the colonies were simply ignored and left to fend for themselves under traditional rule, while the post-independence period could often be characterized as intrusive and anarchistic. The most worrisome development has been the violence of radical Islam in the Sahel region that has led to a fresh round of military coups. More recently the intrusion of Russia and China replaced the European colonialists in their efforts to exploit the continent's resources.

While our unbridled enthusiasm about African independence was naïve, I continue to hope that lessons learned by the very large body of young Africans and a growing middle class could serve to generate good governance with the assistance of the United States and Western Europe.

My second great disappointment was the disappearance of public diplomacy as I knew it. The end of the Cold War was used by Senator Jesse Helms and likeminded Senators as the rationale for ending the existence of an independent United States Information Agency and the attempted integration of its functions into the Department of State. That occurred just at the time when public diplomacy had the greatest potential in a world in which a broad spectrum of African society began to exert its greatest influence. While the traditional diplomacy of the State Department has focused on relating to political leadership, the role of USIA focused on a dialogue with future leaders emerging from academic institutions as well as civil society.

Why do I believe public diplomacy to be so important? We live in a world in which America is in the news worldwide and on a daily basis. Our ideas and culture, events and influence, our successes, and failures, are by far the most followed of any nation in the world. What takes place in Hollywood, Harvard, Nashville, Silicon Valley, New York, and Washington influence people everywhere. What happens there may well presage what impacts lives in the far corners of our earth. While others may be exposed to our news, few will know the context from which those events emerge. Providing context is the essential work of public diplomacy. Without it, foreign audiences will not fully understand where today has come from and where it's likely to take us. But let's face it, the negative impact of American ideas emanating in the age of Trump has caused irreparable damage to our image in the world. Perhaps never again will we regain the respect and influence of the time of Kennedy or for that matter of Reagan, either Bush, Clinton, or Obama.

Prior to the merger with the State Department, our public affairs officers most often managed cultural centers and American libraries as well as English teaching programs and had their own vehicles and representational/entertainment resources. Since USIA's merger with the State Department the role of public diplomacy, predictably has taken a back seat to thc dominance of political diplomacy. Where once our USIS officers overseas had a degree of autonomy, since integration they report directly to DCMs and ambassadors only. While some of those State officers appreciate and cultivate public diplomacy, it appears to me that many subordinate it to the rigidly defined diplomacy of the past. Also, too often the cultural and press jobs have been staffed by former consular or administrative officers who lack the proper background and training to carry out public affairs positions.

I strongly believe in the reestablishment of an independent/autonomous public diplomacy entity that would better manage our relations with foreign audiences and provide improved public affairs guidance to the leadership of our embassies and to State Department officers in Washington. While public affairs officers would be, as in the past, accountable directly to their Washington agency, they would also continue to be accountable to ambassadors. Also, as in the past, the policies they would support would be those defined by the Department of State.

My third disappointment relates to the fate of democracy in the world. My work in the 1990's with USIA, and in the twenty years after my retirement from government, involved encouraging democracy's expansion and consolidation both in Africa and throughout the world. One example of a particularly painful reversal was that of Hungary. Our impressive board member, Mark Palmer, as ambassador to Hungary was exhilarated by the transition from Soviet domination and Hungary's ascension to NATO membership. Mark had been close to Victor Orban who had been a major leader in Hungary's struggle for democracy. That manifested itself in Hungary's founding role in the Community of Democracies. But once in power Orban turned his nascent democracy into an authoritarian regime. Poland too, after its democratic transformation fell victim to authoritarian characteristics. After working in Italy for six years to counter the rise of Communism in that country, it has been painful to see a neo-fascist come to power there.

One especially painful, indeed tragic, reversal for me was that of Mali, a country I was fond of for its people and their culture which had been successfully transformed into a model democracy. But Mali has been unable to sustain its democracy in its confrontation with Islamic fundamentalism in the north which has led to a military regime following a coup. Military takeovers have also been a feature of other West African countries.

While the return of Nigeria to civilian rule and the end of apartheid in South Africa under Mandela, arguably the two most important African countries, seemed to mark the zenith of democratic change for the continent, both countries have failed to live up to expectations. Nevertheless, Nigeria's return to civilian rule is a positive step even though its elections have been flawed. Former military leaders have been elected and massive corruption continues to swallow most of its petroleum earnings. Despite all of its many problems, Nigeria has made some progress subsequent to military rule. The Nigerian situation is however fraught with instability based on pervasive corruption, Islamic fundamentalism, crime, and internal disorders, especially in the oil producing Eastern region.

After South Africa's brilliant transition and what was thought by many of us as the golden age of Mandela, there followed the less than effective presidency of Mbeki and the corrupt reign of Zuma. At this writing, there remains hope under the presidency of Cyril Ramaphosa. Ramaphosa was the ANC point man in negotiations for the transfer of power from apartheid to majority rule and was said to be Mandela's choice to succeed him. Regrettably, the ANC leadership insisted that an ineffectual Mbeki would be his successor. The peaceful transition to majority rule has been splendidly portrayed by Allister Sparks in his *Tomorrow is Another Country: The Inside Story of South Africa's Road to Change*. His subsequent account of the early period of majority rule under Mandela Beyond the

Miracle: Inside the New South Africa, recounts the early successes and failures of majority rule. Sparks, in 2016 assessed the new government's impact. He noted that despite problems in meeting all of its goals: "South Africa still is a much better place than it was under apartheid." That appraisal must be seen in light of subsequent water shortages, power failures, unchecked crime and massive scandals under President Zuma who was nonetheless supported by many influential ANC members before Ramaphosa came to power.

The model of South Africa as a successful example of transition to democracy was diminished when my friend and member of our network, Paul Graham, was obliged to shut down IDASA. Paul had led IDASA when it had been the Institute for Democracy in South Africa during the years in which it fought against apartheid. When the struggle against apartheid ended, Paul rightly believed the organization could help solidify democracy elsewhere in Africa and accordingly changed its name to the Institute for Democracy in Africa. It drew on its lessons in helping South Africa achieve majority rule to help other African countries. Most regrettably, sufficient U.S. funding for South Africa was lacking, just as support for CCD was lacking in the United States.

Perhaps the most dramatic threat to democratic change came when Russian tanks invaded Ukraine on February 24th, 2022, crushing the hopes of the Ukrainian people to become part of a democratic Western Europe. That invasion was seen by those countries liberated from Soviet domination as a threat to their efforts to preserve their own hard-won freedom.

Throughout my diplomatic career and my work on supporting democratic transitions, I held the belief that it is in the interest of the

United States that democracy prosper around the world. Accordingly, I sought to draw upon American institutions, however imperfect, to serve as examples to help others support press freedom, rule of law, representative government, the rights of women and minorities, and other freedoms. I believe people everywhere regard those attributes as essential for a healthy society in the modern world. While it appeared that the Arab Spring, the fall of the Berlin Wall, the liberation of Soviet control of Eastern Europe, and the democratic developments in Africa in the 1990s profoundly transformed the world for the better, two things were cause for pessimism. They were the failure of the Community of Democracies to live up to its promise, and the decline of democracy in my own country with the election of Donald Trump and his political authoritarianism.

It is difficult to see the U.S. maintain its role as the world's most powerful democracy when its reputation for democracy at home has been diminished and its own role as model is no longer as attractive as it once was. The image and idealism of a country in the world is so easily tarnished by the cynicism of it leaders and their policies, and especially their narrow nationalism which fails to consider the impact of such policies on their friends, neighbors, and allies. Mr. Trump's dalliance with dictators Vladimir Putin, North Korea's Kim Jong Un, and China's Xi Jinping, and his admiration for such other miscreants as Hungary's Victor Orban who abandoned his government's hard-won democracy in favor of authoritarianism have sullied our reputation as the world's most powerful democracy and weakened the creation of a more democratic world.

To once again be the "shining city on the hill" we Americans need to reinforce our weakened infrastructure, not just our roads and bridges but the fundamental institutions of democracy. We must end the powerful influence of money in politics, reduce the economic gap between hyper-rich and very poor, eliminate the nefarious role of jerrymandering, broaden the base of voters, provide meaningful education for democracy to all our young people, combat racism and domestic terrorism and the prevalence of guns, among other reforms. Clearly four years of Trump severely damaged the image of America in the eyes of the world and such damage will take many years to overcome. But for goodness sake let us begin.

# Acknowledgements

I am most grateful to my daughters, Florence, Alisa, and Therese LaGamma who labored many hours on editing the manuscript.

The work of Professor Larry Diamond has been a font of ideas as has the late Crawford Young and former Ambassadors Robert Hunter and the late Ambassador Mark Palmer and Canadian Ambassador Jeremey Kinsman as well as Admiral Dennis Blair for his work on democracy and the military.

Important contributions to ideas of democracy education were provided by innovative human rights advocate, South African professor David McQuoid Mason and former director of South African NGO IDASA Paul Graham.

Also to my colleague and friend who led CCD, Dick Rowson and the members of our Board of Directors who have been tirelessly dedicated to the course of democracy who continue to work for its promotion.

While I cannot list them all, I am in debt to the continuing work of the CCD network of NGO leaders who have made great sacrifices to overcome authoritarianism and tyranny sometimes at great expense.

Finally, I have been especially grateful to the leadership of Ambassador Herman Cohen, and his work in advancing relations between Africa and the U.S.

And to my late wife Anita of 58 years who motivated, inspired, and made joyous the life and work described in this book, I owe everything.

# About the Author

Robert LaGamma joined the Foreign Service of the United States Information Agency (USIA) when it was directed by Edward R. Murrow, during the Kennedy Administration in 1963 working in Africa for twenty-three years and retiring after concluding his diplomatic career as Director of USIA for African Affairs and Public Affairs Officer in South Africa during the Mandela presidency. Besides South Africa, his other African diplomatic posts were in Southern Rhodesia, Zambia, Niger, Ivory Coast, Togo, Senegal, and Nigeria. Upon his retirement from USIA he received the Edward R. Murrow Award for Public Diplomacy. He later led missions for the National Democratic Institute in the Congo and the Carter Center in Nigeria. Subsequently, he led the non-governmental Council for the Community of Democracies in its worldwide democracy promotion campaigns. He was married to his wife Anita for 58 years before her passing. He has five children and he resides in Reston, Virginia. Bronx-born Robert LaGamma is a graduate of Brooklyn College who earned a master's degree in international relations from Boston University.

www.ingramcontent.com/pod-product-compliance
Lightning Source LLC
LaVergne TN
LVHW091250150826
845673LV00006B/1375

* 9 7 9 8 8 2 2 9 4 9 1 6 4 *